The Lady Of Beauty (Agnes Sorel)

Frank Hamel

THE LADY OF BEAUTY

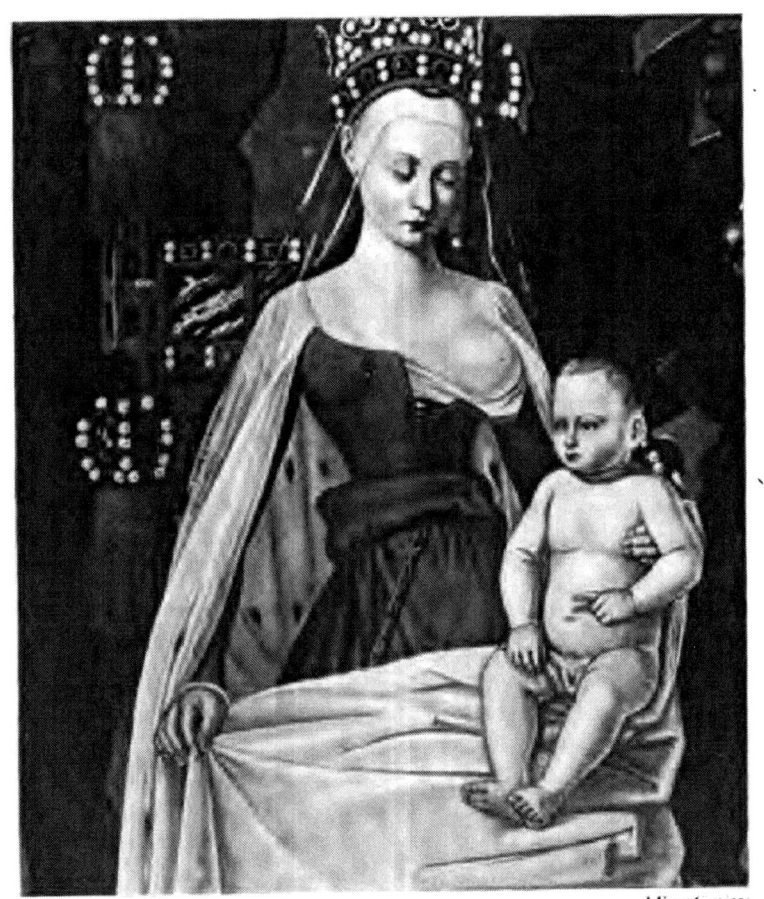

[*Frontispiece*

THE LADY OF BEAUTY

(After the painting by Fouquet in the Museum at Antwerp)

THE
LADY OF BEAUTY

(AGNES SOREL)

BY

FRANK HAMEL

WITH SIXTEEN ILLUSTRATIONS

BRENTANO'S
NEW YORK

CHAPMAN & HALL LTD.
LONDON

1912

RICHARD CLAY & SONS, LIMITED,
BRUNSWICK STREET, STAMFORD STREET, S.E.,
AND BUNGAY, SUFFOLK.

PREFATORY NOTE

AFTER studying the statements of the most learned and authoritative historians on the subject of Agnes Sorel, I sympathise with them to some extent in their endeavour to deprive the Lady of Beauty of the exaggerated sway and charm she possesses in the eyes of more romantic writers. On the other hand, I have read all the traditions that have grown up around her with a sense of enjoyment that serious history alone can never give.

If in writing her biography I have been unduly influenced by the less important works, I can only say, in extenuation of these lapses from the path of authenticated fact, that the feeling inspired by Agnes Sorel's lovable personality tends to disarm the criticism and defy the analytic judgment which should be indispensable weapons in the historian's armoury.

FRANK HAMEL.

LONDON,
   Spring, 1912.

CONTENTS

CHAPTER I

AN HISTORIC PASSION 1

PAGE

The place of Agnes Sorel's love-story in history—Difficulty
of sifting inaccuracies—Question of dates—Was she an
Egeria?—Meeting of the lovers—Opinions of the historians
—Her personal power—Temperament of the king—Period
of her sway.

CHAPTER II

THE LEGEND OF HOW AGNES CAME TO COURT . 7

Birth of Agnes Sorel—Her parents and family—Career of
her brother André—Upbringing of Agnes—Was she at the
Château de Maignelais?—Her friendship for Antoinette—
She is sent to the Court of Lorraine—Isabelle's visit to the
King of France—The lovers' first meeting.

CHAPTER III

THE KINGLET OF BOURGES 25

Appearance of Agnes—Her character—A charming daughter
of France—Her first impression of Charles VII—A royal
puzzle—Appearance and character of Charles VII—Birth
of the king—Isabeau de Bavière—Murder of Jean-sans-Peur
—Charles resides at Bourges—His marriage—Ironical verses
—His nervousness—His habits.

CHAPTER IV

A FIRST AVOWAL OF LOVE 86

Agnes is invited to stay at court—She hesitates—She falls
ill—Charles pleads with her—She agrees to remain at Chinon.

vii

CONTENTS

CHAPTER V

PAGE

HOW AGNES CAME TO DO THE KING'S WILL . . 40

Agnes is put on her guard—Was she influenced by others ? —Position of Yolande d'Aragon in the matter—Pierre de Brézé—Agnes gives herself into the king's keeping.

CHAPTER VI

THE KING'S SECRET 46

The uprooted floweret—Agnes and the historiographer Jean Chartier—The king's reserve—Marie d'Anjou—Lowly position of a king's mistress—Agnes fears the dauphin—Contemplates suicide or flight—Becomes a mother.

CHAPTER VII

'MAÎTRESSE EN TITRE' 57

An equivocal position—A factor in court life—Difficulties and temptations—A maiden in danger—The queen's jealousy—The decisive step—A problem in the history of France—Celebrated favourites—Cabals and intrigues— Agnes uses her influence for good—Her sweet aggressiveness —Her fascination and faithfulness—Compared to Louise de la Vallière—Her unscrupulous successor.

CHAPTER VIII

AGNES AND JEANNE D'ARC 67

Brantôme's story—A stirring poem by Dubout—Did Agnes carry on the work of the Maid of Orleans ?—Verses by François I—Voltaire's *Pucelle*—A romantic legend.

CHAPTER IX

THE REAL AGNES 82

Agnes emerges from the mists of tradition—The chroniclers write of her—The king gives her the Château de Beauté, from which she takes her name—Chartier's defence— Chastellain's grave charges—The wages list of the House of Anjou.

CHAPTER X

PAGE

THE COURT AT TOURS 92

Treaty of peace between France and England—Betrothal
of Henry VI and Marguerite d'Anjou—Suffolk lands at
Harfleur—A May-Day picnic—Wedding festivities.

CHAPTER XI

THE COURT AT NANCY 99

A révolution de palais—Meeting of the Courts of France
and Lorraine—A brilliant throng—Personality of the Queen
—Margaret of Scotland—Suffolk's second visit to France—
Tournaments and feasting—Departure of the young Queen
of England.

CHAPTER XII

THE COURT AT CHÂLONS 111

Visit of the Duchesse de Bourgogne—She sympathises with
the queen—Conferences and councils—Jacques de Lalaing
—Disagreement among the nobles—Charles VII makes a
pilgrimage—Death of the dauphine.

CHAPTER XIII

RAZILLY 124

The king's *mignons*—The affair of Pierson Sureau—Agnes
pleads for mercy—An inquiry into the death of Margaret
of Scotland.

CHAPTER XIV

LIFE IN THE CHÂTEAUX OF TOURAINE . . . 133

Fashions in the day of Agnes Sorel—Her letters to Mlle.
de Belleville—Chivalry and gallantry—Two forms of love
— Loches — Cheillé — Agnes is generous — Beaulieu — La
Guerche—Diary of Etienne Chevalier—The building of
Roberdeau.

CHAPTER XV

ANTOINETTE DE MAIGNELAIS 152

Agnes gives an invitation—Sends Chevalier on a journey—
Welcomes her cousin—Antoinette's curiosity—Her departure.

CHAPTER XVI

PAGE

THE JOUST 159

Mode of procedure—Expensive equipments—The joust of the great Emprise of the Dragon's Jaws—Forfeits and prizes —The queen's wit—Agnes chooses a cavalier—Death of Louis de Bueil.

CHAPTER XVII

THE LEGEND OF BOIS-TROUSSEAU 175

A romantic château—The king in disguise—Beacon fires— A domestic interior—Agnes's furniture—A visit from Jacques de Lalaing.

CHAPTER XVIII

THE INTRIGUES OF THE DAUPHIN 185

Ambition of Louis—Quarrels with his father—His lavish presents—Plots with Chabannes—Longs for the Lady of Beauty's downfall—Relations between Louis and Agnes— Chabannes makes love to the king's mistress—A disgraceful family scene—Parting of father and son—Agnes retires temporarily from court.

CHAPTER XIX

PIERRE DE BRÉZÉ 206

The dauphin goes to the Dauphiné—His enmity against Brézé—Affair of Guillaume Mariette—Trial of Brézé— Arrival of Agnes—Brézé is restored to favour.

CHAPTER XX

THE ENTRY INTO PARIS 212

Description of Paris in the fifteenth century—Entry of Agnes into the capital—Her house near the river—Her letters to the seneschal—Her capacity for friendship.

CHAPTER XXI

JACQUES CŒUR 220

Birth of Jacques Cœur—His career—His enormous fortune —Introduces cut diamonds—Loans money to the king—A financial budget—Jacques Cœur's house at Bourges—His fall.

CHAPTER XXII

ETIENNE CHEVALIER 229

A romantic attachment—Chevalier's love of Art—Jean Fouquet—Paints Agnes as the Madonna—The wonderful "Book of Hours"—Portrait of Chevalier—Of the king—Representations of the Lady of Beauty—Did she see Fouquet's work?

CHAPTER XXIII

THE CONQUEST OF NORMANDY 243

Agnes consults Etienne Chevalier—Negotiations between France and England—Siege of Le Mans—Progress of the French in Normandy—Scene from *Le Jouvencel*—Agnes goes to Beauté.

CHAPTER XXIV

WHAT HAPPENED AT THE CHÂTEAU DE BEAUTÉ . 249

The king consults Etienne Chevalier—Charles pays a visit to Agnes—Her patriotism burns brightly—She urges him to do battle—A banquet and a parting—Triumphal entry into Rouen.

CHAPTER XXV

JUMIÈGES 258

Agnes takes a perilous journey—An historic abbey—Origin of the name Jumièges—Death of "les énervés"—The prosaic Dibdin—A fair vision—The manor at Mesnil—Penitence—Illness and death of the Lady of Beauty—Her burial and epitaphs—Jacques Cœur accused of poisoning her—His trial—A poem.

CHAPTER XXVI

ANTOINETTE BECOMES MME. DE VILLEQUIER . . 281

Antoinette has a pension—Her want of rectitude—A *Parc aux cerfs*—Blanche Retreuves—Comparison with Agnes to the latter's advantage—Submission of Guienne—Rehabilitation of Jeanne d'Arc—Illness and death of Charles VII.

CHAPTER XXVII

PAGE

THE CHILDREN OF AGNES SOREL 287

Fate of Marie—Her letters—The Comte de Maulevrier kills
his wife—Jeanne marries Antoine de Bueil.

CHAPTER XXVIII

CONCLUSION 292

The Controversy about Agnes.

APPENDIX A

A PORTRAIT OF AGNES SOREL 303

APPENDIX B

AGNES SOREL'S LETTERS 305

INDEX 308

LIST OF ILLUSTRATIONS

To face page

THE LADY OF BEAUTY . . . . *Frontispiece*
(*After the painting by Fouquet in the Museum at Antwerp*)

AGNES SOREL 16

CHARLES VII 32

MARIE D'ANJOU 48

THE LADY OF BEAUTY 64
(*After a portrait by Belliard*)

RENÉ D'ANJOU 96

MARGARET OF SCOTLAND 112

AGNES SOREL 128

CHARLES VII 160

AGNES SOREL 176
(*From an engraving by Petit*)

LOUIS THE DAUPHIN 192

JACQUES CŒUR 224

A PORTRAIT OF CHARLES VII . . . 240
(*From a miniature by Fouquet*)

ETIENNE CHEVALIER 256

LA BELLE AGNÈS 272
(*From the portrait in the album of Mme. de Boisy*)

CHARLES SOREL 304

SOME AUTHORITIES CONSULTED

ANSELME. Histoire généalogique de la Maison Royale de France.

BASIN, THOMAS. Histoire des Règnes de Charles VII et de Louis XI.

BENGY DU PUYVALLÉE. Mémoire historique sur le Berry.

BOUCHET, JEAN. Les Annales d'Aquitaine.

BOUCHOT, HENRI. New York "Cosmopolitan," 1894-5.

BRACHET, A. Pathologie mentale des Rois de France.

BRANTÔME. Vie des Dames Galantes.

BRUGIÈRE DE BARANTE, A. Histoire des Ducs de Bourgogne.

BUEIL, J. V. DE. Le Jouvencel.

CAPEFIGUE. Agnès Sorel et la Chevalerie.

CHARTIER, JEAN. Chronique de Charles VII.

CHASTELLAIN. Œuvres.

CLEMENT, PIERRE. Jacques Cœur et Charles VII.

COHEN, A. Chinon et Agnès Sorel.

COSTELLO, L. S. Jacques Cœur and his Times.

COUGNY, G. DE. Chinon et ses Environs.

DELORT. Essai critique sur l'histoire de Charles VII, d'Agnès Sorelle et de Jeanne d'Arc.

DESHAYES. Histoire de l'Abbaye Royale de Jumièges.

DIBDIN, J. F. A Bibliographical, Antiquarian and Picturesque Tour in France and Germany.

DREUX DU RADIER. Mémoires historiques des Reines et Régentes de France.

DU CLERCQ, JACQUES. Chronique (continuation of Monstrelet).

DUCLOS, PINEAU. Histoire de Louis XI.

DU FRESNE DE BEAUCOURT. Histoire de Charles VII. Revue des Questions historiques, vols. i. and v.

DU GARD, R. M. L'Abbaye de Jumièges.

DUQUESNE, ROBERT. Vie et Aventures Galantes de la Belle Sorel.

DURRIEU, P. La Légende et l'histoire de Jean Foucquet (l'Annuaire Bulletin de la Société de l'Histoire de France).

ESCOUCHY, M. DE. Chronique.

FABYAN. The New Chronicles of England and France.

FOUQUET, JEAN. Œuvre de J. F. Heures de Maistre E. Chevalier.

GABORIAU. Cotillons célèbres.

GRUYER. Chantilly : Les Quarante Fouquet.

HOOKHAM, M. A. Life of Margaret of Anjou.

INTERMÉDIAIRE DES CHERCHEURS.

LABORDE, L. E. S. J. DE. La Renaissance des Arts.

LALANNE, LUDOVIC. Athenæum Français, Nov.–Dec., 1855.

LAVISSE. Histoire de France.

LECOY DE LA MARCHE. Le Roi René.

LERNE, E. DE. Reines Légitimes et Reines d'Aventure.

LEROUX DE LINCY. Femmes célèbres de l'ancienne France.

LESEUR, G. Histoire de Gaston IV, Comte de Foix.

MARCHE, OLIVIER DE LA. Mémoires.

MARTIN. Histoire de France.

MICHELET. Histoire de France.

MONSTRELET. Chronique.

NIEL, P. J. G. Portraits des personnages français les plus illustres du XVI siècle.

NODIER. Voyages Pittoresques et Romantiques dans l'Ancienne France : Normandie.

PEIGNÉ-DELACOURT. Agnès Sorel, était-elle Tourangelle ou Picarde ?

PÉTIGNY, J. DE. Histoire du Vendômois.

RAYNAL, LOUIS. Histoire du Berry.

ROBIDA, A. La Vieille France ; La Touraine.

ROUARD, E. A. François I chez Mme. de Boisy.

SOREL, CHARLES. La Solitude.

STEENACKERS, F. F. Agnès Sorel et Charles VII.

THAUMAS DE LA THAUMASSIÈRE, G. Histoire de Berry.

TOUCHARD-LAFOSSE. La Loire historique.

TOULGOET-TREANNA. Histoire de Vierzon.

TURNER's Annual Tour : Wanderings by the Seine, Letterpress by Leitch Ritchie.

VALLET DE VIRIVILLE. Histoire de Charles VII.

   " Recherches historiques sur Agnès Sorel " (Bibliothèque de l'École des Chartes).

   " Agnès Sorel, étude morale et politique sur le XV⁵ siècle " (Revue de Paris).

   " Agnès Sorel, son introduction à la Cour de Charles VII " (Compte Rendu, Académie des Sciences, Morales et Politiques, Vols. XVII and XVIII).

   Jacques Cœur.

   Jehan Foucquet.

VULSON, M. DE. Le Vray Théâtre d'Honneur et de chevalerie.

THE LADY OF BEAUTY.
(AGNES SOREL)

CHAPTER I

AN HISTORIC PASSION

THE love-story of Charles VII of France and Agnes Sorel deserves its place among the great passions of history. Around the beautiful heroine tradition and legend have been busy for centuries, weaving a romance containing elements of secrecy, of sacrifice, of patriotism, and, unfortunately, also of frailty and infidelity.

The unknown and the mysterious often possess attractions not to be found in a straightforward tale, and if the tale concerns a charming woman who was loved by a king, and much that happened to her is left to conjecture, the interest increases by leaps and bounds. What she looked like, what she did, and what she said are fascinating points to determine, and every shred of available information assumes importance.

In the case of Agnes Sorel it is not easy to sift the inaccuracies from the reality. The cleverest historians of the period in which she lived are unable to discover the exact date when her sway over the king's heart began. They

B

differ as to the time when she was born by as
much as a dozen years. They do not agree as
to whether she was beloved by a youthful monarch or whether she was the darling of a middle-
aged, world-weary king. Was she the Egeria,
the "mysterious Beatrice" who transformed an
indolent and pleasure-loving Charles into a strong
and worthy individual, or had the king won the
great fight already by his own efforts and become
sovereign of France in reality as well as in name?

Did the Lady of Beauty take a real part in
politics, or was she merely the coquettish play-
thing whose realm ended with the domestic
affairs of the reign, and who must be regarded as
a lovely will-o'-the-wisp in the history of her
country?

Perhaps these questions will never be settled
satisfactorily; perhaps the truth lies mid-way
between the two extremes.

Fact often lurks in legend, while scientific
history based on certified documents may lie.
In the stories that father told to son and son to
grandson there are gleams of human nature and
human motive full of revelation, whilst in the
logical deductions from authentic data the lack
of the personal element sometimes tends towards
misrepresentation of the truth.

Although in the life of Agnes Sorel there are
discrepancies which put the historian at a disadvantage, a certain unity in the development
of her story makes it possible for the biographer
to tell a connected narrative. Where and how
the king met his future mistress may be obscure,

but it is clear enough that they did meet, that
they loved intensely, and that their passion
became known to the world.   From 1444 onwards
Agnes was recognised as the first official favourite,
was seen at Court, became the mother of several
of the king's daughters, and was dowered with
estates and other gifts of great price.

Until about 1855 no historian seems to have
doubted that Agnes Sorel was born in 1409 or
1410.   Anselme[1] named these years and was
followed by a number of authoritative writers,
among them M. Vallet de Viriville, whose re-
searches were very exhaustive.   In 1856 he drew
up a chronological résumé of the facts, and gave
this date.[2]   Nine years later, in 1865, he made
out a corrected résumé in his *Histoire de Charles
VII*,[3] fixing upon 1415 as the year of birth, and
confessing frankly the perplexities which assailed
him in coming to this conclusion.

A year later (1866) M. G. du Fresne de Beaucourt, whose *Histoire de Charles VII*[4] may be
regarded as the standard modern work on the
reign of this king, placed the birth of Agnes
Sorel after 1422.[5]

His reasons for this change are many, but he
admitted that the difficulties in the way of prov-

[1] *Histoire généalogique de la Maison Royale de France*,
1726–88, Vol. I. p. 119.
[2] *Séances et Travaux de l'Académie des Sciences morales
et politiques.   Compte rendu.   Agnès Sorel, son introduction
à la cour de Charles VII*, Vol. XVII. p. 876.
[3] Vol. III. p. 28.
[4] 1881–91, six vols.
[5] *Revue des Questions Historiques : Charles VII et Agnès
Sorel*, Vol. I. p. 217.

B 2

ing his contention were almost insurmountable.
It seems probable, however, that his date will be
accepted by future historians.

The chief consequence of his discovery is that
Agnes, if she were barely ten years old at the
time of the death of Jeanne d'Arc, cannot be said
to have carried on directly the great work begun
by the Maid of Orleans, and the charming legend
which gives her credit for this patriotism falls to
pieces.

In the *Histoire de France*,[1] edited by M. Ernest
Lavisse, the date of Agnes Sorel's birth is not
given, but the author explains in a footnote that
the tradition, according to which she influenced
the king to take an active part in the conquest
of Normandy, is confirmed by a passage in
Le Jouvencel.

The conquest of Normandy was in progress in
1449, and this statement may be regarded as
proving that the influence of Agnes was exerted
then instead of at an earlier date.

M. Camille Favre, in his Introduction to *Le
Jouvencel*,[2] referring to M. du Fresne de Beaucourt's suggestion that the relations between the
king and Agnes were not established until about
1443, wisely remarked, " Even if the tradition
is at fault on this important question of date,
it does not follow necessarily that this tradition,
which is already ancient, should be entirely
fictitious, nor that the influence of Agnes, which
was exerted later than was originally supposed,

[1] *Paris*, 1902, Vol. IV. pt. ii. chap. v. p. 229.
[2] *Paris*, 1887, Vol. I. p. cc.

never existed on that account. It appears, indeed, difficult to believe that Agnes did not possess a considerable power over the king's mind during the later years of her life."

The personal power of the Lady of Beauty over her king-lover can never be for a moment in doubt. There has never been a susceptible king who could be stern when the fairest lady in the land to whom he had given his heart asked also that she might share in his intellectual pursuits. Charles was accustomed to have women about him who took an interest in affairs of state. His mother-in-law, who had helped in his upbringing, had a mind as astute as any man's. She had taught him to value the opinion of women.

King Charles had a strange temperament. His life was made up of curious phases outlined by Brachet.[1] His childhood appears to have been normal, and was followed by a period of immense activity. A sudden change occurred at the age of nineteen, when he grew utterly indifferent and suffered apparently from the partial paralysis of his faculties. Seven years later he awakened gradually from this state of inertia with the assistance offered him by the powerful suggestion which the words and actions of Jeanne d'Arc supplied. Then came a relapse, and during the thirties he was once more in a condition of weakness and indecision.

About 1440 he recovered, and for a period of ten years he was his most brilliant self.

[1] Auguste Brachet, *Pathologie Mentale des Rois de France*, 1908.

In 1450 his nervous balance was destroyed, he was led into excesses, and fell into a condition which culminated in disease, hallucination and death.

The interval between 1440 and 1450 covers roughly the period of his relations with Agnes Sorel, and though she may not have been the cause of the restoration of his powers, she certainly contributed to their development, their vigour, and their duration. Her influence in the main was good, in spite of all opinions to the contrary.

In one respect she gains in importance by this alteration in the period of her sway over the king.

Previously it was impossible not to compare her to Jeanne d'Arc—not always to her advantage—but by the light of the recent discoveries she holds a place of her own without a rival, and in a less familiar atmosphere than that which surrounded the Maid at the Court of King Charles VII.

CHAPTER II

THE LEGEND OF HOW AGNES CAME TO COURT

AGNES was born in the little village of Froid-mantel in Picardy.[1] Her father was Jean Soreau, Lord of Coudun, gentleman to the Comte de Clermont. He died in 1446. Her mother was Catherine de Maignelais, and if we may believe the account of Anselme she was alive in 1459, was of gentle birth, and acquired certain lands and a pension from the king which enabled her to spend her last days in very comfortable circumstances.

Agnes was the only daughter, but she had four brothers whose names were Charles, Louis, Jean and André. They all received appointments and gifts of money from Charles VII. Charles was given a post in the king's household in 1446, and his salary was eighty livres per month. Louis was a member of the king's bodyguard, and there is a record of certain sums accruing to him in 1450 and 1451. Three years later he died. The third brother, Jean, became Grand Veneur, always a coveted appointment,

[1] The legendary date is July 1409, the most authoritative date is 1422. The legendary place is Fromenteau in Touraine. See Du Fresne de Beaucourt, *Histoire de Charles VII*, Vol. IV. p. 171.

7

and in 1457 he received an amount of nearly three thousand livres. Agnes had her brothers' interests at heart. Probably she said to her royal lover that she had all she wanted herself, and if he must give he might give to her brothers.

The most interesting of the four was the youngest, André, who forms one of the important links in the chain of evidence as to his sister's age. When she died, the Lady of Beauty left to her pet brother the sum of five hundred crowns in her will. He was then sixteen years of age. If Agnes was born in 1409 or 1410 this made her twenty-four years older than André, a figure in which it is difficult to believe. On the other hand, if she was only twenty-eight or twenty-nine when she died there would be no more than twelve years between her brother and herself, which is much less unusual.[1]

André being a minor was placed in charge of the Bishop of Nîmes, one Geoffrey Floreau (who was more probably a Soreau and closely related to Agnes).[2] After a time André was appointed to a canonry in Paris, and in 1452 the king gave him enough money to establish a fine house in Paris.

It is worth noting that a good many of the

---

[1] No one seems to have made the suggestion that if the earlier date of Agnes Sorel's birth be the correct one, André might possibly have been her son and not her brother. Such things were not unknown at that period. It may be taken as unlikely, however, that Agnes had any other lover but the king.

[2] Vallet de Viriville, *Histoire de Charles VII*, Vol. III. p. 11 *n.*

benefits bestowed upon the Soreau family came to them after the death of the Lady of Beauty in 1450.

Her childhood can only be reconstructed by conjecture. At that date girls brought up in the country, or in town for the matter of that, had little education and few advantages or luxuries. Probably she slept in an attic of the paternal mansion in an antique bed with the family nurse who had brought her father into the world before her, and perhaps his father before him. Presently the nurse would be superceded by a *fille de suite*. Among the duties of these servants would be the care of the child's wardrobe, which was a very modest affair indeed.

Even as a tiny girl Agnes was very much alive, and had many simple pleasures and interests. She did not always seek the company of her elder brothers, but preferred that of the son of a neighbouring lordling who was of her own age, and became her playfellow and childish confidant.

Agnes had been born with the gift of coquetry, and as the two infants toddled hand in hand the servants watched them with amusement, called them a charming little couple, united them by a mock betrothal, and bade them kiss and swear to be true to one another.

In some such manner the love of love was instilled very early into the mind of Agnes, and her sweet and affectionate nature became a fertile ground for seeds of romance.

Fortunately she received more practical training as well, so that in days to come she might know how to serve as lady-in-waiting to some great personage.

"It was then the custom among the lesser nobility," wrote Vallet de Viriville, "for young girls as well as young men, having reached adolescence, to leave the manor-house in which they were born and to go to the court of some more powerful overlord or patron. There, beyond the reach of tenderness of relatives, which was sometimes excessive, they finished their private education under stricter discipline in the service of some illustrious lady. At the same time they passed through an apprenticeship to public life, to which they were called as well as men."

In preparation for this great event—although the nature of the public life she was to be called to cannot then have disturbed her wildest dreams—Agnes was taught to embroider, to sing, to play on the harp, to dance, to write little verses, and to decipher the manuscripts of which there were no great number in her home. She learned to ride well, was taught to hunt at an early age, and knew how to handle a dagger and short spear.

According to several historians, Agnes lost her parents[1] in her youth and was brought up

[1] Anselme's account of the family contains so many inaccuracies that it is difficult to accept any of his statements as reliable. In one place he declared that the mother of Agnes was the daughter of Jean de Maignelais and Marie de Jouy, in another he made Marie de Jouy the mother of Antoinette de Maignelais.

by her aunt, Mme. de Maignelais. This necessitated her separation from the little playfellow whom she had learned to regard as her future husband, and her heart would have been sore indeed but for the fact that she found a new companion in her cousin Antoinette.

Delort[1] was one of the authors who gave credence to the theory that Agnes was brought up at the Château de Maignelais, and M. A. Cohen,[2] following in his footsteps, has based upon it the description in his picturesque work of the relations between the cousins and the incipient jealousy of Antoinette.

In after years the two were rivals in the king's affections, and it strengthens the dramatic aspect of their rivalry to make it a sentiment of long-standing, developing steadily with the progress of years.

Both young girls were beauties. Of the two Agnes had by far the more gentle and pliant character. Her loveliness was more pronounced and of a more perfect type than that of Antoinette. "Tenderness was natural to her," wrote Cohen of the Lady of Beauty. "Sensitive by nature, she loved as thoughtlessly as the brook ripples or as the sun shines. She was born to love, formed to triumph through love, and to die the victim of love."

Whether she was altogether wise in her affections is a different matter. She lavished

---

[1] Delort, *Essai Critique sur l'Histoire de Charles VII, d'Agnès Sorelle et de Jeanne d'Arc*, 1824.

[2] A. Cohen, *Chinon et Agnès Sorel*, 1846.

her love indiscriminately upon those with whom she came daily into contact, and her fondness for her cousin was out of all proportion to that young lady's real worth.

For Antoinette eyed Agnes with an indifference which soon merged into dislike. She was envious of her superior wits and her powers of pleasing everybody. She was annoyed because her own mother seemed fonder of the niece whom she had adopted than of her daughter. Antoinette was not of a generous disposition, and even as a girl she was grasping and ambitious. She grudged Agnes the happiness which came to her through her own lovableness.

Home-life at the Château de Maignelais did not always run smoothly. Pin-pricks were felt by various members of the household. Occasionally open friction occurred between the girls and the neighbours' daughters who played with them. Usually the fault was on the side of Antoinette, for it was not in the nature of Agnes to quarrel.

On such occasions Mme. de Maignelais took her niece's part, saying, " It could not have been Agnes, she is too good-tempered and kind ever to be angry." Then Antoinette fumed inwardly against her mother's attitude in spite of its justice, and added one more grudge against her cousin to those already harboured in her heart. And Agnes, grieved that Antoinette should show sulkiness, would gladly have borne the blame of what had happened for the sake of seeing her smile again. Agnes knew well her own human failings, and had no wish to be regarded as a paragon even by the aunt she loved.

When the girls reached their teens [1] the time came when it was necessary to think about sending them out into the world, as the custom was, to take their chance of making good matches and getting established. Agnes's turn came first, according to M. Cohen's account.

"My dear child," said Mme. de Maignelais to her, "you will soon be fifteen years old, and life in this dull château in the company of one old woman would be but a sad affair. I have made a very different plan for you."

Then she blessed her adopted daughter, and said she had decided to place her in the household of Isabelle de Lorraine, and that she hoped this decision would turn out very successfully.

At first Agnes heard the news with mixed feelings. She had been very happy at Maignelais with her aunt and her cousin. She did not feel at all sure that the change would be for the better.

She appealed to her cousin on this point, but Antoinette was not sympathetic. She thought it was silly of Agnes to refuse, or wish even for a moment to refuse, the splendid chance that was offered her. She would have jumped for very joy had such an attractive opening presented itself for her. The Court of Lorraine was one of the finest courts in France, and life there would be far more gay than at the Château de

[1] Vallet de Viriville gives Antoinette's birth as about 1420. *La Nouvelle Biographie générale*, Vol. XXXII. p. 866.

Maignelais.   Antoinette loved festivities and admiration.

"You will have a much more enjoyable life there than here," she said, with a sigh of envy. "Your good looks are wasted here. Half-a-dozen ineligible old men see them, and nobody else at present.   If I were you I would go without hesitation."

Thinking Antoinette was pleased to get rid of her, Agnes burst into tears.

"You are sending me away from you," she sobbed.   "You are cruel, cruel."

The excitement of packing up for the journey lessened her grief to some extent.   The time that passed between the making of the plan and its execution slipped away like a dream.   Mme. de Maignelais accompanied her niece to Nancy, and left her in charge of the charming young duchess.

At this point the biographer steps once more upon sure historical ground.   The date of Agnes Sorel's advent at the Court of Lorraine is indefinite, but the fact that she became a member of the duchess's household is incontestable.

Bourdigné, in his *Chroniques d'Anjou et du Maine*, said Agnes "was brought up from her youth by the Queen of Sicily, and was so well-beloved by her that she gave her much furniture and property, so that she enjoyed the estate of a princess."

Here again is evidence bearing on the question of age. Although Bourdigné's statement must not be regarded as true in every particular, it is important to note that he wrote as though Agnes had been placed in Isabelle's care, that is to say, as though her patroness were older than herself. Isabelle, or Isabeau as she is sometimes called, was born in 1410, and if the earlier date be allowed for the birth of Agnes was her junior by a few months.

On the other hand, if Agnes first saw the light in 1422, Isabelle had been a wife for more than two years, her father, Charles le Hardi, Duc de Lorraine, having arranged a marriage for her with René d'Anjou, which was solemnised on October 24, 1420. Seven years later, at the age of seventeen, Isabelle became a mother, and by that date would naturally have had an established household and her own women about her.

The Court of Lorraine was a model one. Isabelle's mother, Marguerite de Bavière, was its ruling spirit. She was an aristocratic lady of pious character, who never allowed the attendants at the palace to give way to idleness. She set herself up as an example of industry before their eyes. If there were unoccupied moments, such as happened on feast-days and holidays, she read to the domestics out of the Holy Scriptures. Probably she was a terror to every one about her, as was also Yolande d'Aragon, the remarkably masculine mother of René and Marie d'Anjou.

But Marguerite de Bavière did not make the same mistake as Yolande of suppressing her children's individuality, and Isabelle inherited much of her mother's love of order, possessing as well remarkable courage and conspicuous powers

of statesmanship.   She played an important part
in French history.

Her court was a centre of virtue and culture.
She taught her children and grandchildren herself,
and no doubt Agnes received lasting benefit
from her sojourn in the Lorraine household.

"Even amongst the ruling houses of Christian-
ity," wrote Vallet de Viriville,[1] "it would be
difficult to find a better or more brilliant school.
Isabelle de Lorraine was amongst the most
distinguished princesses of her century."

The courts and the castles were excellent
schools of courtesy, of politeness and other
virtues for the young gentlewomen who were
bred up with the pages and squires.   The simple
graces and tender sentiments for which nature
seemed to have fitted them were here cultivated
to perfection.

"Courtesy," wrote Lacurne de Sainte-Palaye,[2]
"towards persons of low estate was strongly
recommended, as well as respect to the great.
The latter, they were taught, claimed it of right,
and there was no virtue in showing it to them,
but humility and tenderness to inferiors were
testimonies of a good, frank and gentle heart,
and brought real glory to its possessor.   Girls
were taught to speak courteously, but not to
talk or laugh too much, not to be absent or
inattentive, lofty or bold.

"The young gentlewomen were taught also
to anticipate in civility the knights who visited

[1] *Agnès Sorel, son introduction à la cour de Charles VII.*
[2] *Mémoires sur l'ancienne chevalerie.*

[*To face p.* 16

AGNES SOREL

at the castles, to disarm them on their return from the tournaments and warlike expeditions, to provide them with change of garments, and to serve them at table: the examples of which are so frequent, as not to cause the least doubt of this custom, and it was agreeable to the spirit and the sentiment which was universal among women in this age; and to have those generous attentions and cares conferred by those with whom they were afterwards to form an alliance, was, as it were, the seal of knighthood. This also inspired women with fortitude."

In this manner women were affected by chivalric notions. They had to be courageous, for when the knights or squires returned from their frequent affrays, covered with blood and dust, it was the part of the maidens to bathe their hurts, and in general to succour the wounded.

The place of the young women of the lesser nobility to which the fair Agnes belonged was very clearly defined in those days, and for their permanent happiness and peace of mind it was well that they should be contented with it.

A breach of the conventions was not regarded leniently at a court where no word of scandal had ever been breathed, and in Isabelle's time the capital of her little kingdom had a reputation for which its mistress had no need to blush.

When this same court was ruled over by the energetic spirit of Stanislas, ex-king of Poland, in the middle of the eighteenth century, the gaiety there was not quite so innocent, but at both periods it was the home of art and letters, pos-

c

sessed many of the advantages and few of the
disadvantages of the court of the French kings,
and was in every way more free from restraint
and more replete with happiness.

Charles le Hardi, Duc de Lorraine, having no
son, made his daughter heiress to the Duchy.
Her marriage with René d'Anjou united with it
the Duchy of Bar, and presently additional
grandeur was acquired when René inherited
Naples, Sicily and Jerusalem from Jeanne II.
René was brother to the queen, and their mother,
Yolande of Aragon, had a finger in every political
pie. She was an exceedingly ambitious woman,
beside whom even the artistic and clever René
seemed a cipher. Queen Marie had learnt to
efface herself in childhood, and never afterwards
lost the habit of being a nonentity.

With all these individuals Agnes Sorel was
destined to come into daily contact, and naturally
enough they exerted a great influence in her
life.

Yolande, Isabelle and Marie all had their
say in the attitude and actions of Charles VII.
They were all anxious to make the king aware
of his responsibilities, and no doubt Agnes took
her tone from them as soon as she found it
possible to use any personal influence at all.

René's marriage had had the effect of causing
Charles le Hardi to withdraw his support from
the English, with whom he had been negotiating,
and to give a fresh impetus to the Valois cause.
That was one feather in the loyal Yolande's
cap. Another was that, with her usual diplomatic

success, she was able to choose councillors for her
son-in-law who not only won his confidence but
who did the work of the State in a satisfactory
manner; that is to say, very differently to some
he had chosen for himself.

Whilst Charles's mother-in-law was busy with
affairs at the king's court, life was passing tranquilly enough at the Court of Lorraine, and these
years in which Isabelle and Agnes were mistress
and maid-of-honour might have continued
happily enough had not an interruption occurred
with the death of Isabelle's father in 1481.

No sooner had René and his wife become Duc
and Duchesse de Lorraine than the former's
cousin, Antoine de Vaudémont, was prompted
by envy to dispute their claim and to make an
attempt to wrest the country from their grasp.
A *coup d'état* of some sort he achieved.

The " good king René," as he was called by
his subjects, was more artistic, musical and
poetical than manly and bold. He lacked the
sterner qualities which were needful in the barbaric
times in which he lived. The strain of effeminacy
in his character had been increased by his bringing
up under the overpowering personality of his
mother.

Impetuous and foolhardy in battle, his military
tactics were at fault, and though he threw himself
valiantly into the struggle against his presumptu-
ous cousin, he was vanquished and taken prisoner
at Bulgnéville.

He was forced to deliver up his ducal sword
to his captors, and as he did so, according to the

chronicler, he uttered the words, "Save my life and claim a large sum as ransom if you like."

This strain of weakness in René's character was more than balanced by the strength his wife showed at this juncture of affairs. She possessed the courage of a lioness, and it was said by Etienne Pasquier that " in her womanly bosom she bore a man's heart."

No sooner was she made aware of her husband's captivity than she summoned a council, and had the army reorganised at Nancy. Then, aided by her mother, the pious dowager, and by the Lorraine nobles, she succeeded in holding the kingdom against the invaders. At the same time she opened negotiations with King Charles, the powerful Duc de Bourgogne and Antoine de Vaudémont himself, in the hope of obtaining her husband's release and ensuring the safety of her little realm and its loyal soldiers.

The importance of these events in the life of Agnes Sorel was great. They were regarded as the direct cause of her arrival at court. Although this was probably not strictly accurate, indirectly they led later to the meeting between her and her royal master.

It is possible that Isabelle de Lorraine presented herself in person before Charles VII at this date, and that Agnes accompanied her. Good historians have held this view. Vallet de Viriville [1] placed her visit to Chinon in 1485,

[1] Résumé chronologique, etc., p. 876 of *Séances et Travaux de l'Académie des Sciences morales et politiques. Compte rendu*, Vol. XVII. See also his *Histoire de Charles VII*, Vol. III. p. 12.

following the account of Pius II, who believed that the Duchesse de Lorraine went to the château on her way to Naples in that year.

But the basis of this statement is not well founded, and Lecoy de la Marche,[1] describing a visit paid by René d'Anjou to Toulouse, where Charles VII was staying in 1448, wrote, " Isabelle accompanied her husband, and this was, in all probability, her first appearance at the Court of France, for we have seen her constantly occupied ever since her marriage by the cares of government, either in Lorraine or Naples."

Between the capture of René and his wife's journey south several events happened. Having quitted one prison cell, René was unfortunate enough to fall captive a second time, and for something like six years he did not regain his complete freedom. In the meantime he had succeeded to the throne of Naples through the death of his brother, Louis d'Anjou. The country being in a state of uproar it was necessary to establish the king's claim by force of arms. Owing to his inability to start for his new domain, it was thought well that the intrepid Isabelle should take his place. She was appointed *lieu-tenante-générale*, and thereupon set forth for Marseilles to embark for Italy. She did not return to France until 1441.

It is quite impossible to say whether Agnes accompanied her or not. The historians who place her birth in 1422 are those also who date her first meeting with the king about 1448 at

[1] *Le Roi René*, Vol. I. p. 228.

Toulouse, and they presume that Agnes was till then in the charge of Isabelle. When the duchess set sail for Naples, however, Agnes would have been twelve years of age; too young, it seems, to be of much use as a maid-of-honour, or in any other capacity, on a long and arduous journey taken into a strange land, where the people were in revolt and affairs were very unsettled.

Nevertheless, if she did not go, where was she left behind ? History does not say. Isabelle's eldest girl, Marguerite, afterwards Queen of England, remained at Anjou, but no one has suggested that Agnes was there too.

The years that Isabelle spent in Naples are years in which all that concerns Agnes is very dim indeed, and it must suffice to say that one day, before her journey to Naples, or upon her return, the Duchesse de Lorraine arrived at the Court of France with the young Agnes in her train.

The manner of their arrival has been told by M. Cohen.[1]

About two leagues from Tours on the banks of the Vienne stood the imposing old château of Chinon.

This ancient residence of kings was composed of three groups of buildings, constructed at different epochs in varying styles of architecture. The castle was surrounded by a moat, and origin-

[1] *Chinon et Agnès Sorel*, 1846. Du Fresne de Beaucourt called this a " work of fantasy." The author has based his story on a supposed manuscript written by Etienne Chevalier, which he declared he found in an old château of Touraine. See *Revue des Questions Historiques*, 1866, Vol. I. p. 208.

ally had but one tower. Within was the apartment in which some years previously the king had first received Jeanne d'Arc.

One morning a courier was announced who bore despatches to Charles, in which Isabelle proclaimed her desire for an interview. She had halted with her little band of attendants some way outside the town of Chinon to await the king's pleasure.

Charles sent a messenger to beg her to hasten to the castle, where he was waiting to welcome her.

At the drawbridge he stood surrounded by a group of nobles when she rode up and drew rein there.

She dismounted, and having greeted the king, formally begged that she might be allowed to present to him her knights, squires, ladies and maids-of-honour, who had escorted her in loyal service.

The king was graciously pleased to permit the presentation. The members of Isabelle's court approached him, one by one, bowed low or curtseyed, kissed his outstretched hand, and expressed their fidelity and loyalty. All was passing off in the manner usual to such occasions, when suddenly there stepped forth, almost from the end of the queue, a young girl of surpassing beauty.

It was Agnes Sorel.

The king's eyes were riveted on her face, but he did not utter a single word.

Abashed by the king's notice, she attempted

to withdraw into the background, but this was not permitted.

Already the thought had flashed through Charles VII's mind that he did not wish to lose sight of her.

When a move was made into the palace, Agnes was told to remain by the side of Isabelle, and the king stayed close at hand.

A great banquet was served immediately. Etienne Chevalier, the king's secretary, was seated at the royal table near to Agnes Sorel.

When the meal was over the company moved into the adjoining apartments, and dancing went on until the night was well advanced.

Tradition states that the king was unable to sleep a wink that night, for his thoughts were occupied with the young girl who had come to Chinon and conquered his heart by her fresh beauty.

"Pursued by waking dreams the king could not rest," said Etienne Chevalier. "Visions of the graceful Agnes chased one another through his brain like hurrying summer cloudlets passing swiftly in the blue sky."

Charles had a poetic strain in his character. He was convinced that sleep itself could not have offered him sweeter images.

CHAPTER III

THE KINGLET OF BOURGES

THE visions which kept Charles VII awake that night represented a very charming original.

All the chroniclers of Agnes are unanimous on that point. Agnes was surpassingly fair and surprisingly young. Jean Chartier said of her that "amongst all the beauties she was the youngest and loveliest in the world," nor would he allow a word to be said against her innocence and virtue. Olivier de la Marche thought her more perfect in appearance than any other woman he had seen, and Fouquet, the artist who painted her portrait, represented her in the guise of a Madonna. Fairest of the fair she must have been, according to the standards of beauty in vogue at that time.

Her features were well modelled, her eyes clear, melting and blue, with a look of appeal in them which now and then turned to merriment. Her nose was straight, and if anything rather long; her lips were full and curved, disclosing even, white teeth when she smiled. Her forehead was high and crowned with luxurious fair hair. Her eyelashes were long and dark, resting on cheeks which were described as of "the colour of lilies and roses." She was neither tall nor yet too small, and her figure was rounded, of lovely proportions and delicate curves.

Her mental gifts matched those of her body. She was clever, but not obtrusively so. Serenity, calmness, good-nature and sweetness were among her characteristics. Her vivacity was tempered with an air of seductive gentleness, and her gaiety did not exclude common sense nor good judgment.

But no list of her physical and intellectual perfections can give an adequate idea of her personality. She was born a daughter of France, and one of that country's loveliest daughters— which is the same as saying that she was as attractive a young feminine being as any in the world.

According to one account the promise of her loveliness had been evident at a very early age, and her fame spread beyond the borders of the province in which she lived. Delort [1] wrote : " She attracted an infinity of magnificent nobles to her side," amongst them the famous Duc d'Alençon, Charles de Bourbon, Dunois and " a hundred others."

Although it is hardly likely that personages of this importance should have travelled long distances merely to see a young girl who had a reputation for good looks, it was not an uncommon thing for reports of such beauty to reach the Court of France. It is possible that Charles

[1] *Essai Critique sur l'histoire de Charles VII, d'Agnès Sorelle et de Jeanne d'Arc*, 1824. Vallet de Viriville said of it : " This book unfortunately, in spite of its title, is lacking in sound criticism. History and fiction are mingled too frequently in it" (*Histoire de Charles VII*, Vol. III. p. 14).

had not been left in ignorance of Agnes Sorel's whereabouts, and wished to judge of her appearance with his own eyes. Only a century later François I, hearing of the attractions possessed by Mme. de Châteaubriand, endeavoured to persuade her husband to bring her to court. In her case a ruse was resorted to, and a ring was sent her as a signal, purporting to be from her husband, whose command she obeyed.

In the case of Agnes no such lure was required. Circumstances had brought her naturally to the side of the king, who had a right to command the presence of those who called themselves his subjects.

Charles, according to all accounts, was astonished and deeply moved when he set eyes on Agnes, but, because a woman's thoughts are more difficult to fathom, it is not so easy to say what her feelings were when first she beheld her sovereign.

She would naturally regard him as a king rather than a man.

In the hearts of the French the king, next to the Almighty, was an object of devout worship.

" It is not I who am the king," Charles had said some years before to Jeanne d'Arc, who had sought him out to help him to regain his country, and who, in spite of his dissembling, could not be deceived.

" Gentle prince," she replied, " it is you and no other."

And now once again Charles was ready to deny

his kingship.   But for far more personal reasons. He wanted Agnes to like him for himself and not because he was a monarch.

Charles was a strange being.   Odd in appearance, baffling in character, he is one of the royal puzzles in history.

At the time of his meeting with Agnes he was between thirty and forty years of age, probably nearer forty.

His figure was not good.   He was thin and of medium height, and his lower limbs were shrunken and ill-proportioned.   Yet he could assume a noble dignity of carriage, and when he wore the long robes which were usual at court functions he even attained a certain elegance of mien.

His head was large, his forehead broad and prominent.   His face was clean-shaven and his colouring dull red.   Thick and arched eyebrows when lowered almost hid the small grey-green eyes which, troubled at times, were none the less penetrating.   Many a brave man had quailed and lost his assurance before his keen gaze. Charles had a long nose and a strong jaw; his mouth was small, with full lips which in later life acquired a sensual curve.   He usually affected a small felt cap with a turned-up brim, from beneath which not a single hair was allowed to stray.

Externally, then, there was little that was prepossessing in his appearance, but the man's personality was, nevertheless, arresting and full of interest.

His whole aspect was expressive of amenity,

kindness, firmness, which, although tempered to the weak, was inflexible. An indefinable charm mingled in his physiognomy with sadness, anxiety and defiance. His somewhat hatchety features bore an unquestionable imprint of suffering. But his smile, like that of many who have bought their experiences in a bitter school, possessed a rare sweetness and lit up his eyes, transforming his countenance into something lovable.

Apart from rare gleams of happiness, the existence of Charles, which by many of his biographers was said to have been passed in frivolity, carelessness and pleasure, had been fraught with trials and continuous struggle. Few kings of modern times have led a more precarious or troubled life than he.

From the day when he was born unkind fates appeared to be conspiring against him; whilst pre-natal and hereditary influences[1] had been remarkably unpropitious.

Charles was born at the Hôtel de Saint-Paul in Paris, on February 22, 1403. His mother was Isabeau de Bavière; his father, in the question of heredity, must be left out, since his identity was exceedingly doubtful.

[1] Auguste Brachet, in his book entitled *Pathologie Mentale des Rois de France*, already mentioned, has given to the world some valuable information and deductions on this subject. The work, which is intended to elucidate the mental pathology of Louis XI, deals with the period of six centuries between 852 and 1483. The first edition, published in 1896, received honourable mention from the Académie de Médecine. It was not intended for the general public. The second edition, which appeared in 1903 after the author's death, was edited by Mme. Anna Brachet, *née* Korff.

His mother was *une détraquée*, dissolute
and neurotic. She has been described as an
egoist, sensual, frivolous, and a coquette. Of
her twelve children only four or five lived till
they were twenty. Seven of them were born
after Charles VI went mad, and Charles VII
was the fifth born since the first attack of
madness.

Brachet considered the question of the pater-
nity of Charles VII a difficult one to answer.
Was he the son of Charles VI, of Louis d'Orléans,
or of another? Owing to this doubt Brachet
refused to follow the historians like Vallet de
Viriville, who named the king the child of
dementia.

On the other hand, the maternal influences
were pronounced. Isabeau de Bavière was a
very stout woman, ill-proportioned and of dark
complexion. She was usually carried from place
to place in a sedan chair. She was too nervous
to cross a bridge, and this weakness was inherited by Charles.

Apart from certain hysterical tendencies the
mentality of Charles was normal. He was possessed of intellectual vigour and strong political
intelligence.

From the years of his childhood, however, he
had undergone various terrible experiences, which
had left their mark upon him.

At the age of eight or nine, when lodging in
the Louvre, he had seen English soldiers brought
into Paris and quartered in the city, and had

listened in fear to the cries and clamour of the executions by which Jean-sans-Peur had celebrated his triumphs.

Five years later he was obliged to flee from the Hôtel de Tournelles on the night of the massacre of the Armagnacs by the Burgundians, and for nineteen years he was an exile from the French capital, having lost his chief possessions in the North.

By the death of his brother Louis, Duc de Guienne, in December, 1415, followed by that of Jean, Duc de Touraine, in April, 1417, he became Dauphin of France, and endeavoured to grapple, child as he still was in years, with the disordered affairs of State.

In September, 1419, Jean-sans-Peur was murdered before his eyes at Montereau, a murder for which he was held responsible by many historians, and for long afterwards he went about in nervous dread of death by the sword.

Then he was disowned by his mother, disinherited, and by letters patent made to give up the title of dauphin and all claim to be a son of France.

He established himself at Bourges, where in April, 1422, his marriage with Marie d'Anjou, to whom he had been betrothed nearly ten years earlier, was celebrated. This year (1422) was a very significant one in the history of France. On August 31, Henry V died, leaving his infant son, Henry VI, to be proclaimed King of France, in October, on the death of Charles VI.

In spite of the many difficulties under which Charles laboured he showed remarkable activity, both mental and physical, about this time. He had lost his throne, and was known ironically as the Kinglet of Bourges.

The people composed ironical verses about this monarch without a crown, this sovereign dispossessed of his lands—

> "Les Anglais, avec leurs croix rouges,
> Voyant lors sa confusion,
> L'appelaient le *roi de Bourges*
> Pas forme de dérision." [1]

In 1422 the Kinglet of Bourges was nineteen. There was every reason that the energy which he had shown of recent years should be stimulated to greater heights. Henry V had paid him one tribute when he said to the negotiators of the Treaty of Troyes that the dauphin, carried away by his burning ardour, would endeavour to prevent their coming to terms. Suddenly, however, a curious change had come about in his character. He became listless, and neither his marriage nor the fact that the throne should by rights have been his seemed to have power to wake him from his apathy.

[1] A legend is told that one day when Agnes was particularly anxious to urge Charles to do his duty she paid a group of singers to chant some of the derisive songs outside the castle windows. Charles flew into a temper, and threatened to hang the offenders, being goaded by their taunts. When Agnes confessed to him what she had done he owned that she had stirred him into activity.

CHARLES VII, ROI DE FRANCE,
SURNOMMÉ 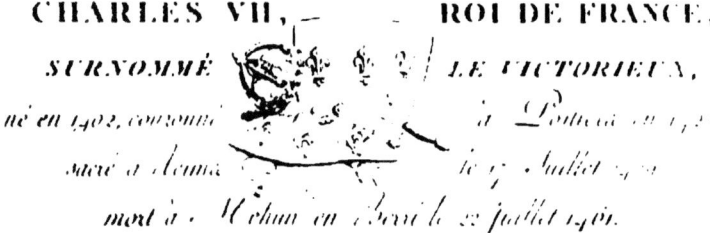 LE VICTORIEUX,
né en 1402, couronné à Poitiers en 142..
sacré à Reims le 17 Juillet 1429.
mort à Mehun en Berri le 22 Juillet 1461.

[To face p. 32

CHARLES VII

Where the historians failed in giving a reason for this breakdown, the pathologists believed they had discovered one.

Only a few days before the mad king's death Charles had suffered a serious shock to his system, which apparently paralysed his faculties. This accident, which happened at La Rochelle, shattered his nerves, which had already been unstrung by the death of Jean-sans-Peur.

Whilst lodging in the bishop's palace, where he was holding a council meeting, the floor of the hall in which the company was assembled gave way, and all present were precipitated into the room below. Several were killed, but Charles, who had been seated on a cushioned throne which broke his fall, was only slightly wounded.

His terror, however, was great, and from that day he could not cross the floor of any room without an effort.

He inherited this nervous temperament from his mother, and a very strong spur was required to restore him to a natural condition. Seven years later he found it in the potent suggestions made to him by Jeanne d'Arc. But the awakening was but temporary. A relapse succeeded the slow restoration of his faculties.

"The sovereign of France," wrote Vallet de Viriville,[1] "had reached his thirtieth year, and the question arose as to whether the son of an adulteress and a madman was not himself under

---

[1] *Revue de Paris*, Vol. XXVIII., Oct. 1855.

D

a curse. . . . What designs had Providence upon this royal head; a vessel fragile and holy as the grail of the legend, for it bears the burden of the whole country ? "

The same author pictured the young king as half demented, surrounded by unworthy favourites, and rocked into ease and indifference by grasping mistresses, but Du Fresne de Beaucourt refuted most of these charges, and proved to his own satisfaction that the king, at least in these early years, was sane, active, moral and temperate. Perhaps the halo with which he crowned his hero's head shines somewhat too brightly, but Charles was not without his good points. At table it was said he ate and drank little, taking but two meals a day. His piety was extraordinary, and religion played a large part in his daily life. Superstition had also a hold upon his mind, and soothsayers, astrologers and necromancers were always sure of a welcome from him, as they were from many other people at that date. He had great conversational gifts, told a good story, and gave his protection to letters and art. He loved horses and the chase, and though he did not possess great personal courage he seems to have been able to inspire others with the physical bravery in which he was somewhat lacking.

Such was the man—a lonely and disappointed man—who confronted Agnes. It was natural that her youth, vivacity and loveliness should appeal to him strongly.

To her his contradictions were not visible. To her he represented all there was of power, of influence, and of majesty. How was she to resist his influence if he should choose to exert it ?

CHAPTER IV

A FIRST AVOWAL OF LOVE

CHARLES, having fallen under the spell of the fascinating Agnes, was not likely to contemplate her departure from court with equanimity. He knew that as soon as Isabelle de Lorraine had completed her business at Chinon she would prepare for her return journey, taking her retinue with her. It was his intention to delay this event as long as possible.

On her arrival Isabelle had demanded a secret audience of the king in order to solicit his help in obtaining the release of her lord and master.

Charles did not hasten to her assistance. He gave her an evasive answer and promised to consult his ministers on the matter, begging his sister-in-law to extend the time of her visit.

The opportune arrival of ambassadors, intent on negotiations for a continuation of the truce with Burgundy, gave rise to a series of festivities which postponed the departure of the duchess.

At length, however, Charles was unable to prevaricate any longer. He was obliged to give a definite promise to Isabelle, at the risk of losing Mlle. de Fromenteau, as Agnes was then called.

At this juncture, according to Cohen's account, it was Marie d'Anjou who came to the king's aid.

Fascinated by the lovable and gentle ways of the young maid-of-honour, she suggested to Isabelle that if she could spare Agnes she would gladly take her into her own household.

Isabelle was naturally aggrieved by such a proposition, but it was difficult to give a direct refusal to the queen, and she said that she would put the matter before Agnes and let her decide her future for herself.

At first Agnes refused to abandon her original protectress in this off-hand manner. The Duchesse de Lorraine had trained her, had helped her with good counsel, had indeed been her true friend. To leave her thus, seemed an act of base ingratitude. It would be wrong, quite wrong, she thought.

"On the other hand," wrote Cohen, "Charles gazed long and sadly at her, and his glance had been full of eloquence. His eyes had spoken, and Agnes trembled."

At last the moment came when she had to choose between staying at the Court of France, in the service of Marie d'Anjou, or of returning with the duchess to the Court of Lorraine. Winter was drawing on apace, and any day snow might render the rough tracks utterly impassable.

At the critical moment Agnes fell ill and took to her bed. Probably her ailment was a simple cold; but in the account given by Etienne Chevalier "des physiciens vindrent iceluy iour en grand nombre au châtel de Chinon."

The Duchesse de Lorraine, finding it impossible to delay her departure, set forth for Nancy, leaving instructions that Agnes should follow at the earliest opportunity after she became well again.

As soon as her health was re-established, Mlle. de Fromenteau, mindful of the wishes of her mistress, prepared to follow her. But the king would not let her go without a protest. He drew her to an embrasure and showed her an expanse of country buried in snow. The roofs of the houses were white, and the few people who ventured out into the freezing temperature were wrapped up in the thickest furs and were so powdered with the falling flakes that to those who watched them from the castle they appeared to be mere phantoms.

" Gentle Agnes," said Charles, " how can you think of leaving here ? You must not go. The distance between Chinon and Nancy is great. You might perish of cold by the way, and I should not be there to protect you. Promise me you will not go."

The young girl looked at him and her eyes were troubled. She did not know how to reply. The tones of his voice moved her strangely.

" Sire," she said, " you are my king, my lord and my master. I must obey you."

" I am your king, but I am not a tyrant," responded Charles. " If my presence troubles you, Agnes, I will not try and persuade you to stay. Two things you will leave with me, the memory of your sweetness and your beauty, and the memory of happy hours spent in your company."

He was about to kneel at her feet when the door opened suddenly and one of the guards entered the room.

" *Ciel!* " cried Agnes.

And, rushing from the king's presence, she fled to her own apartment.

That evening, meeting the same guard, she was attacked by a sense of discomfort because she felt that in his eyes she must be compromised.

" Simple maid though I am," she said to him, " the king will not find it easy to win me. I revere and honour him, but I would not do anything to displease the queen."

Thus it came about that Agnes remained at Chinon and made friends on every side. She was beloved for her beauty, her grace, and her playfulness.

As time passed a whisper was heard in court circles, " The king adores the queen's new maid-of-honour."

CHAPTER V

HOW AGNES CAME TO DO THE KING'S WILL

AGNES was put on her guard by the king's first attempt to make love to her, and determined to give him no further opportunity of expressing his feelings. She avoided meeting him, and never lingered in the apartments of the palace where he might enter unexpectedly. If she became aware that he was approaching the room in which she was working at her embroidery, and it was possible for her to escape, she fled to her own chamber, where he could not follow.

In public she greeted him with the cool and ceremonious curtsey that the meanest subject must offer to her sovereign.

But Charles grew impatient at her indifference. He thought her bashfulness assumed and her modesty excessive. He grew bolder in his wooing.

Charles VII was always considerate in his behaviour towards women and especially to Marie d'Anjou. During the early years of their marriage he spent as many hours as he could with his wife, and he gave money to her liberally and as many comforts as were possible in times that were straitened and unsettled.

If not remarkable for her beauty or her wit, the queen was a lovable woman and a devoted mother. Charles had probably never been in love with her, but he lived with her happily enough at first.

The names of one or two other ladies were mentioned in connection with that of the king. But such matters were chiefly gossip or conjecture. Du Fresne de Beaucourt would have posterity believe that before his relations with Agnes Sorel, Charles VII had been a faithful husband.

If that be so, what were the causes which led the king into a breach of the marriage vows he had respected for a matter of something like twenty years ?

The origin of royal love affairs is never a very easy one to discover. Often politics play almost as large a part in the affair as sentiment.

Instances have been known in which ambitious courtiers have thrown into the arms of an amorous king some charming woman, who might serve them as a tool when favours were required.

On the other hand, in a number of such affairs affection on both sides has been the only factor of importance. Thus Louis XIV wished to be loved for himself alone, and Louise de la Vallière loved him passionately.

In the case of Louis XV a shameful intrigue was the beginning of a profligate career.

Charles VII loved Agnes Sorel, and he probably pursued her by inclination rather than because he was urged thereto by designing courtiers. Agnes possessed many of the virtues of Louise de la Vallière. She was generous, unselfish and devotional, and she used her influence for the king's good.

It is difficult to judge those who fall into the position of mistress to a king because they bear a genuine affection for him.

Agnes was young, but she knew the ways of courts; she was pure in heart, but she saw the dangers of the interest the king showed in her doings. She was beautiful and realised that personal beauty is a great gift, but she was not vain, and she was not personally ambitious.

What can have led her to take the step which was to brand her for ever as a king's mistress? In later centuries such a thing was not unusual, and many were willing enough and proud enough to fill the anomalous position. But in the time of Agnes Sorel, when the morals of the day were elementary, it was almost an unknown thing for the king to keep up a grand establishment for any woman besides his queen. Such a state of affairs could not pass without criticism.

Perhaps, like Louise de la Vallière, Agnes hoped that the king's love might be kept a secret. And for a time it remained a secret.

But she could not have expected it would always be so, because the life of a king cannot be hidden from his people. Everything he does, and everywhere he goes, is known.

Perhaps she was influenced by those about her. Many historians stated that the queen herself and her mother connived at the king's passion, though they gave no adequate reasons for this belief. Sismondi [1] wrote: "Far from being jealous of this young beauty, they (Yolande d'Aragon and Marie d'Anjou) favoured the sovereign's latest passion; Marie d'Anjou begged her sister-in-law to allow her to keep Agnes Sorel and employ her as a personal attendant." Michelet [2] expressed much the same idea. "The king's mother-in-law, Yolande d'Anjou, mother-in-law also of Isabelle, had the mind of a man. They thought it well to bind Charles VII for always to the interests of the house of Anjou-Lorraine. They gave him as a mistress the gentle creature, to the queen's entire satisfaction, for she wished to put La Trémouille and other favourites out of court."

The historian, H. Martin, [3] expounded the same idea even more fully. "The dowager of Anjou was little scrupulous," he explained, "and Charles VII was no Saint-Louis. She could not govern him through her daughter, the queen, his legitimate wife; she could not hinder him from keeping mistresses; she gave him one herself, and influenced him by means of this strange intermediary."

It is not easy to believe the statement that a mother could be so unnatural as to desire to set up a rival to her own daughter.

Another suggestion bears a different character. Among his personal followers Charles had

[1] *Histoire des Français*, Paris, 1881, Vol. XIII. p. 208.
[2] *Histoire de France*, Paris, 1876–78, Vol. VII. p. 8.
[3] *Histoire de France*, Paris, 1878, Vol. VI. p. 821.

signalled out one for especial favour, a young man of the House of Anjou called Pierre de Brézé. Step by step Brézé was raised from a simple squire to be a member of the council and Seneschal of Poitou. A brilliant knight, a witty courtier, he was as skilled in statesmanship as he was handy with the sword.

The speedy advance of the young squire synchronised with the growing influence of the Lady of Beauty.

References to this effect appear in the chroniclers. " The seneschal spoils everything, destroys everything," wrote Guillaume Benoist; " he keeps the king in subjection by means of Agnes, who is the queen's woman;" and in a secret report addressed to the Duc de Bourgogne the significant phrase appeared : " The said seneschal enjoys himself mightily with the king, in part through the influence of Agnes, from whom he obtains whatever he wants."

Perhaps it was true that in the background some one had something to gain by expediting matters between Charles and the woman by whom he was deeply attracted. A hundred eyes were watching the trend of events, and their owners were ready to reap advantage out of the new combination of factors.

If strings were pulled at court to bring about the submission of Agnes Sorel to the king's will, she at least was innocent of all intriguing.

What she did she did of her own free choice. She loved, and in her loving she forgot prudence, virtue and restraint. But she remembered that if she could be of service to the king and to France, her offering would not be wasted.

So she gave herself into the king's keeping, and he, enamoured of her generous impulse, valued her sacrifice the more.

CHAPTER VI

THE KING'S SECRET

CHARLES had discovered a little floweret, modest, attractive and fragrant. Having set his heart on so precious a treasure, he was not likely to forgo the pleasure of gathering and wearing it. But the humble blossom had been accustomed to sheltering leaves, and to pluck it forth into the full glare of publicity without a transition stage might be to subject it to a form of torture which would cause it to wither speedily.

Therefore he adopted the plan of uprooting the plant and of changing the soil by slow degrees, until his cherished floweret might in the end bloom forth in fullest perfection in the humid, sunny court of le Roi Victorieux.

Agnes was still in her extreme youth. Her eyes were full of innocence, her skin gave off a glow of childlike health, her golden hair was fine-spun as lustrous silk, her voice was adorable, and the words she spoke with it were always gentle, kind and full of charm.

" Grace, even more beautiful than beauty "

was hers.

Many men had discovered this truth, many

46

men had hoped to bask in her smiles, but that was impossible, for one who was higher than they had cast glances in her direction, and it was for the others to efface themselves. They could not rival their king.

Whether weeks or months passed before Agnes yielded to the king's entreaties cannot be ascertained positively. Sovereigns are not usually slow in their wooing. They do not suffer embarrassment to keep them from their purpose, and they have means of coercion, without seeming to coerce, which are lacking to lesser people.

No biographer of Agnes could succeed to-day in following in the footsteps of Jean Chartier, who sheltered her from the consequences of her own act by attempting to prove her innocence. She entered into illicit relationship with the king, and at times she gloried in the fact, whilst at times she deeply and sincerely regretted it. In the end she candidly confessed her fault, and no doubt through her pious works gained peace and consolation.

But when Jean Chartier declared that he never in public saw any sign of familiarity between the lovers, he was no doubt describing what he knew of the beginning of their relations.

Charles, unlike some of his successors, did not seek notoriety in his love affairs. When, urged by the passionate love which Agnes inspired, he overcame the resistance offered to his advances and won Agnes for his own, he was chary of sharing the knowledge of his good fortune with the world. Thus the king's secret was known only to himself and to her. That it must have been suspected by others anybody may guess who has studied the complex life of courts.

But Charles was reserved and circumspect. He was satisfied with his own company and did not always welcome intrusion into his solitude. He was not given to the habit of confiding everything he did to those about him. The age fostered secrecy and mystery. He did not relax his attention to religion for a moment. Had he done so, there would have been many who would have inquired into the cause of this falling from faith.

Charles attended many church services daily, and he closeted himself too with astrologers and others who might direct his path. He lived at this time, it was said, *une moult saincte vie.* Outwardly, then, there was no clue to the inward tumult which was shaking the very foundations of his being.

It is difficult at all times for a man gripped by a passionate love to appear so calm that no one shall suspect, but for a king upon whose every movement the fire of many eyes is turned the feat is well-nigh impossible. Yet no one knew more about the dangers of intrigue and scandal at court than Charles himself. There must, there should be no room for calumny.

Marie d'Anjou must be left in ignorance that there was a rival to her in his affections. She had never been made to suffer for his passing whims,

[To face p. 48

MARIE D'ANJOU

but it would not be so easy now that he really loved. Everything that could be done must be done.

He did not care to face midnight scenes or to find her anxiously considering why he had been so long absent. She would shed tears, and he hated tears. Then there would have to be a reconciliation, and that was no less unpleasant to him; for she would throw her arms about him and tell him she loved him whatever he did to her or however much he despised her.

Her excessive meekness annoyed him, and in thinking of new gifts to please her he would despise himself on seeing her once more made childishly happy. She did not realise that the king's affection had never been true love, and even if she suspected rivalry she would never listen to court gossip or permit any one to spy upon the king on her behalf.

There was another side to the question. If once the power of Agnes over him were known she would be surrounded by a pack of ambitious sycophants ready to regard her as a political factor and to profit by her position. He reckoned on her reserve and her disinterestedness to help him in concealing that which he did not desire should be common knowledge.

Many women—women who did not love him for himself—would have used their influence to obtain benefits from their lover which by their very munificence would proclaim the truth. Agnes was content to remain lowly and to wait;

E

she acquiesced entirely in Charles's plan to keep their understanding hidden.

The king, though generous to a fault, still bore the lean years of poverty too closely in mind to find it possible to give largely, and Agnes was a maid-of-honour at a small stipend and had as yet received no love-tokens of price. A few jewels perhaps were hers, a few trifling fripperies, which it was not difficult to conceal in her little room in the upper chambers of the castle. But her life, though it fluttered with future possibilities, was narrow and ordinary enough. She had to wait on her mistress; she had to answer her beck or call.

When she caught sight of the king in public, knowing him so near, she turned sick with anxiety. Suppose that she betrayed herself, suppose that others should catch the gleam in his eyes as he turned them on her, for he did so now and again ! That nearness which was more like separation, though the barrier was invisible, seemed to her one of the cruelest things she had ever had to suffer. Proud and hitherto honest, Agnes felt the restraint of her position acutely. She desired secrecy above all, yet the limitations it imposed upon her galled her beyond all bearing.

One of a merry company in the banqueting-hall, she felt as though she must stand forth and shriek out the whole truth that she loved the king, that he loved her, and that they claimed their share of the world's happiness before it was too late. Only a knowledge of the consequences deterred her from so mad an act! A sudden hush would have fallen upon the assembled company as they listened to her crazy speech, and then—ah, that she could not face!—there would be a buzz of derision, and they would point out her shame with scornful fingers.

Undergoing the torture of indecision, she would leave the queen's side at the earliest moment and rush to her room to pour out her misery in bitter tears. And sometimes in the night she would start out of her sleep with the mocking laughter of the dream-crowd still ringing in her ears.

The king and the king alone could ease her distress. He guessed something of this trouble and urged her to be patient, to try to be happy for his sake. And while she was with him she was unfeignedly happy. He was kind, considerate and full of understanding. He soothed her so gently, and assured her so freely of his undying love. To be with him was to be in paradise, but the moments of such bliss were necessarily few.

As yet there were no subterranean passages leading from the châteaux to some sheltered manor-house, which made frequent rendezvous the easiest thing in the world. The smaller rooms in the palaces, where it was possible to have occasional stolen meetings, were built so that all communicated, and, though none followed when the king had signed he wished to be alone,

E 2

an element of uncertainty gave the zest of tantalisation to the snatched kiss, the hand-clasp, the hurried embrace.

In the gardens by the artificial lakes it was possible to wander separately, meet, and leave again by different paths through the thickly growing plantations, and in the woods, when riding or hunting, there were hours together which required few words to account for them.

Only a love-sick young king could resort to the expedients which Charles did to gain his way. Near the châteaux there were usually residences where Charles stayed for luncheon or a deep draught of good red wine. It was easy to make some cavalier take his cloak and his plumed bonnet, while he wore a forester's plain jerkin and rode off to the spot where he had told his lady-love to be in waiting for him.

Such things might be done once or twice without much mischief, but always some one guessed much, if they did not know much.

Agnes was probably the first of the two to discover that whispering can sound very ominous, and that silence can be full of meaning. On the one hand were those haughty dames who passed her, their heads held high, their noses apparently aware of an unpleasant scent, their eyes never turning once in her direction. On the other hand there were men, and women too, who smiled at her and tried to draw her into conversation, although they had not regarded her as anything better than a servant before.

As time passed these mannerisms were more accentuated still. The haughtiness became more proud, the smiles more cunning. Agnes knew not how to meet the first without wincing, nor the second with a dignity that discouraged familiarity.

Both attitudes disgusted her, and she learnt to dread the approach of any one. She divided people into two classes, and feared or despised them. Only the queen was uniformly kind and natural. Perhaps because she did not know; perhaps because she knew and had learnt to discipline her natural feelings.

Then there came a day when Agnes grew so self-conscious that she could not enter a room in which two people were in intimate conversation without imagining that they were talking of her—and often she was right. At other times she wished the queen would scold her, strike her even; in short, do anything rather than that she should be so good and so blind. And when she happened to meet Louis, the dauphin, who was not very often at court, she shrank away until she seemed a very insignificant person indeed in her own eyes.

Louis, now grown up, greeted her usually with a crafty leer, which she could not, nay, dared not, analyse. She knew him for cunning, for dishonest, and for base. Her instinct told her that he must either love or hate. She had seen gleams in his eyes of both passions, and she preferred the latter to the former, but realised that both were

dangerous. If he should discover the truth!
What harm he might do!

She went to the king with her fears and her
alarms, but he only laughed and pooh-poohed
her anxiety. The dauphin was his son and must
obey. And then he turned the conversation to
more personal matters, and for a while Agnes
was happy, her terrors being allayed.

When she was left alone again, the black
thoughts which had assailed her returned with
double fury, and for one mad moment she contemplated an act of folly. She remembered the
cool lake in the grounds, lying still and serene
under the stars—for night had fallen—could not
she too lie still and be at rest in its waters?

She dared not die. She had not that kind of
courage. Life called to her strongly. She was
young and joyous; death was silent and awe-
some. With it she had nothing to do.

But she could run away! Leave all the
mingled pain and happiness, start fresh, and find
new pastures where she might win after long
years happiness of a better and more satisfying
kind. Many an erring woman has thought the
same, many of her sisters went so far as to attempt
the plan. So Louise de la Vallière fled to the
convent at Chaillot in February, 1662, only to be
fetched back ignominiously the following day by
her imperious young lover.

Agnes had not the strength of despair which
actuated Louise. When the morning dawned
she felt her spirits revive, and when next she saw

the king alone she told him of her intended flight with a smile instead of a tear.

" If you had left me like that, ma belle, do you know what I should have done ? " cried Charles, straining her close to him.

" No," she whispered, and her heart beat so loudly that she could barely speak. Visions of his anger and punishment passed through her quick brain.

" I would have proclaimed aloud that you were mine. And I would have sent out the whole of my bodyguard to scour the country till you were found, and the man who found you would have carried you back and placed you in my arms, and I should have borne you into the hall before the assembled courtiers and seated you on the throne itself."

And at this terrible threat Agnes hid her face anew.

But fate was working to disperse the secrecy. A new bond was coming to unite still closer the king and his fair Agnes, a bond that the world would not ignore. Agnes, about to become a mother, was filled with anxiety as to her future position. Charles, already the father of a number of princes and princesses, was a little perturbed by the thought of bringing into the world this offspring of an illicit passion.

Agnes must cease to live in the apartments of the queen's ladies, and should be given a dwelling-place of her own. After many months, which had perhaps stretched into years of mutual love, the time had come to free his mistress from her subordinate position and to acknowledge her definitely as his official favourite, insisting on the fact that she must in future be regarded as a great lady, and be looked up to and courted by all who expected or treasured his consideration.

CHAPTER VII

'MAÎTRESSE EN TITRE'

NEVER in the world's history has any woman's position been more criticised than that of a king's mistress. Never have mistresses been more discussed than those of the French monarchs. The powers and possibilities, the advantages and disadvantages which surrounded these women have been considered from the point of view of policy, diplomacy, expediency and morality, but rarely of humanity.

The *maîtresse en titre* was a factor to reckon with in court life; at the same time she could not be of official importance. She spent more hours in the intimate society of her lover and received more of his confidences than any other, yet where his actions in affairs of State were concerned she was supposed to know nothing and to possess not the smallest influence.

She could make or mar not only the king's happiness, but his usefulness (since kings like other men are led and moulded through their passions), yet her interference was deplored and her power decried.

It is true that her position was equivocal and that from its nature the good she might be able to do was not unmixed with evil. But her want of standing hampered her in doing such good as she might have done.

She was beautiful and loved beautiful things about her—without these qualities her fascination would have diminished and she would have ceased to exist—but because she indulged in tastes which were expensive she was blamed and condemned.

Whatever happened she was in the wrong. The difficulties and temptations in her path were left out of account, the private griefs, the twinges of a troubled conscience, the pangs of jealousy, the long misery which had perhaps to be faced after a short and merry reign—none of these things was placed to her credit to balance the weight of censure that appeared on the debit side of her account.

She was never subjected to fair criticism without the cries of " Shame " which prejudice had prepared against her. Her personality was never discussed without reference to the dubious aspect of her position. She existed and might surely have been contemplated as she was, not as she ought to have been.

Picture a fair maiden of perhaps eighteen, very sweet, very loving, inexperienced, but perhaps ambitious and rejoicing too openly in her beauty. She might have noble blood in her veins or she might be of the people, but at all events she would be much below royalty in rank.

Suppose she were brought by design or even by accident into a corrupt court by a woman older than herself, who was a born mistress of intrigue and who knew that substantial gains were to be obtained by pandering to the tastes of a vicious king. Suppose she were left unguarded, perhaps even ignorant—though that is unlikely—certainly guileless, to face the wiles and blandishments of one who had never been thwarted in a wish, who had power, riches, persuasion, and perhaps even a pleasing appearance and a winning personality on his side.

The king, gloomy and restless, wearied with bought pleasures, turns a jaded eye upon those who surround him and sees amongst them a fair face, a beautiful figure, charming manners, a modesty and coyness which urge him to attempt a capture. He is inspired indeed with a deep passion.

The maiden will not yield to the king's wooing, but if at first it shocks her virtue, she grows to regard it as less and less reprehensible.

How is she to escape his attentions? Alone she cannot fight against him. If she does not find him positively distasteful, her own heart is quite likely to betray her. If his love is sincere and more than the passing whim of an hour, he may teach her to return his love. And then her last defence has gone. She stands on the verge of giving all, for she feels that she is winning glory rather than deserving shame.

At that hour courtiers turn their eyes upon her with meaning glances, sycophants surround her in the hope of deriving benefit from her possible future power. Women who pretend to be her best friends urge her on, forecasting the probabilities of her future good fortune.

Only one thing terrifies her. It is the fear of the queen's jealousy. Perhaps the queen will not know. Perhaps—for the queen has been well schooled and such things have been done—the queen will know and still admit her to her presence.

There are reasons of State for this, reasons of policy, reasons even that make one mistress, if she be modest and well-behaved, a preferable alternative to a round of debauchery.

For good or for ill the maiden takes the decisive step. La Vallière took it, Gabrielle d'Estrées took it, Agnes Sorel took it. All these three loved honestly, and therefore retained something of their soul's purity. All three became the mistresses of kings, and, because they were honourable women, all learned what suffering meant; for to be a king's mistress is to throw much misery into one side of life's balance and to hope that the meagre joy in the other will bring down the scale.

In the history of France these problems were raised and were discussed in every reign. They were never solved, but were succeeded by similar problems again and again.

How many women found the problem too difficult for them and dared not attempt the solution cannot be estimated, but the number of those who spent their lives in the hope of solving it can be guessed, and a large proportion is known.

Whether they were happy, whether they regretted, will never be disclosed.

Many left behind them a celebrated name, more celebrated often than that of the queens they rivalled; for the queens were foreigners who did not understand the people, and knew not how to win their love.

But of them all, including such favourites as the Duchesse d'Étampes, Diane de Poitiers, Mme. de Châteauroux, Mme. de Montespan, la Pompadour and la du Barry, none had greater popularity than the Lady of Beauty. The fascination which she wielded over Charles VII was supreme.

The mistress of the King of France was a second power in the State, abnormal, unacknowledged, impudent in her frankness, restless, agitating, intangible, but still unquestionably a power.

The influence of the *maîtresses en titre* was naturally accompanied by cabals and intrigues. It formed a kind of dangerous internal conspiracy. A struggle between the right hand and the left hand took place, it has been said, at the conjugal hearth of the sovereign. It was well if the infidelity in the household did not become the infidelity of the State Council, and if the faithless husband did not become the forsworn king who in turn betrayed his ministers.

In 1440 such complex corruption was as yet unknown. Agnes took part in the reign beside the monarch much, it has been suggested, as a relative or an affectionate, disinterested friend might have done. The question of sex, however, would appear to make such a possibility an illusion. The French view was that instead of being a menace and a danger to public affairs, the union of two beings in harmony added a certain amount of stability and repose to the State. The grandeur with which the mistress was surrounded added, it is true, to the gorgeous pageantry of royalty. In cases where the *maîtresse en titre* was not too grasping, nor her demands too exacting, periods of creative activity in the monarchy were the rule. The reverse held good, and without her the king frequently showed himself to be cruel and destructive. The worst deeds of the reign of Charles VII were the abandonment of Jeanne d'Arc and of Jacques Cœur. The first occurrence took place before he knew Agnes, the second after her death.

During her lifetime she helped the king as only a clever and tactful woman could do. She had to preserve the charm of variety and elusiveness. She had to baffle him as to the depths of her feelings, the extent of her intellect, and the permanence of her affections. The man who is all ardour when he sets out in pursuit of a mistress, may grow cold enough when once she is his. Then her capacity to guide him would be gone. With a mistress who has it in her power at any moment to be off and away, even a king does not feel secure.

If Agnes had hidden herself in one of her strongholds, Charles might have sent his men to fetch her back by force and bring her to his side again. But the king did not care to hold his mistress by any other force than the compelling one of personality, which gives the illusion of choice. Agnes appeared to have her own will, and when the dauphin offended her, she chose to withdraw from court, and that gave a fresh spur to the king's love.

The Lady of Beauty knew well how to control her moods in the king's presence. She was as different from the queen as it was possible to be. Where Marie d'Anjou was willing to efface herself, Agnes chose to be sweetly aggressive. She demanded gently more new dresses, more beautiful furs, more elaborate tapestries. She knew that if she set the king fresh tasks he would not get weary of doing things for her, and so she racked her brains to think of something new, something extravagant, even exorbitant, although she was not really grasping, which should make all the courtiers wonder at her daring and her originality and say how clever she was.

Charles gave orders to his workmen to execute marvels which taxed their skill and resources to the uttermost. It would never have done for the king's mistress to assure her lover that she was wholly satisfied.

She would appear to be utterly and blissfully content with a new possession, and then, before her lover was wearied of seeing her with a smile of pleasure on her lips, she would change of a sudden and sigh. ᶜ

Such moods must follow as quickly as sunshine and rain, as cloud and limpid blue. It was only the queen who could afford to be the same every day—because she was queen.

The king's mistress has often been an object of envy merely because it was thought that she had nothing to do but to sit still, be gracious and wait for benefits to be poured into her lap. The truth was very different.

She had always to be devising some new way of making herself enchanting. She could not use the simplest weapon of all, because she could not be the first. That was the queen's privilege. The king had a wife and children already; he had tasted the joys of parentage, and to them she could add little. If he loved her and had ceased to love the queen, that was all she could hope for. She could never have the gratification of being the only one.

When he fell in love with Agnes, Charles was not altogether a bad man. He had probably lapsed temporarily from the strict path of virtue, but to her he was sincere and faithful.

She repaid him with faithfulness on her side. In mind and body she was as loyal as Mlle. de la Vallière. These two perhaps alone of the French kings' mistresses may be said to have been on the whole good women. They alone probably had been true to one man and had never felt love for another.

Pius II threw a doubt on the Lady of Beauty's character, suggesting that she may have been a " light woman." But this opinion is worth very little. It was asserted by other writers that Agnes knew well how to check the freedom and to

To face p. 64

THE LADY OF BEAUTY

(*After a portrait by Belliard*)

the end, although he was then beginning to waver. She had something of the gaiety and joyousness of the Duchesse d'Étampes, without that lady's over-assurance.

It is strange that the two women who exerted the best influence upon their royal lovers should have been succeeded by others who were very designing. More unscrupulous mistresses than Mme. de Montespan, who usurped the privileges of the Duchesse de la Vallière, and Antoinette de Maignelais, Duchesse de Villequier, who ousted her cousin Agnes, it would be hard to find.

Fortunately for the ultimate triumph of virtue over vice it is the gentlest of the mistresses who obtained the strongest hold upon the imagination of the people, and that Agnes won a foremost place in their hearts is proved by the many traditions which were woven round her name.

CHAPTER VIII

AGNES AND JEANNE D'ARC

THE legendary atmosphere which surrounds her was created largely by a story which Brantôme re-told from a popular author of the sixteenth century, Bernard de Girard, Seigneur du Haillan.[1]

"Lovely Agnes," wrote Brantôme, "seeing that King Charles VII was becoming wildly enamoured of her and cared for nothing but to make love to her, and grown lazy and ease-loving, no longer looked after his kingdom, told him that one day when she was still a mere girl, an astrologer prophesied to her that she would be loved and served by one of the most valiant and courageous kings of Christendom. When the king had done her the honour of loving her she thought he must be the valorous monarch concerning whom the prophecy had been made. But seeing him so lazy, and taking so little interest in his affairs, she saw that she must have been mistaken, and that the courageous king was not he but the King of England, who made war so beautifully and snatched so many towns from under his nose. 'And,' she went on, ' I

---

[1] *L'Histoire de France,* 1576.

am going forth to find him, for it is of him
the astrologer spoke.' These words stirred the
king's heart so deeply that he began to weep,
and from that time, plucking up his courage, he
left hunting and his gardens alone, took the bit
between his teeth, and by good fortune and
courage succeeded in chasing the English out
of his kingdom."

M. Cohen paraphrased the story of the astrologer dramatically.

"One day," said Etienne Chevalier, "they
told me that the king wanted to see me in the
apartment in which he generally worked, and
when I entered the said apartment, he said to
me :

"'Etienne, my friend, I have need of your
help.'

"'Speak, Sire,' I replied, 'I am ready to do
all that you are pleased to command.'

"'Then hear me,' replied the king. 'I love
very dearly a demoiselle who is maid-of-honour
to the queen, the demoiselle de Fromenteau.
And on this account I wish to see a seer who can
foretell to me the success of my love.'"

It was, therefore, by the express orders of
Charles, and not merely chance, that a few days
later an astrologer appeared at the door of the
Castle of Chinon and demanded to see the
king.

No sooner had he set eyes on him than he
said :

"Tell a servant to go for Agnes Sorel at

once and bring her here. It is the king's wish."

Agnes, unable to disobey a command so urgent, laid down her embroidery and entered into the king's presence.

" Come hither, sweet Agnes," said Charles; " the fortune-teller wishes to reveal to you your future."

Agnes sat down. The wise man looked at the palm of her hand, then he drew forth a little flask and anointed her forehead with some drops of the liquor it contained. He brushed from her brow her hair, which she wore in loose ringlets, and gazed into her eyes.

" Your destiny is a fortunate one," he said in a solemn voice. " Mademoiselle, a great king will love you, and you will be the mistress of a great king."

When Agnes heard these words she rose hastily from her chair and turned to the king.

" Sire," she said, " you heard my fate. Do you understand it ? "

" There was nothing very difficult to understand about that," said Charles, endeavouring to keep the note of triumph from his voice.

" Let me pass then, Sire," said Agnes, trying to make her way to the door.

" Pass ? What do you mean, Agnes ? "

She spoke low, but every word was distinct.

" If I am to become the mistress of a great king I must go to the King of England. It is not to you the prediction refers. You have lost your crown and are but a kinglet. The King of England will soon be master of your realm, and will be a far more powerful monarch than you."

From that instant the king awoke to a sense of duty.

Unfortunately the illusion of the tale is destroyed by the fact that at the time when it might have taken place Henry VI, King of England, was a child not yet in his teens, and therefore not a possible rival to Charles in the affections of the Lady of Beauty. But in spite of inaccuracy in this particular the central idea that Agnes stirred Charles up to do great deeds inspired many historians, biographers, novelists and poets to write of her patriotic attitude.

Alfred Dubout composed a poem on this subject in which he told of the time when the English, allied with the Burgundians, were masters of half France.

Charles VII awaited in his palace of Chinon news of the Comte de Clermont's success against the English, who were besieging Orleans.

Agnes, panting and agitated, entered the royal apartments hurriedly.

" Non, Sire, c'en est trop : une défaite encore ! "

" This is too much, Sire—still another defeat," she began.

" Sire—m'écoutez-vous ? je parle de la France,
    Par Sainte-Anne ! quel calme, ou quelle indifférence ! "

Then she begged him to bestir himself.

" Soyez donc un vaincu, mais non pas un fuyard !
Un fuyard ! qu'ai-je dit ?—Non, la douleur m'emporte !
C'est qu'en ces temps maudits il faut une âme forte !
Et je suis femme, moi ! je suis . . . Ah ! Monseigneur
Accusez la raison d'Agnès, et non son cœur ! "

Wringing her hands she worked him up to a high pitch, imploring him to save his country :

" Hâtez-vous ! hâtez-vous de sauver la Patrie ! "

and pictures to him the battalions marching against the enemy :

" S'avançant vers l'Anglais sous l'Oriflamme en feu,
Le Roi—devant son peuple ; et devant le Roi—Dieu ! "

At her stirring words the young king is re-born, a hero :

" Ainsi parlait Agnès au roi Charles Septième ;
Et, sous l'éclair jailli des yeux charmants qu'il aime,
Sous ces mots enflammés de vaillance et d'amour,
Le jeune roi, surpris et conquis tour à tour,
Sentait de longs frissons secouer tout son être :
L'enfant disparaissait, un héros allait naître,
Superbe de valeur, d'audace et de fierté !
Ses doigts nerveux, déjà, pressaient à son côté,
La garde de son fer à l'étroit dans sa gaine.
Quand, voici qu'au dehors une rumeur lointaine
Monta comme une mer qui s'en vient grossissant :
' Noël ! Noël ! ' criait le peuple, frémissant.
Agnès en tressaillit ; le roi dressa la tête.
La foule s'approchait avec des cris de fête . . .
Et soudain, accouru des profondeurs du parc,
Vendôme, sur le seuil, annonça : Jeanne Darc ! "

In this version it would appear as though Agnes began the work of regeneration and Jeanne d'Arc carried it on, but in most of the legends Agnes is given the credit of completing what the Maid began.

" Charles VII," wrote Mr. Henry James,[1] " was yet a rather privileged mortal, to stand up as he does before posterity between the noble Joan and the *gentille Agnès;* deriving, however, much more honour from one of these companions than from the other."

Gaboriau [2] said much the same : " The throne under Charles VII was saved by two women—the one was an inspired virgin, who, her miraculous standard in her hand, conducted the soldiers to war herself; the other was the king's mistress, the Lady of Beauty, who always thought of glory before thinking of love.".

Capefigue [3] was still more emphatic :

" The services," he wrote, " which she rendered to the king and to France were of great importance : Agnes had decided Charles VII on his patriotic crusade against England : she had made him shake off the troublesome yoke of the undisciplined captains of the great Companies, and instead raise up a regular and stable government, which would give force and impulse to the poor monarchy of the Kinglet of Bourges. Agnes Sorel dominates the history of Charles VII's reign; Jeanne d'Arc was but an episode of it.

" A right consideration of the legend of Jeanne

[1] *A Little Tour in France.*
[2] *Les Cotillons Célèbres.*
[3] *Agnès Sorel et la Chevalerie.*

d'Arc shows us that the Maid of Orleans exercised but a transient influence on the destinies of Charles VII's monarchy; hers was but one of those camp legends destined to raise the sinking courage of soldiers.

"Agnes Sorel, with the help of Jacques Cœur, reconciled the king to the great feudatories of Brittany and Burgundy, and to the House of Anjou, which henceforth were the mainstay of his cause : strengthened by this assistance Charles VII entered Paris again, reconquered Normandy and Guienne, and finally delivered the territory from the hateful presence of the English. Still, the legend of the Maid of Orleans has remained with us, and is better loved, more celebrated and much more popular than that of Agnes. The former was connected with a holy mysticism, a wonderfully romantic life; an inspired daughter of the people, leading the king to Rheims to have him crowned, formed an episode capable of appealing to the imagination of the fifteenth century, while, on the other hand, the career of Agnes Sorel never went beyond the simple conditions of chivalry, and even, perhaps, of politics. This is just what we frequently find in history; we attribute to a wonderful accident something that is but the result of a combination, the action of which has been prepared by events. It will be noticed that after the siege of Paris, by the men-at-arms under Jeanne d'Arc, the standard of France remained quite as low as before the consecration of the king at Rheims.

The Maid had even fallen into the hands of the English ! Discouragement was as profound as ever in the camp of Charles VII. Who, then, was it that revived the courage of all ? Who was it that made the bewildered monarch take energetic resolutions ? Who gave him the wise advice to negotiate with the great feudatories of Brittany and Burgundy ? And at last, when the king was restored, who was it that urged him against the English in Normandy and Guienne ?

"The modern soldier's song, ' Il faut partir, Agnès l'ordonne,' is but an adaptation of the verses of François I,[1] a connoisseur in honour and courage ! "

[1] The original lines were written by François I in the album of Hélène d'Hangest, Mme. de Boisy, which is now in the library at Aix. (See Appendix A.) They have shared with Brantôme's story the honour of perpetuating the legend of the Lady of Beauty.

Various versions of the original are to be found, of which the best known are taken from the *Histoire de Vierzon*, by E. de Toulgoet-Treanna, 1884, p. 217.

"Gentille Agnes plus de los tu méryte,
La cose estant en France recouvrer
Que ce que peut dedans un cloistre ouvrer
Close nonain, ou au désert hermite."

"Icy dessoubz des belles gist l'eslite
Car de louange sa beauté plus mérite
Estant cause de France recouvrer
Que tout ce que en cloître peut ouvrer
Close nonnain ny au désert hermite."

"La belle Anys [*sic*]
Plus de louange son amour sy meryte
Etant crsoe [cose] de France recouvrer
Qui n'est tout ce quan cloytre peut ouvrer
Clouse nonnayn ou au désert ermyte."

The verses in question are of world-wide fame, and have been rendered in English as follows :

"If to win back poor captive France be aught,
  More honour, gentle Agnes, is thy meed
Than ere was due to deeds of virtue wrought
  By cloistered nun or pious hermit-breed."

In comparing Jeanne d'Arc with Agnes there is a distinct danger of confusing divine love with human love—the sacred with the profane.

They had, however, certain qualities in common: kindness, gentleness, generosity and the spirit of sacrifice.

They also had some passions in common: love of monarchy, an ardent patriotism and pride of race.

Women have inspired men in many ways, through intellect, through noble aspiration, and through physical passion.

The last method has not always brought about the worst results. Jeanne, being purity itself, deserved all praise. She was more than human. Agnes, in the weakness of her love, was very human indeed.

" I am Agnes," she cried. " Long live France."

Voltaire, who dared to write the *Pucelle*, improved upon this phrase thus : " I am Agnes— long live France and love." He described her as very fascinating and Charles as very fascinated.

"One Easter-tide, good Charles in youthful prime
  At Tours renown'd, thought fit to spend his time;

Where, at a ball, for much he loved to dance,
It so fell out, that for the good of France,
He found a maid who beggar'd all compare,
Named Agnes Sorel;—Love had framed the fair:
Let your warm fancy youthful Flora trace,
Of heavenly Venus add th' enchanting grace,
The wood nymph's stature and bewild'ring guise,
With Love's seductive air and brilliant eyes,
Arachne's art, the Syren's dulcet strain,
All she possess'd; and, in her rosy chain,
The sage and hero each might have been proud,
And monarchs link'd, before her beauty bow'd.
To see her, love her, feel the kindling fire,
The ardent flame, the soft, the fond desire.
To tremble and regard with dove-like eyes,
To strive to speak and utter nought but sighs,
Her hands, with a caressing hand to hold,
Till panting all the flames her breast enfold."[1]

Translation by W. H. IRELAND.

Vallet de Viriville maintained that those who loved France loved Agnes Sorel, and that those who despised and hated her also despised and hated their country.   Among the latter were the

[1]   *   *   *   *   *   *

"Jamais l'Amour ne forma rien de tel.
Imaginez de Flore la jeunesse,
La taille et l'air de la nymphe des bois,
Et de Vénus la grâce enchanteresse,
Et de l'Amour le séduisant minois,
L'art d'Arachné, le doux chant des sirènes:
Elle avait tout; elle aurait dans ses chaînes
Mis les héros, les sages, et les rois.
La voir, l'aimer, sentir l'ardeur naissante
Des doux désirs, et leur chaleur brûlante,
Lorgner Agnès, soupirer et trembler,
Perdre la voix en voulant lui parler,
Presser ses mains d'une main caressante,
Laisser briller sa flamme impatiente,
Montrer son trouble, en causer à son tour,
Lui plaire enfin, fut l'affaire d'un jour."

Burgundian chroniclers, who received favours from Philippe de Bourgogne and the dauphin. These writers who condemned Agnes said evil also of Jeanne d'Arc.

One author drew a picture of the Lady of Beauty seated in her boudoir, working diligently at a tapestry which represented Jeanne d'Arc entering Orleans. The idea of the king's mistress labouring to depict in wool-work the woman who by her inspiration and virtue had won for the king the freedom of his kingdom—and this in order to give pleasure to her royal lover—is quite idyllic. Unfortunately, however, such a piece of tapestry has never been known to exist except in the imagination.

Nevertheless, the flagrant inaccuracies and contradictory assertions about Agnes have failed to this day to crush the legendary part of her story, and it has even gathered beauty with the passing of the centuries.

All that belonged to her, her castles and lands, her house at Orleans,[1] the Abbey of Jumièges graced by her presence, the walls over which she

---

[1] In the Rue du Tabour is a house which tradition attaches to the name of the Lady of Beauty. Its wide stone frontage is pierced by ornamented windows. The front door folds back in the fashion frequently found in this city. Before it are pillars, and the top of it is adorned with figures which represented the triumph of Charles VII, or the triumph of Love.

Within is a courtyard, round which an arcade is built, with more carved pillars and the medallion of Charles VII. Female heads, daintily portrayed, may or may not have represented Agnes.

peeped, the towers from which she gazed forth, the bridges she crossed, the alleys she wandered down, the battles to which she urged the soldiers, the jousting at which she clapped her hands in glee, the gowns and jewels she wore, the portraits that more or less misrepresented her beauty; in short, all that was hers and all that was said to be hers, is wrapped in a glamour of romance which is as real and living as it is illogical and indefensible.

There is one pretty scene in the *Romance of the French Abbeys* [1] which cannot be spoilt by the fact that it is purely imaginary. It takes place between the young Charles and Agnes at Jumièges in the days when Nicolas Leroux, of Jeanne d'Arc fame, was Abbot there.

During a hunt in the forest the prince's pony was lamed, and this accident took place near the Manor of Mesnil. A servant was sent to the stables to see what could be done, and he received the offer to lend Charles Agnes's own palfrey, which was wild and untamed. Seeing its mettle the prince feared to mount until Agnes, then a mere slip of a girl, sprang to the side of her pet, quieted it by a word and a pat, swung herself on to the horse's bare back and rode round the orchard. Charles regarded her with mingled shame and admiration.

" You need not fear to ride my palfrey now," she said, dismounting near him.

" Nay," he replied, " I do not fear to do that which a maid can do."

[1] By Elizabeth W. Champney. Putnam's Sons, 1905.

When he looked at her he saw she had not meant to ridicule him, and his ill-temper vanished. He added, more pleasantly, " I mean, pretty damsel, that if you will show me the way I will do anything you please."

Before the prince left the Abbey he managed a meeting with Agnes to bid her farewell.

" Sweet mistress," he said, " will you not leave this wild forest and dwell at court ? "

But she shook her head and said sagely, " The court is more dangerous for maids than the forest for princes." And so they parted, but Charles promised to return.

Agnes remained at Mesnil, and one day Leroux told her that he was going to Rouen to take part in the trial of Jeanne d'Arc.

Agnes was overjoyed. " You will save her," she exclaimed, " even as she saved France. For after the victory at Orleans and the crowning of Charles, the safety of the country is assured. But where is the king ? He boasted he could do anything a maid could do. Why did he not follow Jeanne's teaching ? "

" Pardon, sweet mistress," said the Abbot, " the young king said he would do anything—if you would but show him the way."

Lady Agnes laughed. " Ma foi, he has better councillors than I, and if he be so slothful and will not heed the voice of his own heart, he would assuredly not listen to me. Go forth, Lord Abbot, and champion the saviour of France."

And thus encouraged Nicolas Leroux set forth

on the journey which was to bring him much shame, for he helped in the awful condemnation which led to the death of the Maid.

When he reached Jumièges once more, Agnes on her white palfrey was waiting at the landing-stage where his barge arrived after its journey down the river.

" What tidings of the Maid, my Lord Abbot ? " she cried as she greeted him.

And when he told his news her indignation knew no bounds. " You who call yourself a man suffered this ? " she cried in a passion. " And the king ? Did he raise no hand to rescue one so valiant and fair ? Oh shame ! Since manhood is dead, France must be saved by its womanhood."

And so she left him, and for many years the manor-house at Mesnil knew her no more. But the two were to meet once again after a long interval when province after province had been won back from the English, and the King of France had earned the name of the Victorious.

At the time of the Conquest of Normandy, the poor half-crazed Leroux, who had never forgotten the stench of the burning pyre on which Jeanne d'Arc had been done to death, set eyes once more on his king.

And by his side, fair and buxom, her gown glittering with jewels and her horse dressed in rich trappings, rode the king's mistress, in whom the Abbot was startled to recognise the little country maid he had known as Agnes Sorel.

She looked at Leroux gravely, and his eyes fell before hers.

" The work you hindered is nearly done," she said simply.   That was all.

G

CHAPTER IX

THE REAL AGNES

In 1444 Agnes Sorel emerged from the mists of legend and became a personality to be reckoned with in the works of the gravest historians. Historical documents throwing light on her position and her whereabouts are dated in that year.

The passion that had been drawing the king and the Lady of Beauty more and more closely together was openly admitted. Agnes was acknowledged at court. She had her own residences, her own income, a large retinue of servants and ladies, beautiful gowns and superb jewels. She reigned not only in the king's heart, but as a personal power in the land.

Courtiers and chroniclers, the noble ladies of France and the queen herself were aware of a fact which had only been hinted at previously. There may have been gossip, there must have been shrewd guesses, but the king's secret had been so carefully guarded that never a written word had revealed it.

The first episode of the great passion was closed, the second and more public part was about to begin. The sweetness of secret love had become the triumph of mutual passion.

For the woman it is a triumph with bitterness in it, a triumph that may turn at any moment to shame and despair.

Her compensation must be found in the fact that her lover is of the highest possible rank, that her position is unique and cannot be disputed.

The chroniclers began to devote their attention to the favourite in 1444. Thomas Basin, Bishop of Lisieux, declared that Agnes came into favour " at the time of the truce between France and England." [1] The truce was concluded on May 28 of that year.

Olivier de la Marche [2] referring to the voyage of the Duchesse de Bourgogne to Châlons in June, 1445, wrote that the king " had recently raised up a poor girl, a gentlewoman called Agnès du Soret, and put her in a position of such triumph and such power that her station might be compared to that of the great princesses of the kingdom.

" In faith," he went on, " she was one of the most beautiful women that I have ever seen : and she did, according to her station, much good to the kingdom of France. She advanced in the king's favour young men-at-arms and gentle companions by whom the king was afterwards well served."

To Monstrelet's successor we owe the information that the loveliest lady in the world was called

---

[1] Thomas Basin in *Histoire des règnes de Charles VII et de Louis XI*, published by Quicherat.

[2] *Mémoires.*

G 2

" damoyselle de Beaulté " because the king had
bestowed upon her the Château de Beauté.
This castle was near Vincennes, and was described
in the *Journal d'un Bourgeois de Paris* as " the
most charming and lovely and the best-situated
that there was in the whole of the Ile de France."
It had been a royal residence since the early
days of monarchy.

In 1489, during the troubled times following
on civil warfare, it fell into the hands of the Duc
de Bourbon, but was retaken by the Comte de
Richemont and thus was once more owned by
the king. That he bestowed it upon Agnes, and
that she took her title from it in or before the
year 1444, is confirmed by an inscription which
accompanied her gift of an image of Saint Mary
Magdalen which she gave to the Church of
Loches.[1] It ran: " In honour of and reverence
for Saint Mary Magdalen, the noble lady,
Mademoiselle de Beaulté has given the image in
this church of the Castle of Loches, in which
image is enclosed a rib and the hair of the said
saint, and it was the year fourteen hundred and
forty-four." [2]

The evidence contained in these documents
was confirmed by one of the contemporary
authorities, Jean Chartier, who said that Agnes
at the time of her death had been in the service
of Marie d'Anjou for five years or thereabouts,
" where she had enjoyed all kinds of worldly
delights and all the amusements and pleasures

[1] Charles VII was canon of Loches.
[2] La Thaumassière, *l'Histoire de Berry.*

imaginable. That is to say that she wore grand and extravagant clothes, had superb gowns, furs, necklaces of gold and of jewels, and possessed all other desirable and charming things, being herself young and beautiful.

"On this account it was commonly reported that the king maintained her in concubinage; for to-day the world is more inclined to think and speak evil than good."

Whatever Chartier may have thought, the fifteenth century was not the only uncharitable one, though people at that date had good cause to look askance at their neighbours' deeds. His position as historiographer to Charles VII made it expedient for Chartier to refute the scandals that were rife, and he did it with so much will as to defeat his own ends.

"For this reason," he continued, "I desire to write the truth and have taken great pains to reveal the inaccuracy and to obtain the exact verity of this affair. And I have discovered, as much from the tale of knights, squires, councillors, physicians, doctors and surgeons, as from the report of others of diverse estate, who have been examined on oath, as is the rule of my office, in order to disperse and remove the wrongful statements of the people, that during the said five years in which the lady in question has remained in the queen's household, it is said that the king never omitted to remain by the queen's side and has had many beautiful children by her.

"It was often quite against his wish that the said Agnes held such high estate, but this was the queen's pleasure, and so he procrastinated as much as he could, even though he recognised and perceived that the matter did not redound to his credit and was opprobrious. And those questioned said also that when the king went to see the ladies, or if the belle Agnes came to see him in the absence of the queen, he always had a large number of persons present, and no one had ever seen him touch her below the chin. Every one returned to his apartments each evening after the usual sober amusements instituted by the king, and Agnes went likewise to hers. The king's affection in this quarter, as every one said, was on account of the follies of her youthfulness, the enjoyment and gaiety she evinced, as well as for the virtuous and polished speech she employed, and also that, among the fair, she was the youngest and most beautiful in the world, and as such she was regarded.

"Nor was it likely that the king was behaving or had behaved in such manner, for during the period he had practised and restored justice which had previously perished, he had removed every pillory from the kingdom, had provided against dissension in the universal Church, so that peace, unity and happy concord were observed as the result of his actions.

"Wherefore God desired to recompense him by the recovery of his country of Normandy, occupied and violently and unlawfully retained by his former enemies, the English. And thereupon he reconquered in two years as much as the said English had originally won for themselves in the space of thirty years.

"And those making deposition also declared that the said Agnes had always lived a very charitable life, had given liberal alms, so long as they had known her, and distributed her goods freely to the poor churches and to the order of mendicant friars, and if she had had carnal relations with the king, which no one could believe, such a thing having been cautiously carried on and in secret, she being then in the service of the Queen of Sicily, that is to say before she had passed into the queen's household with whom she had lived for some years.

"It was true that the said Agnes had a daughter who only lived a short while, and whom she wanted to make out was the daughter of the king, as was the most likely thing to say, but the king always denied it."

And his historian was evidently advised to do the same.

On the other hand, Georges Chastellain, the chronicler, who held the appointment of *indiciaire* in the household of the dukes of Burgundy, had nothing to say in extenuation of the king's conduct, and he doubtless represented a large class of people who refused to condone profligacy or extravagance.

He declared that the king was utterly infatuated by the Lady of Beauty, and "was put to great and innumerable charges against his honour, and he was seriously to blame for the footing on which he placed her; for in Christendom there had never been princesses so richly garbed, nor who kept up such state.

"From all quarters a hundred murmurs were heard against her and not less against the king. She wore trains a third longer than any princess of the realm, had a larger wardrobe by half, and more expensive gowns.

"She had her apartments in the king's hôtel better furnished and appointed than the queen herself. She was served by a bevy of women, many more in number than hers. She had all the estate and royal formalities for herself as though she were actually queen; finer bed-hangings, more beautiful tapestry, finer linen and covers, more valuable dishes, richer rings and jewels, a better kitchen department and everything else to match, and she expected the queen to suffer her to sit at her table and do her honour."

Then he went on to describe the unusual daring of the clothes she wore, which she designed herself and had specially produced. She wore her shoulders bare as well as her bosom, in the most unsuitable fashion. She studied vanities night and day, and generally endeavoured to corrupt the morals of both men and women.

It would have been as well, perhaps, if Chastellain, chronicler of the notorious duke who had twenty-four mistresses and countless bastards, had begun his crusade against immorality at home, or had taken to heart Chartier's remarks about those who preferred to think and write evil rather than good. His testimony also is of very little value where dates are concerned, the matter of interest regarding Agnes Sorel which is most debated.

Jacques du Clercq, who lived at Arras in the last half of the fifteenth century, wrote that before the peace with Philippe de Bourgogne the king " led a very saintly life and never failed to recite his office." But since the Peace of Arras had been signed in September, 1485, although he continued in the service of God, he had a love affair with a young woman, who came from a little spot near Thour, called Agnes, who since then has been called lovely Agnes. No great importance can be attached to this historian's statements, and the same may be said to apply to the " Commentaries " by Æneas Sylvius, who later became Pope Pius II, in which the author wrote that Agnes Sorel accompanied her mistress Isabelle to court, and that the latter on departing left Agnes behind among the queen's ladies, in spite of a certain rumour that she had a bad reputation. The uncertainty lies in the fact that Pius II referred to Isabelle's journey from Marseilles in October, 1485, and there is no evidence that she was at the French court about that date.

" As she possessed extraordinary beauty," continued the author, " and most charming conversation, the king fell in love with her. In a very short time he was so madly infatuated that he could not be without her for an hour. She was always admitted to his presence whether he was at table, in the council, or in his private apartments."

One of the most important documents relating to Agnes is the wages list of the ladies and officials of the Queen of Sicily, wife of René d'Anjou, for the six months ending July, 1444,[1] on which her name appears :

Madame Marie de Maillé, damoiselle de Montejan.	lx	Livres
Madame Jehanne de Manonville, damoiselle de Beauveau	lx	,,
Madame de Coudray	xxv	,,
Isabeau de Lenoure	xii	,, x s.
Phelice Charno	xvi	,, x s.
Catherine de Serrière	xx	,,
Catherine de Serancourt	xv	,,
Goffeline Garelle	xv	,,
Odille	xii	,, x s.
Jacquette Chanteur	xii	,, x s.
Lyonne	xv	,,
La nourrice de la bastarde de Mons. le Comte du Maine	vi	,,
Agnès Sorelle (dix livres)	x	,,
Jehanne Girante	x	,,
Barbeline, premiere damoiselle d'honneur de la reyne d'Angleterre . . .	xv	,,
Hervée, l'une de ses damoiselles . . .	vi	,,

It is a strange thing that Agnes, who had already borne a daughter to Charles VII, should appear upon a list of Isabelle's household accounts among maids-of-honour and servants for a sum so small as ten livres. While the document throws an important light on dates, it nevertheless adds confusion to the position of affairs. Is it possible that as Agnes is mentioned with those

---

[1] Published by Vallet de Viriville, *Bibliothèque de l'École des Chartes*, Series 8, Vol. I. Paris, 1849, p. 804.

who served Marguerite d'Anjou (the negotiations for whose marriage with Henry VI began in May, 1444), and as she was known to be temporarily attached to the princess's retinue, the sum was in payment of some service done for her ?

This point cannot be determined, but it is clear at all events that Agnes, from being an insignificant nobody in the household of Isabelle de Lorraine, had emerged slowly through a chrysalis stage of secret love-making into the full glare of official favouritism.

Life had changed for her since the day when she had been beholden to the extent of ten livres on the bounty of the duchess. Now she had only to ask to receive many hundreds, nay, if she cared for them, thousands of livres and all other worldly goods her heart might desire.

CHAPTER X

THE COURT AT TOURS

FROM 1444 onwards Agnes was never far from court, and she accompanied the king on his journeys.

Charles had mastered the indignities that had been heaped upon him as Kinglet of Bourges. A truce was declared, and with truce came a time of pleasure and prosperity.

A passage in *Le Jouvencel* [1] pictured the terrors that were passing away. The country had been *moult dessolé et desert.* There had been war for a long time, and the people had grown very poor and were scattered far and wide. Their dwelling-places seemed more like receptacles for savage beasts than habitations fit for human beings.

Some time passed before a sense of security followed on the incessant miseries and perils of warfare, but at last a change for the better was noticeable throughout the kingdom. People flocked back to the villages, agriculture began afresh, trade was brisk, and it was possible to find life pleasant once more. Nowhere was this

[1] *Le Jouvencel,* par Jean de Bueil, Vol. I. p. 19 (Société de l'Histoire de France), 1887–89.

revival of confidence more apparent than at court, where poverty and hardships had been the chief characteristics of the reign.

Charles had done his best to draw up a final treaty of peace with England, but finding, on May 20, that any conclusive agreement was out of the question, he gave power to his pleni-potentiaries to sign a truce.

A preliminary contract was made with the king's consent on May 22, between the King of Sicily and the English ambassadors, stipulating the conditions of the marriage between Henry VI of England and René's daughter, Marguerite d'Anjou.

The betrothal took place on May 24, and four days later the Treaty of Tours was signed, which established peace temporarily from June 1, 1444, until April 1, 1446.

During these negotiations special entertainments and the hospitalities which usually accompanied diplomatic conferences were showered upon the English visitors.

Suffolk's embassy landed at Harfleur on March 18. Conferences were opened at Vendôme on April 8, and a week later Suffolk was at Blois, where he met the Duc d'Orléans, who was interested in the bringing about of the proposed marriage.

From Blois the ambassadors took boat upon the Loire, and, landing at Tours, were presented on April 17 to Charles, whose court was then at Montils-les-Tours.

They were received with the affability and

graciousness which had gained for the King of France a certain renown.

The assembly at the palace was a notable one. Suffolk had been accompanied by the Comte de Dunois as well as the duke. The King of Sicily, with his son, Jean d'Anjou, Duc de Calabre, was there in his capacity of father of the bride, and he was supported by many brilliant personages, among them his brother, the Comte du Maine, and the Comte de Vendôme.

The Connétable, Arthur de Richemont, had unexpectedly brought his nephew, the Duc de Bretagne. The Duc de Bourgogne, who was represented by the ambassadors, was not present in person, but the Duc d'Alençon, the Comte d'Étampes, and many other important people were there.

The beautiful and high-born ladies must not be forgotten. The Queen of France was the central figure, and by her side was the gentle dauphine, Margaret of Scotland, who had been married to the dauphin many years before. Among the queen's forty ladies was the most beautiful woman in the kingdom, the fair Agnes. Every eye was turned upon her, for the king's secret was known to all.

On May-Day a picnic was organised, and all the lords and ladies, to the number of many hundreds, set forth from the castle to gather boughs of the may-tree, symbolic of the coming spring. The queen and the dauphine rode on horseback, and were followed by three hundred *galants*, nobles and men-at-arms.

Joyous, though wearied, the tuneful merry-makers returned as the twilight fell, laughing, singing and bearing the burden of sweet-scented flowers. The king rode beside his mistress, lagging behind all the rest, and he whispered in her ear that the fairness of the white blossom was as nothing compared to her fairness, and that the scent of the petals was not half so intoxicating as the scent of her hair.

She laughed in reply and teased him for a flatterer, and for a time they forgot the cares of the world and the burdens of kingship.

Three days after this excursion the duchess-queen, Isabelle, in company with her daughter Marguerite, left Angers and settled in a part of the Abbaye de Beaumont, about a league from Tours. The English ambassadors hastened thither to pay their respects to the young princess whom they had come to fetch to be their king's bride.

For a short time Agnes Sorel was attached to the household of the Queen of England, as Marguerite was already styled.

Before the final conditions of the great wedding could be decided upon a less important one took place between the Comte du Maine and Isabelle de Luxembourg, who was the sister of the Comte de Saint-Pol. This event was made the occasion of tournaments and feasting. The king, his fair mistress, and all the court were present to witness a joust, arranged by Suffolk and Pierre de Brézé, between the French archers and the English archers. The prize of a thousand crowns was won by the Scottish Guards.

From pleasures it was necessary to revert to business.[1]

Suffolk was charmed with the young Marguerite, who was then just fifteen years of age. Her youth had not been without vicissitudes.

During the absence of her father and mother she had been brought up by her grandmother, Yolande d'Aragon, chiefly in Anjou.[2] She was first betrothed to the Comte de Saint-Pol, then to the Comte de Charolais, son of the Duc de Bourgogne, then to the Comte de Nevers. After these false attempts to climb the matrimonial ladder, it was proposed that she should acquire a royal crown by marrying the King of England. She thus became a political pawn in the game of truce which the two countries were playing. At the same time she offended the sense of national patriotism, and risked being utterly estranged from her family.

On May 24, Suffolk, as proxy for Henry VI, was betrothed formally to Isabelle's daughter in the Church of Saint Martin at Tours.

Charles VII, hand in hand with his brother-in-law René, marched up the aisle, followed by the Duc d'Alençon, the Duc de Bretagne, and

[1] The plenipotentiaries who treated with the English ambassadors were the Duc d'Orléans, the Comte de Vendôme, Pierre de Brézé and Bertrand de Beauvau. Regnault de Chartres, the Chancellor of France, had died suddenly at the beginning of April.

[2] As already stated, no one has suggested that Agnes was left behind with Marguerite. This seems more likely than that Isabelle took her to Naples, and might explain how it was that money was owed to her by the House of Lorraine after she was the king's mistress.

[To face p. 96

RENÉ D'ANJOU

other princes of the blood. The queen followed, hand in hand with Isabelle, and escorted by the dauphine and the Duchesse de Calabre, René's daughter-in-law.

Then came the young bride, on the right the dauphin Louis, on the left her uncle, the Comte Maine.

So she was led before the king.

Charles, removing his cap, took Marguerite's hand and conducted her to where the papal legate stood waiting to pronounce a provisional dispensation. Future husband and wife were closely related, and the actual dispensation enabling them to marry could not be obtained without a long delay.

After certain questions had been asked, and satisfactorily answered, Suffolk was pronounced to be betrothed to Marguerite in lieu of the English king. Then the people pressed round the altar and burst into transports of noisy joy. They clapped their hands and cried " Noël, Noël."

The timid Marie d'Anjou had so far played no part in this gorgeous ceremonial. Now she took the future Queen of England by the hand and led her to a place on the right of her mother, Isabelle.

From that moment Marguerite was treated as though she were in reality Queen of England, and the equal of the Queen of France.

A procession was formed, and the guests made their way to the Abbaye de Saint-Julien, where a banquet awaited them. The two queens were

H

served simultaneously with each dish as it appeared.

Entertainments and dancing followed. A curious masquerade was performed by two giants holding trees in their hands, followed by camels bearing towers on their backs containing men-at-arms, who did battle with lances. The French, in those days, loved an element of the grotesque in their pageants.

Dancing was prolonged to so late an hour as to be *intempestive*, or unwholesome, and then every one rode home to bed.

This was the most important court ceremony at which Agnes had been present since she was acknowledged *maîtresse en titre*.

On the 28th the truce was signed, and the following day the English ambassadors started on their way to England.

Suffolk's progress was one continued triumph. Everywhere he was hailed with the rapturous shouts of "Noël, Noël," already heard at the church during the betrothal. He reached London on June 27, and temporary peace was ratified immediately. His reward was a marquisate.

The real marriage did not take place until the following year, and, in the meantime, various changes had taken place at the Court of France.

CHAPTER XI

THE COURT AT NANCY

THE alterations in the *personnel* at court were perhaps not unconnected with the growing influence of the Lady of Beauty.

In the autumn of 1448, while the king was at Saumur, Pierre de Brézé, Jamet du Tillay and Jean de Maupas became members of the Government, whilst Admiral de Coëtivy was dismissed from court. The princes of the blood grumbled at the ascendancy which these newcomers obtained over the king's actions. Certain letters written by the Comte d'Angoulême, who had been a prisoner in English hands since his youth, referred to this discontent. The release of the French captive had been under consideration at Rouen before Suffolk left there on his way to England. Pierre de Brézé and Jean Havart had been despatched on a special embassy to treat with the English on this and other important matters.

Pierre de Brézé, who was Agnes's friend and one of the men of the moment, was born about 1410, and in his youth became an attendant upon René d'Anjou and his mother. He was related to Jean de Bueil and with him learned military tactics in the struggles against England in Maine, Touraine and Anjou. He gained some fame as a soldier. In 1433, in company with Jean de Bueil and Prégent de Coëtivy, he was instrumental in helping Yolande d'Aragon and Richemont in bringing about the downfall of La Trémouille. This *révolution de palais* gave him his first step in a successful career. The House of Anjou and the Connétable were now growing powerful at court. Brézé knew how to take advantage of every opportunity.

From 1436 onwards he had a place in the king's council. The following year he won renown at the siege of Montereau, and was made Seneschal of Anjou and Governor of the Castle of Angers.

He strengthened his alliance with the nobility of Anjou by arranging a marriage between his sister and Bertrand de Beauvau, one of the king's chief councillors. During the Praguerie Brézé won the king's gratitude and the undying hatred of the dauphin, by taking a prominent part against the troops of the latter. From 1442 he advanced by leaps and bounds in the king's favour, thanks, it has been said by some of his biographers, to the influence of Agnes Sorel.

From 1444 to the time of her death, except for one short interval, he held a principal place in the Government, which he owed, no doubt, to his masterly statesmanship. He took part in the negotiations for the marriage of Henry VI with Marguerite d'Anjou, and later accompanied the king to Metz, and helped to bring about peace after the conclusion of the campaign in 1445.

The dauphin had left court early in June to lead an army against the Swiss. A month later Charles departed from Montils-les-Tours for an expedition in the East. Pierre de Brézé accompanied him in the capacity of lieutenant of the king. The flower of the nobility composed the expedition. René and the Comte du Maine, the Comte de Vendôme, Richemont, the Duc de Calabre, La Fayette, Marshal of France, André de Laval, who was also a marshal, Prégent de Coëtivy, the treasurer Jean Bureau, Bertrand de Beauvau, the dauphine's friend Jean d'Estouteville, her enemy Jamet du Tillay, and a number of others set forth on the campaign, which had for its purpose the subjugation and unification of the country between Tours and Metz. Passing by way of Orleans, Troyes, Montargis, Bar-sur-Aube and Chaumont, Charles traversed the country of Jeanne d'Arc, Pierre de Brézé bringing several towns under the royal protection by the way.

For three or four months this successful progress through the country continued, and on September 20 Charles arrived at Nancy, where he installed his court during the operations of the siege.

From the moment of the arrival in the capital of Lorraine the warlike attitude of the nobles gave way once again to a mood of festivity and amusement.

René d'Anjou, the fifteenth-century master of pageantry, could not welcome his brother-in-law, the King of France, as his guest without making the most of his opportunity for display and entertainment.

For a long time royalty had been deprived of pomps and ceremonies. Lean years had made simplicity a feature of court life, and the necessity of moving from place to place had deprived it of the formalities and etiquette usual to the surroundings of a throne. At certain intervals fêtes had to be held, for instance, at Easter, Pentecost, All-Hallows and Christmas.

At these seasons a full court assembled—*cour plénière*, as it was called—and all the princes, nobles and fine ladies gathered in solemn concourse. This was the time for a general distribution of court robes. There was much feasting, dancing and pantomime. The women exhibited their most valuable jewels, and the men were almost as much curled, scented and bedizened as the fairer sex.

Even the poor had a share in the festivities, for they were invited into the halls to watch their betters feed, and to scramble for the liberal gifts of money which accompanied the cries of "Largesse! Largesse! Largesse!" Nor were they the only recipients of the king's bounty, for all the guests received fine presents, and no king was more generous to his favourites than Charles when he had land or other property to bestow.

For the first time in his difficult reign the king was able to enjoy the splendours of a royal residence, to carry out the traditions of courtly life in the most extravagant manner, and to realise that the prestige of a great and powerful crown was his once more.

Round the throne a very brilliant throng gathered. In all France there could not have been a greater show of splendour than was to be found in the union of the king's court and that of Lorraine. Charles and René were delighted to have a large number of charming and well-dressed ladies present. Henri Baude said of the King of France that he loved ladies " en toute honnêteté et portoit honneur à toutes femmes." Moreover, at this date, " les dames avoient bruit en France et loy d'elles monstrer," as Olivier de la Marche expressed it.

This was the hour at which Agnes Sorel, according to some authorities, was transferred from the Lorraine household to that of the queen.

Marie d'Anjou was now in her fortieth year. She was not strong, and owing to the number of her children she had been compelled to live a somewhat retired life. The loss of several of her babies had saddened her. The recent death of her mother had still further enhanced her natural melancholy. Her two chief interests were to read books of piety and to make frequent pilgrimages to holy shrines. The most human bond which united her to this earth was her love for her eldest son, Louis. Usually she dressed in black, and during the forty years of her married life she appears to have been the good-natured but colourless individual her childhood had foreshadowed.

A year had passed since the birth of her little

daughter Madeleine, and in that year she learnt for certain that her husband had left her for a younger and far more attractive woman. But she did not show resentment. In her heart no doubt she grieved, but outwardly she was always kind and gracious to the maid-of-honour who had usurped her rightful place.

Another gentle but more charming personality was the dauphine,[1] Margaret of Scotland. Betrothed to Louis at the age of three, when still in her native country, she had travelled to France some nine years later and been brought up in the charge of Marie d'Anjou. She was described as beautiful and of a good figure, gifted with all the charms that should naturally belong to a lady of high rank. But there was a pathetic note in her life. Her tastes were not shared by the dauphin, and he never bestowed upon her the faintest semblance of affection. She loved poetry and art, whilst her husband dreamed of nothing but his ambitions and his chances of personal advancement.

A well-known legend is told of a kiss she gave to Alain Chartier. When discovered in such an unconventional act she said hastily, " I did not intend the caress for the man himself, but for the precious lips which have uttered so many beautiful and virtuous phrases."

The queen and the dauphine joined the king at Nancy towards the close of the year. The latter had with her her women, Jeanne Filleul and Marguerite de Salignac. The cultivated

[1] See *The Dauphines of France*, pp. 66–85.

Prégente de Melun, one of the queen's maids-of-honour, was her friend and composed rondeaux for her pleasure. It was said that Agnes, too, was able to write little poems, and, if so, her gaiety and wit must have recommended her to the dauphine's notice; but, on the other hand, Margaret did not approve of the easy morals of the day. She had an uncompromising sense of honour and purity. When by the intrigue of vulgar courtiers a breath of scandal touched her own name she suffered deeply and faded away into a decline. Perhaps, however, she refused to listen to gossip about one whom she met every day in close intimacy, as she must at this time have met the Lady of Beauty. Perhaps she accepted Agnes as a young and lovely woman whom she pitied for being led by others into dubious paths. Perhaps in her heart of hearts she envied her the happiness of being loved, a happiness which was denied to herself. None can tell what passed between these two young women, who, in spite of frequent intercourse, were as wide as the poles asunder.

The days passed pleasantly at Nancy that autumn, and preparations for the wedding of Marguerite d'Anjou went on apace.

On November 5, Suffolk left London once more. Accompanied this time by his wife and a retinue of lords and ladies, he made his way straight to Nancy. Oddly enough, Isabelle and her daughter were not there to receive them. No doubt it was more impressive to arrive later and separately. They had left Saumur together on November 8, and then mother and daughter parted, the former reaching Nancy in December, the latter not till February. Marguerite was attended by Bertrand de Beauvau, by Moreau, René's treasurer, and by other councillors.

The central figure of the assembly was, of course, the bride, who was just sixteen, and who was described by Chastellain as " un des beaux personnages du monde représentant dame."

Among the English nobility were Lady Suffolk, Lady Elizabeth Grey, Lady Elizabeth Hall, Beatrice, Lady Talbot, Emma, Lady Scales, Lord Clifford, Lord Greystock, Sir Richard Roos, Sir Robert Harcourt and Sir Hugh Cokesey. They were accompanied by a bishop, four chamberlains, fifty squires, and one hundred and eighty attendants.

The ceremony was solemnised by Louis de Harancourt, Bishop of Toul, and was followed by festivities which lasted for a week and included every form of gaiety. A joust occupied four days, and the most prominent exponents of the art were the Duc de Calabre, the Comte de Saint-Pol, de Beauvau and Pierre de Brézé.

René entered the lists and vanquished King Charles, who bore on his shield the serpent of Melusina. The Comte du Maine, uncle of the bride, particularly distinguished himself in the field.

Bertrand de la Tour entered the lists preceded by André de Laval, and followed by Coëtivy and Saintrailles. He rode a magnificent charger, caparisoned in cloth of gold and ornamented

with little golden bells. The ten gentlemen
who rode with him were dressed in white satin,
and they fought a dozen bouts, three against
Pierre de Brézé, three against the Comte de
Saint-Pol, and six against Jacques de Lalaing.[1]

Many of the knights wore garlands of daisies,
the modest flower being the emblem of the fair
Marguerite. Marie d'Anjou and Isabelle de
Lorraine bestowed the prizes upon the victors.

But the real Queen of Beauty was Agnes,
rejoicing in her new lands and new title.
According to the romantic account of Barante
she appeared that day in a fanciful riding-habit,
which was blazing with jewels, and was made
in the style of a man's suit of armour. She rode
a fine horse with rich trappings. At that date
such horses were very valuable, and a gentleman who possessed the best *chevaux de
parage* was very proud of his equipment.

[1] The chroniclers have given rather confused accounts
of the jousts which took place in 1445 at Nancy, at Châlons,
and at Montils. The passage-at-arms described by Jacques
de Lalaing probably took place at Châlons and not at Nancy,
in spite of the accounts of the *Livre des faits de Jacques de
Lalaing* and of Olivier de la Marche. Lalaing gave an
account of jousts taking place at Nancy on June 10, 1444.
This year is inadmissible, and on June 10, 1445, the
king was at Châlons. It was improbable that a second series
of fêtes took place at Nancy after those at the marriage of
Marguerite d'Anjou. For one thing, René accompanied his
daughter to Bar-le-Duc, and only rejoined Charles VII at
Châlons. The queen left Nancy at the end of April, and
news of Radegonde's death at Tours on March 18 arrived
at that time. The Comte d'Angoulême was said to be
present, but he had only been released at the beginning of
April, 1445, and he could not have reached Nancy. He met
the king at Châlons.

According to Olivier de la Marche no one spoke of selling a good animal unless he could get an enormous price for it. The horse Agnes rode was priceless.

All the men admired the laughing, joyous face of the king's mistress, and the ladies envied her her rich clothes and the vast amount of attention she received. But that did not save her from ill-natured remarks, and there were many who whispered about her anomalous position.

But though her presence may not have gladdened the hearts of the virtuous matrons who beheld her—they would not have missed the sight for worlds—it certainly added to the splendour of the scene. There was no doubt in any mind about that.

Of the well-known people present, two or three took but little part in the warlike games. Suffolk, who was no longer a young man, thought his share of the proceedings ended after he had arranged the marriage. He refused to enter the lists against the gay young French sparks who knew every trick of the tourney and the joust.

The dauphin indulged in one of the fits of sulks to which he occasionally gave way. According to one account he had fallen ill at Nancy, and was thus debarred from taking a part in the rougher sport.

Ferry de Lorraine, the son of Antoine de Vaudémont, was very preoccupied during these events. His story provided the underlying note of human interest to a scene of pageantry where people are not supposed to give way to their personal feelings because the occasion is a purely public one. Ferry had been in love with his cousin Yolande for nine long years.

King René, full of animosity against his one-time enemy, was strenuously opposed to a marriage between de Vaudémont's son and his own eldest daughter. But the lovers enlisted the sympathy of some of the adventuresome young cavaliers, and a secret marriage was arranged which threatened to break up the harmony of the gaieties at Nancy, had it not been for the timely intervention of Charles VII and Marie d'Anjou, who insisted on a general reconciliation.

So with ballets in which princes and princesses took the chief parts, with a *basse danse de Bourgogne* in which Isabelle de Lorraine, the Duchesse de Calabre, the dauphine and the Duc de Bourbon danced the varied figures, with pastoral banquets and concerts arranged by troubadours and *jongleurs*, the week at length came to an end, and the hour struck when the Queen of England's departure for her adopted country could be delayed no longer.

Charles VII accompanied her two leagues out of Nancy, and her father went as far as Bar-le-Duc. Tearfully the young queen proceeded on her way in the care of Lord and Lady Suffolk, tearfully the King of France and the King of Sicily returned to the court that had been so gay. Charles embraced his niece several times, and his parting words were, " I am doing little for you, my daughter, in placing you on one of the greatest thrones of Europe, since there are none worthy of possessing you." They never met on earth again.

Marguerite arrived at Paris on March 15, and a few days later spent a night at the château at Vernon, of which Agnes Sorel was soon to be in possession. The entry into Rouen on March 28 was made in triumph. On April 22 Marguerite's marriage with Henry VI was solemnised in England, and the queen was crowned at Westminster on May 80.

From the affairs of the Lady of Beauty her one-time mistress was severed. Yet one link in later days connects them. When after eighteen years of anguish and misfortune the Queen of England journeyed to France to beg for help from Louis XI, or from her father and her brother, her own people utterly failed her in her adversity. But a friend of Agnes, Pierre de Brézé, who had broken a lance for her at Nancy on her wedding day, enlisted in her service with two thousand followers. By that time Agnes was dead and Brézé's son was married to the Lady of Beauty's daughter.

CHAPTER XII

THE COURT AT CHÂLONS

THE tears that Charles VII had shed at parting with Marguerite d'Anjou, not far from Nancy, were followed by tears more bitter still only a few days later, when the news came from Tours that his eldest daughter, Radegonde de France, was dead. Born at Chinon in 1428, Radegonde was betrothed at the age of two to Sigismond of Austria. Her death at the age of seventeen overwhelmed her parents with grief, and even Agnes was unable to bring consolation to the heart of her royal lover in this unexpected trouble.

At the close of April a move was made from Nancy, where many emotions grave and gay had been lived through. The queen with the dauphin and dauphine went to Châlons, where they arrived on May 4. The king joined them on the 29th. He had broken his journey at Toul, at Commercy, at Louppy-le-Château and other places. Agnes being one of the queen's ladies ought to have accompanied her mistress, but the détour made by Charles was not a long one, and probably she accompanied her lover.

The king stayed at Sarry-les-Châlons in the bishop's residence there. He was very busy indeed with affairs of war, and he entertained a number of foreign envoys and ambassadors. The Duc de Bourgogne had despatched his wife Isabelle on a diplomatic message to the King of France.

The negotiations had been begun at Rheims, but as soon as the queen was settled at Châlons, the duchess hied her thither.

She did not make her descent upon the court alone. She had her nephew, Adolphe de Clèves, in her train, as well as a couple of nieces and a large retinue of gentlemen and ladies. They were used to invasions of this kind at the court. The palaces were large enough to hold all the ministers, attendants and other individuals who swelled the king's household until it became a very unwieldy one.

The usual formalities were gone through when the duchess arrived.

Seigneur de Créquy, her *chevalier d'honneur*, arrived first at the queen's residence and inquired whether Marie d'Anjou would be pleased to receive her guest. An answer in the affirmative being given, the duchess dismounted from her palfrey and accompanied by the Comte de Clermont advanced to pay her respects to the queen.

Her train was borne by maids-of-honour; that was one of their duties, as Agnes Sorel had long since learnt. When the little procession neared the entrance to the queen's apartments the duchess took hold of her own train, allowed it to sweep the ground, and gave a low curtsey in

[*To face p.* 112

MARGARET OF SCOTLAND

the fashion of the day. Then she advanced with stately mien to the centre of the apartment, and curtseyed a second time.

The queen was standing beside her bed. When the duchess advanced and made a third salutation, Marie d'Anjou stepped forward, laid a hand on her friend's shoulder, and then drew her into an upright position. The duchess kissed the queen's hand. It was all very formal.

Olivier de la Marche said that the queen received the duchess with great warmth and did her " moult grand honneur et privauté." He went on to say that neither lady was young nor beautiful, that they shared a certain grief and misery, which was jealousy, and that this common cause of complaint against their respective husbands for being unfaithful bred much sympathy and familiarity between them. "The king," said the same chronicler, "had recently taken unto himself a young lady,[1] and in a trice had placed her in a position of such triumph and such power that her estate was comparable to that of the great princesses of the kingdom."

From this it may be gathered that the visitor at court was not too well disposed towards the fair Agnes, and that when they met, as must have been a daily occurrence, the good duchess opened wide her eyes, though she may have retained enough good breeding to keep her mouth shut. Her own husband had been renowned for his flirtations for some time. One of his pages

[1] Olivier de la Marche calls her " une pauvre demoiselle."

I

described him quite neatly as " le prince le plus dameret et le plus galant de son époque." The word " dameret " is so expressive that it would be a pity to give it an inadequate English equivalent. In short, the Duc de Bourgogne was rather proud of his natural children, and thought no shame attached to them. It was in part due to him that the fifteenth century has been known as " the age of bastards."

The queen and the duchess were able to open their hearts to one another, and to mingle their sighs over this mutual cause for complaint.

The poor dauphine, Margaret of Scotland, was also a neglected wife; even more so than her mother-in-law and the haughty duchess, for her husband, Louis, had long since refused to associate with her at all. What must the Lady of Burgundy do but spend much time and dine almost daily with the dauphine and help her to bewail her woes. As it was not etiquette for the duchess to take her meals at the table with the king and queen, she had plenty of opportunity of inflicting her presence on the young princess. To entertain so virtuous and depressing a lady visitor in the palace for two months was no light matter. She instigated Marie d'Anjou to level complaints at the king for his infidelities, and it is not surprising that Charles, wearied by his wife's attitude, found the company of his mistress all the more exhilarating.

Affairs of State were, however, deeply engrossing. A marriage was projected between the king's daughter, Madeleine, and the eldest son of Richard, Duke of York.[1]   On August 21, 1444, Henry VI had sent letters to Charles in which he had expressed a wish for a " final conclusion of perpetual and loving peace between the two kingdoms," and at the same time he promised to receive and welcome the French ambassadors burdened with the duty of arranging the proposed betrothal.

One of Charles VII's first acts after arriving at Sarry-les-Châlons was to issue letters patent empowering the ambassadors to set out on their expedition. The Comtes de Vendôme and Laval, Jean Jouvenal, Archbishop of Rheims, and Etienne Chevalier amongst others set sail from Calais on July 8, 1445. One result of the embassy was to arrange for an extension of the truce between England and France until April 1, 1447. It is important to notice that Etienne Chevalier went to England at this time. Some historians have given him an important part to play by the side of Agnes Sorel. The ambassadors did not return to France before the beginning of 1446.

No sooner had the King of France sent his embassy to Henry VI than he found himself obliged to receive a number of foreign ambassadors from different parts of Europe. The Duc de Milan had business with France, so had the Duc de Savoie, who was presently to abet the dauphin in his marriage with his daughter against the wishes of Charles VII. The King of Castille, the Electors of the Empire, and the

[1] Later Edward IV. The negotiations came to naught.

I 2

Duke of York, who was concerned about his son's marriage, all sent messengers to the King of France.

Although the days were filled with conferences and councils there was time for festivities too. Agnes, who was established in the palace in apartments which for luxury far excelled those of the queen, took a prominent part in the gorgeous fêtes which were the rule at court.

The tournaments were well described by a young squire of Hainaut, the Jacques de Lalaing [1] already mentioned, who was a member of the Duchesse de Bourgogne's suite.

One evening, after supper, the King of France and René d'Anjou went out to enjoy themselves in the fields and meadows, gathering plants and flowers, and finding innocent pleasure in other rural pursuits. Charles d'Anjou, the Comte du Maine and the Comte de Saint-Pol, accompanied by a number of knights and squires, joined them. They were chatting with all the fair ladies, and vying with one another who could tell the most entertaining stories. Those who were acquainted with the Court of Burgundy told remarkable tales about the marvellous jousts, tourneys and combats which took place there.

The nobles of Charles VII's court listened enviously to these wonders, and declared that never had such a fine and courtly prince been seen in France as the Duc de Bourgogne—never one so good, so debonair, so powerful !

[1] *Le Livre des Faits de Jacques de Lalaing. Œuvres de Georges Chastellain*, 1866, edited by Kervyn de Lettenhove.

Listening to these opinions the Comte du Maine and the Comte de Saint-Pol were struck by an idea. They moved aside and discussed the matter privately. They agreed that it would never do to tell the ladies all about the festivities, jousts, dances, tourneys and such-like amusements in Burgundy, whilst they themselves at the Court of France spent the day sleeping, drinking and eating, and never organised warlike games, and that it was shameful they should spend their days in idleness and ease.

The Comte de Saint-Pol, after considering the position carefully, said to the Comte du Maine that he would like to devise some exhibition of skill at arms. He suggested that they should open the lists for a joust to all comers, that the king and all the ladies should be present. This plan was much to the taste of Saint-Pol, who began to smile and said it pleased him greatly. Without wasting words on the matter he called a herald and had the fact of the jousts cried in the presence of the kings, the queens, the princesses and ladies.

Because Jacques de Lalaing came from the Burgundian court he was given the privilege of arranging the tourney for the Comtes de Saint-Pol and du Maine, and they took him into the king's presence to settle matters of detail.

Charles was in the apartments of the queen, where they found Marie d'Anjou, Isabelle de Lorraine, the dauphine, the Duchesses d'Orléans and de Calabre, Agnes Sorel, and quite a bevy of duchesses, baronesses, dames and damsels.

Permission was given for the tournament to be held, and the preparations went on apace. The Comte de Foix, the Comte de Clermont, Pierre de Brézé, Poton de Saintrailles and others distinguished themselves. The Comte de Saint-Pol won the prize.

One day two unknown knights, richly garbed, entered the lists to a blare of trumpets so loud "that it seemed as though earth and sky were about to enter into a combat."

After the knights had fought four rounds and broken two lances each, it was discovered that they were no less distinguished personages than the King of France and Pierre de Brézé.

Every evening there were banquets and dances. Trumpets and fiddles never ceased to sound until day was dawning. It was all very festive indeed.

On July 2 another marriage took place. The Comte de Richemont, who had previously been married to the Duchesse de Guienne, and after her death to Jeanne d'Albret, had been left a widower in September, 1444. Now he was wedded to Catherine de Luxembourg before nine months had passed.

This alliance was productive of a re-arrangement of officials at court. Pierre de Brézé, now Seneschal de Poitou and Comte d'Evreux, was growing in power as quickly as the fair Agnes. He was convinced, or pretended to be convinced, that the strengthening of relations between the House of Luxembourg, the Comte du Maine and the Connétable, was responsible for certain signs of revolt among the princes, René, the Comte du Maine, the Comte de Saint-Pol and Richemont. A great stir was caused by the breaking out of a quarrel between these influential persons. The position became acute at Châlons, and Charles saw fit to make a clean sweep of the disputants. Several of the nobles were ordered to depart, and the king gave his personal orders to them not to return until he gave them permission.

King René withdrew to Anjou, where he remained for eighteen months before he left for Provence. In the meantime his son, the Duc de Calabre, returned to Lorraine as lieutenant-général, his brother, the Comte du Maine, ceased to be a member of the Council, and the only prince of the blood who was allowed to remain was the Comte de Vendôme.

By the end of the stay at Châlons the people most in favour with the king were the friends of Agnes Sorel, Pierre de Brézé, Jacques Cœur, Etienne Chevalier (soon to return to France), Bertrand de Beauvau and Jean de Bueil.

The result of the clearance of the court was quickly apparent. The affairs of State which had kept the king busy were completed. The Duchesse de Bourgogne had departed for Flanders, all the ambassadors had left, and the queen, wearied with the festivities and bustle, was in poor health, and suggested that she should retire to some quiet spot and live the simple life in which she found happiness. Charles himself was preparing to relax his strenuous attention to public matters and spend more time in the company of the Lady of Beauty, when an event occurred which caused fresh sorrow at court and altered the plans of those who had made any.

On August 7, King Charles, influenced by his piety, set forth on a pilgrimage to Notre-Dame de l'Épine, a church not far from Châlons. It would not have been suitable for Agnes to accompany him on such an expedition, and he took with him his daughter-in-law, Margaret, for whom he had always shown a deep affection.[1]

The unhappy dauphine, having allowed her husband's neglect and other troubles to weigh on her mind, was not in good health. She took cold that day, sat down on her return in one of the stone halls of the palace without changing her clothes, and developed inflammation of the lungs.

Perhaps she did not care to make an effort to live. Perhaps, because there was no likelihood of her giving birth to an heir to the throne, others were not so anxious to save her life as they ought to have been. For many months she had suffered greatly from calumny, which had spread about her at court. The story is a well-known one and has nothing to do with the affairs of Agnes Sorel, except in so far as the death of the dauphine removed from court one of the

[1] Only a short time previously he had spent two thousand francs on silk and furs for her use.

influences upon the king towards virtue and devotion.

One winter evening, whilst the court was at Nancy, one of the king's councillors, Jamet du Tillay, who had never been friendly towards the Scottish princess, entered her apartments at dusk and found her lying on her bed, surrounded by her ladies, chatting with Jean d'Estouteville, Seigneur de Blainville, and another young noble. The room was almost in darkness. Jamet du Tillay placed the worst construction upon what he had seen. He was instrumental in spreading scandal which compromised the dauphine, openly discussed her *amours*, and said her manners were more like those of a courtesan than of a great lady.

Probably the affair was the outcome of certain intrigues which had been woven round this rather helpless princess. Marguerite de Ville-quier, one of Margaret's women, seems to have been a traitor to her mistress, and the queen and Agnes Sorel had endeavoured to get rid of her and replace her by Prégente de Melun, who was chosen by Brézé as loyal to the party of favourites.

The dauphine was certainly not the most discreet of women, considering her isolated position. She was warm-hearted and impulsive, and the story was told of her that whilst at Châlons she presented a simple squire who had done well in the tournament with a purse containing six hundred golden crowns. Such trifles were magnified a thousand times at a court where intrigue and gossip fed on the most scanty fare. It was said also of the dauphine that her taste for poetry had led her to spend whole nights in versifying when she ought to have been asleep. Undoubtedly she was innocent, but the accusations against her virtue were worse than death to her.

"Ah, Jamet, Jamet," she cried, when near death's door, "you have worked your purpose. If I die, you and the words you have spoken of me without any foundation in truth will be the cause." Pierre de Brézé, who was present at this pathetic scene, came out of her chamber, full of grief and anguish. "The trouble and misery this lady suffers," he said, "are a thousand pities."

On the day she died the dauphine swore, as she had sworn before, that "she had never wronged her husband." In the end she forgave her enemy, and expired on August 16, 1445, breathing her last pathetic thought, "Fie upon this life. Never speak to me of it again."

Whether Agnes Sorel was at the death-bed or not is uncertain. Very probably she was. La Belle des Belles was much too good-natured to bear the dauphine ill-will because that lady's strict views must have been against her interests.

The power of Agnes was growing far too strong for such considerations to affect her. She had won the king's whole heart; she was all in all to him, and her wishes were his law.

The death of the dauphine was a terrible blow

to both Charles and Marie d'Anjou. The queen
became quite ill. The king left Châlons hurriedly
on the 17th of the month. He went to Montils-
les-Tours and from thence to Razilly, two
leagues from Chinon, where he spent the autumn
in the company of his mistress.

CHAPTER XIII

RAZILLY

THE Lady of Beauty was now in Touraine, the country with which she has the closest associations. A couple of leagues from Chinon lay the Château de Razilly, a glorified manor-house in which there was room for the king and all his court.

Jean, seigneur de Razilly, one of the king's chamberlains, had been commanded by an order dated December 17, 1489, to fortify his castle and make it ready for residence.

Within solid outer walls rose the parapets and battlements of a substantial dwelling-place. A huge gateway led into the precincts of the castle. South of the main block of buildings stood the chapel surmounted by a rectangular dome, pierced by three embrasures, each topped by a gable. In this secluded spot Charles saw fit to dwell for more than eight months. If he was required for business matters he had to be sought out by those who were anxious to obtain his ear. The dauphin knew that he was quite accessible and that " every one had the right to enter Razilly who desired to do so," [1] and presently

[1] Duclos, *Recueil de Pieces pour servir de Histoire de Louis XI*, p. 64.

intended to make use of this knowledge for his own ends. He was staying at Chinon, and the queen, who was awaiting another confinement, was there too. She visited Charles occasionally, and when her youngest son was born in December, 1446, the king gave her some magnificent presents.

But Agnes was queen of his heart, and the object round whom all his actions centred. Since the time when he had openly acknowledged her as his mistress, a little group of gay and brilliant young men became satellites at court and were called the king's *mignons*.

Among these one of the most important was André de Villequier, a squire of Normandy, who, it was said, mounted fortune's ladder more speedily and to greater heights than any other of his day. One of his two sisters had been lady-in-waiting to the dauphine, and both were favoured at court. From the beginning of 1444, de Villequier was in receipt of the king's liberality. In July, 1445, he became the king's chamberlain, and presently he was to be found constantly in the company of Charles, was loaded with presents of money and land, was known as " Monseigneur de Villequier," and before many years had passed was the husband of the notorious Antoinette, cousin of the Lady of Beauty.

A young squire attached to the Comte du Maine entered the king's service about the same time as de Villequier, and, like him, received large bounties. His name was Guillaume Gouffier, and it appears over and over again in the accounts, now for expenses at Tours, now at Troyes, for a new costume to wear on Christmas Day, and for expenses in connection with a tournament held at Razilly. Gouffier was intimate with Agnes, escorted her to Paris, and was present at her death-bed.

A number of young men were hangers-on at court, and recipients of presents above and beyond their fixed wages. Not the least prominent were Jean and Charles Soreau, brothers of Agnes—Bouchot [1] accused her of nepotism—Guillaume Gazeau, who seems to have hunted in couples with Gouffier, a younger de Beauvau, and Antoine d'Aubusson, called *Petit Trignac*, who married Marguerite de Villequier.

But Charles was not satisfied to be surrounded by popinjays and no others.

In the unsettled state of affairs it was necessary to have a very efficient bodyguard. The Scottish guard, called the *grande garde*, consisted of a number of archers and their captain. It had been organised at the beginning of the reign by Cristy Chambre, and his son Nicole commanded a company numbering forty-eight archers and twenty - five men - at - arms. In January, 1444, Charles bestowed a seigneurie upon Nicole Chambre, and both he and the queen were friendly towards him. He was mixed up in the inquiry made into the cause of the dauphine's death.

Another body of soldiers was drawn from the young men of the king's household, and in all

[1] *Cosmopolitan*, New York, Vol. XVIII., 1894-95.

his personal protectors must have numbered several hundreds at this time.

Surrounded by a small army of courtiers awaiting his slightest favours, jealous of one another, ready to pick quarrels on the slightest pretext, none of them above scandal and gossip if such weapons could be turned to account to further their own interests, Charles must have found it no easy matter to rule those who came in personal contact with him, without considering the larger proportion of his subjects at all.

The Court of France was a little city in itself, composed of a hundred discordant elements, in which intrigue, sedition, disloyalty, jealousy, and many other disintegrating influences seethed freely. Personally popular, the king seems to have been wanting in firmness and strength where his own household was concerned. He was too fond of distributing presents, a dangerous habit where scores of hands were outstretched to grasp them. Whilst his own affairs went exactly to his taste Charles was easy-going, but if any one ventured to interfere, woe betide the rash adventurer.

His own life made it impossible for the king to object to the conduct of others. Nor could he altogether expect to avoid the criticism which his relations with Agnes Sorel were bound to awaken.

Apart from her influence over him for good, apart from her gentle and sincere ways, and her generous employment of the liberalities bestowed upon her by Charles, the fact of her constant presence at court gave rise to certain evils which could not be altogether ignored.

She drew him into culpable irregularities, wrote Du Fresne de Beaucourt, she had a bad influence on the manners of the times, and even on public affairs.

" What abuses, what evil examples, what scandals! Passion is a bad councillor; where Agnes was concerned Charles VII would listen to no one. More than one intrigue, more than one split in the royal camp had their origin in the scandalous favouritism. When a courtier wished to ruin a man in the king's sight, it sufficed if he accused him of speaking ill of Agnes. Honest souls could not look upon this public and triumphant adultery without indignation. It was a pity, they said, that such an example should exist on the steps of the throne itself, and the results could not be other than disastrous."

In spite of the easy morality of the day on the one hand, and the respect for royalty on the other, ugly murmurs were certainly raised against both king and favourite, and many contemporaries gave voice to the expressions of an outraged public conscience.

Apart from unavoidable harm brought about by the irregularity of her position, Agnes's influence was ever exerted on the side of good. Her generous gifts to the poor have already been spoken of, her sympathy with those in trouble, her desire to rescue those who were in danger or dread of punishment, and her intervention on behalf of those who had offended against authority must be counted in her favour.

One such little incident is cited by Vallet de Viriville,[1] which may be taken as representing the Lady of Beauty's love of justice and mercy. It occurred at the beginning of 1446, when the court was at Razilly.

On April 10 a peasant of the little village of Rosoy-sur-Serre in Picardy was killed by the thrust of a spear in a quarrel with two other peasants. One of the murderers was called Pierson (or Pierron) Sureau, and he had thrown himself into the struggle to save his brother Jean, who was trying to punish his adversary for a wound he had received at an earlier date. Pierson had done his best to persuade his brother not to bear malice against his enemy. He had only joined in the affray in order to save his brother's life, but this was not sufficient justification in the eyes of the law to prevent him from being condemned to death as a murderer.

Aged eighteen, Sureau's record had till then been stainless. As he was on the way to execution a young woman of good family, seeing his anguish and moved by pity, in conformity with a custom then in vogue, claimed him as her husband. Temporarily, at least, this gained a respite for the condemned man, the girl's appeal was sent to the king and discussed in council.

Rosoy was the property of Charles de Bourgogne, a cousin of the all-powerful duke, which made jurisdiction in this case a delicate matter.

[1] *Histoire de Charles VII*, Vol. III. pp. 100–101.

K

But the accused was a native of Picardy, and the fact that he was a compatriot and a namesake of the favourite emboldened that lady to plead for his release. A young girl had already done much to save the accused. Agnes, as ruling lady of that part of the country, was deeply interested in the fate of unfortunates and those who suffered from judicial harshness. Exactly what passed is unknown, but her intervention appears to have been productive of immediate results. Pierson was set free by letters dated at Chinon June 22, 1446, his character was re-established, and he was permitted to wed the young girl who had offered herself as his liberator.

One of the most important pieces of business to which King Charles gave his attention at Razilly was the inquiry into the conduct of Jamet du Tillay, with regard to his slander of the dauphine. Gérard le Boursier, the *maître des requêtes*, and Guillaume Bigot, *conseiller au parlement*, were appointed commissioners and commanded to proceed in the matter. There had been an addition at court recently in the persons of Jane and Eleanor of Scotland, two of Margaret's sisters, who had been sent for to live with the dauphine. They landed on the shores of Flanders at the very moment when their sister lay dying at Châlons, and her death must have grieved them intensely.

The inquiry lasted from October, 1445, to August, 1446. Agnes Sorel's name only occurs once in the papers relating to it, and that was when Jamet du Tillay was interrogated and swore that he knew nothing of the queen, the dauphine and the king's mistress having tried to displace Marguerite de Villequier from the princess's household, and replace her by Prégente. The doctors bore witness, the dauphine's ladies made depositions, the queen was cross-examined, and Jamet du Tillay underwent the ordeal of being questioned twice. The evidence was considered in council, but no decisive conclusion was given. Jamet remained in the king's favour.

The time which Agnes spent at Razilly must have been a very happy one on the whole. She found life pleasant enough when the king dallied in the beautiful châteaux, enjoying leisure and security consequent on the truce with England, and feeling younger at forty than he had appeared to be at twenty.

Du Fresne de Beaucourt did his best to destroy the accusation which had been levelled against the king for many centuries, and which attributed to him an excessive love of ease and pleasure.

To this accusation Bussy-Rabutin referred in a letter to Mme. de Sévigné, written on February 28, 1678, concerning Mme. de Montespan. " I remark," he wrote, " that although the king loves her deeply and that he has good reason to do so, he loves himself still better, and he does not act as did Charles VII, who instead of taking La belle Agnès to the army, lived with her at Mehun-sur-Yèvre or at Bourges while his kingdom was being fought for."

K 2

And then he told the well-known story about La Hire.

" Apropos of that, Madame, I must tell you a little story about Charles VII which does honour to the king in comparison. The celebrated La Hire having been sent by the Comte de Dunois to Charles VII, who was then at Bourges, to tell him some bad luck which had befallen and to hear what His Majesty wished done in this misfortune, found the king at a dance. He heard the reason of his journey, said he would think over the matter, and with a joyous countenance asked what he thought of the fête, and if he did not think he was spending his time well. La Hire, enraged to observe the want of feeling and baseness of the prince, did not reply, and the king pressing him again to give his opinion, La Hire answered with a bitter smile that it was true he seemed to be amusing himself splendidly, and that no one could lose a kingdom more gaily than he was doing. Do you not love La Hire, Madame, and despise Charles VII heartily ? Nevertheless, admire the flattery of history. The king was called le Victorieux."

During the years he lived in Touraine Charles was certainly not idle. He was busy preparing for the activities which were to win him this complimentary title, and Agnes did her best to point out to him where his duty lay and urge him to its performance.

CHAPTER XIV

LIFE IN THE CHÂTEAUX OF TOURAINE

DOTTED upon both banks of the smiling river are the old castles of Touraine. They were residences of kings long before Versailles or even Fontainebleau had been thought of as royal palaces.

From Bourges to Angers, from Orleans to Chinon, a number of places are connected with the name of the fair lady whose exquisite beauty and sweet nature cheered the heart of the troubled King Charles, sovereign of the land of France from 1422 to 1461.

In a setting of wild nature, forest, stream, meadow and tangled thickets, feudal towers peeped here and there through the clearings, and denoted the homes of warlike nobles. As the times grew more secure these edifices possessed an architectural elegance and interior luxury which had been impossible during the previous barbaric period.

When Agnes knew Touraine the worst of war was over and the country had taken on a new lease of peace and prosperity. The frugality which had marked the days when Charles VII, wearing common garb, sat down to a scrag end of cold mutton for his dinner was past and forgotten.   No longer could his guests laugh over the old story of a visit from the captains of his army :

> " Un jour la Hire et Poton
> Le viendre voir, pour festoiement
> N'avoit qu'une queue de mouton
> Et deux poulets tant seulement."

There were not only chickens in plenty, but greater delicacies still.   Hares, pheasants, partridges and the magnificent peacock graced the festive board.   Drinking was as important a part of the banquet as eating, and good red and white wines flowed abundantly, threatening to drown the brains if not the persons of the assembled company.

The costumes of the day were not only very costly, but very cumbersome.   It was said that a lady's gown was worth the whole revenue of a duchy.   The armour and velvets, the silks and cloth of gold with which the nobles adorned themselves and their horses were worth untold fortunes.

Usually the women wore the huge conical caps nearly a yard in height called *hennin,* and stiff brocaded gowns which cased in their figures so tightly that it was an effort to breathe.   Agnes Sorel had quite different ideas of comfort and beauty in dress.   She placed the simplest cap over her luxuriant curls, or, better still, left them to cluster round her head at their own sweet will, tying them loosely in the nape of her neck with a bow of ribbon.   Her gowns were all cut low in front to show her white throat and the curve of her bosom.   The satin and silk of which her robes were made were lined with rich furs[1] and fastened with a girdle set with a cluster of cut diamonds, the present of Jacques Cœur.

She had dainty linen undergarments instead of those of woollen material then in fashion. Her shoes were ornamented, embroidered and lined with various kinds of fur.

In every detail of her costume she was as neat and careful as any fine lady could be, and all accessories were in harmony and in the best of taste. Her gloves were fringed, notched and stitched with fancy silks, as was usual in that day among the exquisites.

They were not a cheap commodity, and she valued them so greatly that when some pairs were lost on the way to Razilly she was very troubled and wrote a letter from that castle on September 8, 1446, about them. The letter was despatched to Mlle. de Belleville [2] by an

[1] Among the documents " relatifs à la personne d'Agnès Sorel," published by Vallet de Viriville in the *Bibliothèque de l'École des Chartes*, Series 3, Vol. I. p. 309, is one which states that a piece of fur formerly belonging to the Lady of Beauty, deposited with Jacques Cœur, was sold by Etienne de Manné. It was described as " ung manteau de dos de martres sébelines qui fut à feue Agnès Sorelle, en son vivant damoiselle, dame de Beauté, en unes manches ouvertes." "Manteau" at this time was not the shape of a garment but the size of the fur, and the one in question was used by Agnes in the form of "unes manches ouvertes." In Jacques Cœur's house was a large store of jewels, precious stuffs and furs.

[2] Mlle. de Belleville was the daughter of Charles VI and Odette de Champdivers. Charles gave Odette the estate of Belleville in Poitou. Leroux de Lincy said Odette's daughter was Marguerite de Valois, legitimated 1427 and married to Jean de Harpedenne. She died before 1458.

attendant of the name of Cristofle, who was responsible for the loss.

" Mademoiselle, my good friend," she began, " I greet you with all my heart. Kindly give to the bearer of this letter, Cristofle, my grey gown faced with white and all the pairs of gloves that you can find in my apartments; the said Cristofle having lost my glove-case in which there was a large number.

" Please receive by him my greyhound Carpet, and keep the dog with you. We could not let him go hunting with us for he obeys neither whistle nor call, which is the reason why I am sending him back; for he might otherwise have got lost, which would have been a great grief to me. God send you grace. Your very good friend,

" AGNES."

It was not surprising that personal luggage, such as boxes containing gloves or fripperies, should disappear during the flittings from castle to castle. The prince or noble who possessed a number of residences and journeyed from one to another was obliged to transport not only his personal belongings but the furniture, tapestries, beds and bedding, and indeed everything that he possessed.

He stripped one castle almost bare in order that he might make the next one comfortable, for the ornaments and furniture of the day were costly and scarce. It was impossible to have enough for every residence. Their owner, too, liked to be surrounded with all that was dear and familiar to him. Every time a journey was taken it meant that most of the goods had to be carried on horseback, or in the most primitive wagons through districts where the roads were mere tracks. Often disasters worse than the loss of a box of gloves occurred by the way.

Hunting was a favourite sport, and was one of the causes which led to frequent changes of scene. Razilly was one of the hunting centres near Chinon.

Charles was not as passionately devoted to the chase as most of the French kings. But he loved horses and went out riding almost every day. He never mounted a mule nor a palfrey, but rode " un bas cheval trotier d'entre deux selles." [1]

Agnes was an accomplished horsewoman, and when the king hunted she accompanied him. A second letter she wrote about this time to Mlle. de Belleville tells of an accident to one of her pet dogs :

" You must know that I am very surprised at the report which you have sent me by young Dampère,[2] and I am sending him back that he may help you to throw off the great ennui you must have suffered.

" You must know also that we are enjoying ourselves as much as we can in these quarters, and you ought to come here as soon as possible

[1] Henri Baude.
[2] François de Clermont, Seigneur de Dampierre.

in order to get away from the said ennui, which will be soon, I hope.

"Yesterday we hunted a boar of which your little Robin had got scent, and the hunt turned out badly for the said little Robin, for he was struck by a stone which one of the hunters had flung at the boar in a thicket. He was wounded rather badly by it.

"But I hope he will soon be cured, and I shall have him well looked after. Meanwhile, if I can do anything for you in view of your coming here let me know, and I will do it with pleasure."

She knew that Mlle. de Belleville, whatever she might suffer, would recover from her ennui at court.

Agnes was never behindhand in trying to help her friends, and she asked little of them in return. All she expected was kindliness and justice. She hated flattery and the double-faced dealings of the courtiers.

Life was a complicated affair in the châteaux. Hundreds of people kept coming and going, each with their own private interests and motives. Every one had an axe to grind, a log to roll, or an intrigue to hatch. Relatives, connections, allies, neighbours, travellers and pilgrims, arriving and departing, made up a shifting population. For every guest festivities were instituted, and holidays proclaimed. The buffet in the hall was always loaded with food and drink. Whole calves and sheep were roasted on the huge hearths, and game and poultry were cooked in profusion.

The courtyard was the scene of joyous movement. There the younger portion of the community exercised their horses and themselves in feats of war. Quoits, ninepins, pitching the bar and shooting at the popinjay were some of the amusements indulged in. In the evening the dance, the oft-repeated tale, the songs of the troubadours, or a concert of trumpets, pipes and cymbals took place. This luxury and extravagance were carried on at the expense of the peasantry, who had to labour day and night to provide the wherewithal to pay the heavy taxes.

Nor was this contrast between the wealth of the nobility and the poverty of the lower classes the only surprising discrepancy in the affairs of the fifteenth century. There was quite as wide a gulf between piety and vice. It was said that the name of the Almighty appeared in all the charters, and the words " bastards " and " mistresses " in all the genealogies.

Under the laws of chivalry which flourished there was an elaborate code of honour on the one hand, and actions of bare-faced deceit and circumvention on the other. Formality and etiquette struggled side by side with a striking coarseness of manners. Great luxury often accompanied a lack of the most ordinary decencies.

In chivalry the true knight must be loyal to his king, but he occasionally betrayed his dearest friend. He must worship his lady-love, but he behaved like a scoundrel to less-favoured women.

Platonic love and extravagant expressions of sentiment did not interfere with passion of a much coarser kind, indulged in especially by the powerful nobles, who had no scruples in demanding letters of legitimation for natural sons.

The ideas of gallantry in the chivalric system were far-fetched and absurd, although they were at the same time romantic and picturesque. The young squire who set out to find his mistress, to serve her with valour and virtue, was on a level with the great lady ever on the watch for a young cavalier whose fortune she could build up so that he might become a distinguished man and do her honour. She was to be his *dame par amours*.

Usually she appropriated him while still young and unspoilt, showered kisses and presents upon him, and taught him all the mysteries of amorous feelings, of which until then he had no knowledge. All this was carried on with an air of secrecy and mystery which was part of the game. Directness would have destroyed the glamour and poetry of such affairs. If a meeting were to be arranged it must take place in the most unlikely spot, perhaps in a bosky dell whither the guiltless partners made grand show of going undetected. If a letter were to be delivered it must be hidden in some niche where no one would think of looking for it, perhaps between the cushion and the seat of an upholstered chair, or pinned to the back of a hanging tapestry.

If a few words were to be said in the ear of the chosen one, though they be so innocent that all the world might hear and think no shame, certain manœuvres were necessary and a pre-arranged signal must be given. " Quand vous me verrez que d'une espingle je purgeray mes dens," said one famous lady [1] to her attendant lover, " ce sera signe que je vouldray parler à vous." What could be more descriptive of the odd manners of the day! The high-born dame, ashamed to beckon her squire-lover to her, picked her teeth with a jewelled pin in public in order that he might know she wanted a word with him.

The tears, the sighs, and the groans that accompanied the exercise of chivalric love far outweighed the laughter and joy. The attitude which was correct was to be pensive rather than happy, desirous of attaining something more than was offered, rather than grateful for what had been bestowed. But perhaps for the attendant there was a reason for these dolorous moods, he was for ever subject to the whims of his fair lady, for ever dependent upon her bounty, and for ever at her beck and call like the veriest slave.

The student who reads of the platonic love-affair of the days of chivalry cannot help wondering how frequently the make-belief suddenly broke down and the realities of life stepped in, and then whether the exponents of the art of love were not affrighted by their own temerity in playing with fire. That accidents of this sort happened occasionally may be gathered from

[1] *L'Histoire du petit Jehan de Saintré et de la Dame des Belles Cousines.*

the warning which Jacques de Lalaing received from his parents before he set forth to master the real business of life.

"My son," said his father, "to acquire glory and good fame, you who are to take up your abode at the court of a prince, it behoves you to follow the good manners that you see there.

"First of all, above everything it is necessary that you should flee from the sin of pride, if you wish to achieve good and acquire the grace of your well-beloved lady; for you must know that few gentlemen have achieved great heights of valour and fame if there is not a dame or damsel whom they love; but, my son, so that you may know with what kind of love you must love them I will tell you. If it should occur, in all honour, that you fall in love with any dame or damsel, take care, if you wish to reach the heights of valour, that it is not with a mad love, for you would be led into great villainy and shame for ever."

Two forms of love thus ran side by side like a tiny rippling brook trying to keep pace with a roaring river in flood.

Firstly, there was the courtly love between knight and lady. The latter was always perfect, for she could do no wrong. To think of her as lovable was to experience more joy than could be derived from the possession of any other woman's affection. The knight's every thought was a longing to serve her, a desire to be in her presence. The breeze that had fanned her cheek made him thrill as it came to him, for it had enjoyed the privilege of touching her. If she smiled, if she spoke to him, if she laid her hand on his, these were real gifts, and he had no need to ask more of her. To see her face was like life, to endure her frown was worse than death. He would not tell her of his love nor ask of her the tiniest favour. It was enough to worship her in silence and at a distance.

The second kind of love occurred when the empty forms of a boundless devotion became changed into a tumult of passion.

A proverb of the day ran : " There is no lady who does not wish to yield, and none who will not if wooed sincerely enough." Customs and conventions went to the wall, sighs changed to hot vows, a servile obedience became of a sudden fiery mastery. The lady who had dallied with a pretty sentiment of which she had read in romances and heard recited by the troubadours in beautiful verses, was swept off her feet by a force of which she was unable to calculate the dangers. Where before she had languidly raised a little finger to command she now found herself down on her knees to obey. It was only by giving her all that she once more regained a sway over her lover, but her position had changed. She was no longer the flawless angel, the perfect, unattainable ideal, but a woman with human faults, a comrade whose love was of the world worldly.

Since the love of kings must always transcend that of ordinary mortals, the passion of Charles for Agnes was a thing apart. It was made less

turbulent by his unique position, and less sentimental by her practical view of things. He had
no need to win renown and valour for love of a
fair lady, and she could not make him stand
gaping and shuffling his feet in the attitude of
the knight who awaits the fair one's pleasure.

The sunny days in Touraine were calling them,
and life seemed joyous. Spring kept the blood
in their veins young. They moved from château
to château, and found each one delightful.
Chinon was the stage on which some of the
warmest scenes of their courtship had been
played, and there the king built Agnes a house
called Roberdeau opposite the tower d'Argenton.
He had a vault made under the terrace, one of the
underground passages so famous in the history
of that day, so that he could go to her from the
château without being seen. Roberdeau was
surrounded by six acres of park.

Loches was her favourite castle of all, and
there, as an addition to the huge fortress, were
the finer erections of the fifteenth century, the
apartments of Charles VII and the turrets of
Agnes Sorel's tower.[1]

Near Tours by the Château d'Usage stood a
pavilion called Bonaventure, which served as a
night's resting-place when the chase led in that
direction. There was a more pretentious hunting-
lodge with fortified towers at Candes, from which
Agnes wrote one of her letters to Mlle. de Belleville. It became later the residence of Louis XI.

---

[1] According to one legend Charles used to lock Agnes up
in her tower on the occasions when he went hunting.

When, as dauphin, he conspired against his father in 1446 a commission was held at Candes to discover who were the guilty plotters.

Cheillé was another of the *rendezvous de chasse*. Agnes had the rights of a châtelaine over La Chesnaye. In a letter written to the Provost of that spot, from Du Plessis near to Chinon, she expressed her sympathy with the poor, and begged, nay commanded, that they should not suffer for depredations made upon the trees, since they must be very much put to it to find firewood. The forest laws in France were very strict, and were sternly enforced. Agnes was exerting her prerogative with a will in remitting punishment.

" It has come to my ears," she wrote, " that certain persons of the parish of La Chesnaye have been summoned by you on a suspicion of having taken wood from the forest in this neighbourhood, and that a day has been fixed for an inquiry to be made into their innocence.

" Whereas, having been informed that some of the said individuals are poor, unfortunate folk, and that they find it very difficult to make a living for themselves and their families, I wish that no further steps may be taken with regard to the said information and days of inquiry, and that the said individuals should not be detained in person or their goods confiscated, but that on the other hand the matter be let drop entirely, and in carrying out my wishes without delay you will be doing me a favour.

L

" Praying God, Sir Provost, that He will give
you health and keep you in His care,

"Your good mistress,

" AGNES.

" Du Plessis this 8th day of June."

Du Plessis[1] was a residence near to Vaugandré,
and was connected by vaulted passages under
the bed of the Vienne with one of the towers of
the Château de Chinon.

At Beaulieu, not far from Loches, with which
it was connected by a series of bridges crossing
an arm of the Indre, Agnes possessed another
hôtel, which had been beautifully decorated with
frescoes and paintings. Later the place went by
the name of the Maison de la Reine.

Another of her favourite dwelling-places was
the Château of La Guerche not far from Loches,
on the right bank of the river Creuse. This
building was erected specially for her, and completed as speedily as possible. The apartments
were all decorated with frescoes and gilding.
The paintings represented hunting subjects with
life-size figures and gilded costumes. The king's
tastes were allowed full play in the ornaments
of decoration, which included mottoes, allegorical
devices, interlaced initials, and other fanciful
designs inspired by love.

La Guerche was a truly royal residence. Two
immense machicolated towers protected the
gates. The main body of the building was

---

[1] Touchard-Lafosse, *La Loire Historique*, 1840–44, Vol.
IV. part i. p. 275.

flanked by towers. A drawbridge spanned the river, which flowed at the foot of the solid masonry. Beautiful gardens surrounded the two-storied block in which the chief apartments were situated. Charles, in order to cut off some of the distance between La Guerche and Loches, had built a beautiful stone bridge [1] over the Creuse, and this saved time when he paid visits to his mistress.

Alas that earthly joys should be so fleeting! After the death of the Lady of Beauty La Guerche became the possession of her successor, Antoinette, and remained in the family of the de Villequiers. A mausoleum consecrated to the memory of Agnes was found in the Church of La Guerche.

In every charming corner of fertile Touraine Agnes had a manor-house, a château, or a residence of some sort. Most of them had been specially built for her, or at all events they were newly decorated. Charles loaded her with presents of this kind. Beside those already mentioned she had Rocqueczière in Rouergue,[2] Issoudun

---

[1] He could not summon up his courage to ride across a wooden bridge.

[2] Two receipts concerning this estate are in existence, one for the year 1446–47, dated February 12, 1448, and another in April, as follows:

"We, Agnès Sorelle, Lady of Beauté and of Roquecezière, admit having had and received from Master Jehan le Tain-turier, notary and secretary of the King our Lord and his treasurer of Rouergue, the sum of two hundred and seventy-five livres tournois, on that which he owes or will owe on account of the revenue of the said Roquecezière. With which sum of two hundred and seventy-five livres tournois we are content, and give quittance to the said Lord Treasurer, and

L 2

and Vernon-sur-Seine. The first château bestowed upon her was Beauté-sur-Marne, near the
Bois de Vincennes, and the last in which she lived
was Mesnil near Jumièges.

All these houses and lands seem plentiful
provision for one small woman, and cause wonder
as to what she did with them beyond draw their
rents. Perhaps they were empty half the year
or more, and servants looked after them and
prevented them from going to rack and ruin.
It was the easiest thing in the world for the
king to say, "Have another house," and give
instructions for one to be built.

Cohen, in his *Chinon et Agnès Sorel*, printed
a portion of a diary alleged to be by Etienne
Chevalier,[1] in which he tells of the arrangements
made by the king for a gift of landed property to
his mistress.

"April 25, 1433 : This morning, said Etienne
Chevalier, the king called me to come to him.
When I entered the room he said, 'Etienne, I

wish to be held as having given quittance everywhere and to
every one whom it concerns.

"In witness whereof we have signed this receipt with our
own hand, and had it signed also by Pierre Dardaine, notary
royal in the seneschalship of Rouergue, 18th day of April,
the year 1448.

"AGNES AND DARDAINE."

[1] The manuscript was entitled :

"Des faicts et moult mémorables et grandes choses
avenues en le royal chastel de Chinon l'an de nostre seigneur
MCCCCXXV et jusques en l'an MCCCCL, ou se voient les
gestes de ma dame Agnès Soreau, dame de Beauté sur
Marne, de Roquecezière et d'Issoudun, escrites par son très
fidède serviteur Etienne Chevallier, secrétaire de nostre très
amé et redoubté seigneur le roi de France."

have to leave Chinon in a few days, perhaps to-morrow. Look after Mlle. Agnes Sorel with scrupulous care, forestall her every desire, grant her every wish. I charge you specially with this delicate mission. Prove that you are worthy of my confidence.'

" April 26 : I have seen Mlle. Agnes Sorel and found her extremely sad. I offered her my services and told her of the king's wishes. ' My friend,' she replied, ' I thank you, but I have need of nothing but calm and repose.'

" I informed her of the king's intention to leave the château on the following day, and to betake himself to his estates in Poitou.

" ' What—so soon ? ' she replied, and her cheeks became suddenly suffused with a blush.

" April 27 : The king departed at ten o'clock, accompanied by Messeigneurs de Chissay and de Gaucourt. The queen came to say farewell to him; Mlle. de Fromenteau stood a little way behind the queen. The king sought her eye and made a sign to her. The queen perceived it and turned round. Agnes fled.

" April 28 : I was in the queen's cabinet, and she dictated a letter to me to her Intendant in Languedoc. As I went out I saw Mme. la Gouvernante go in, and heard her say to her mistress that the king had an inclination for Mlle. de Fromenteau. I do not know whether it is true. But the queen's reply was admirable. ' The king is my Lord and Master. He has command over me. It is not for me to interfere in his deeds.'

" May 2 : I received a letter from the king, in which he informed me that the summer must not pass before a certain residence was built in order that it might be offered to Mlle. Agnes Sorel, for that was his good pleasure.

" The king left the choice of the site to me. I shall consult Mlle. Agnes on this topic.

" May 4 : Mlle. Agnes Sorel has just received a letter from the king, dated from Poitiers. Mademoiselle has said nothing to me, except that the king has given her the Comté de Penthièvre. It is much—yet it is little enough if it be true that the king has been happy enough to win her love.

" May 5 : We went to-day to examine the spot where the residence is to be erected. It will be situated in the park which extends beside the castle on the left.

" The garden of Roberdeau has lovely groves."

Here the journal breaks off, but enough has been said to call up a vision of " la belle des belles," in pretty enjoyment, watching her new residence grow day by day. At last the crenellated towers were completed, the terraces stretched before the frontage, and a haughty peacock, borrowed from the château near by, strutted on the newly laid lawns. With her dogs gambolling round her feet Agnes walked between the gay parterres and thought of her royal lover, hoping for his return.

When at length he came, life resumed its normal course, the evenings were spent in banqueting, in playing chess or dice, whilst subdued strains of music were heard rising from the outer hall where the troubadours gathered. This was the lazy, the luxuriant side of the *vie de château*. Cares were put aside and love was allowed full sway. No one in their senses would have changed it for the strenuous ways of a noisy modern city. Not those, at least, who can derive joy from the inner spirit of romance.

CHAPTER XV

ANTOINETTE DE MAIGNELAIS

WHILST she was staying at Chinon Agnes was indiscreet enough to invite to court her cousin, Antoinette de Maignelais, in the hope that she would be a pleasant companion in the lonely hours which now and again befall the mistress of a king. Unwittingly she was nourishing a viper in her bosom. Beautiful and ambitious, it soon appeared that Antoinette hoped to become the rival of Agnes.

Cohen [1] told a romantic story of the manner in which the Lady of Beauty sent for and introduced to the king's notice the woman who was to succeed, if not to supplant, her in his affections.

No sooner was Agnes settled in the new château of Roberdeau, whilst Charles was still in the north of France attending to the affairs of the kingdom, than his mistress began to feel the isolation of her position, and longed for the company of one she had known in her girlhood.

She despatched a messenger to Etienne Chevalier, and when he appeared in answer to her summons she begged him to be seated near her.

[1] *Chinon et Agnès Sorel.*

152

"Sir," she said, "if I have understood the king's wish rightly, it seems to me that it would please him if I should find in you a sure and faithful friend, ready to brave every difficulty if you could be of use to me."

"I have understood the same thing, Mademoiselle," replied Etienne, "and I will gladly prove my belief."

"Then listen to me," continued Agnes. "If you serve me in the manner I wish, I can assure you my gratitude will be lasting."

She fell into a fit of abstraction.

"The memory of the happy days of my early youth cannot be erased from my mind. I shall never forget the pure and sweet affections I indulged in at that time. Oh, do not be surprised," she went on presently, her eyes filling with tears, "it was the affection of an innocent girl. . . ." Then she recovered her composure and spoke quickly in even tones.

"My cousin Antoinette was brought up with me. Next to my aunt I loved her most dearly, and for seven whole years I have not seen her. I do not think she loved me as whole-heartedly as I cared for her, but time and absence will have changed that, and if I could embrace her, I feel I should have one friend the more."

Etienne sat silent. He thought he saw whither this conversation pointed, but it was not for him to speak until she had opened her mind fully to him.

"Go to Picardy for me, will you?" she pleaded after another pause. "There on the banks of the Oise you will find a lovely fortified château, surrounded by hills and woods and bosky dells. In the Château de Maignelais dwells Antoinette. There in childhood's days I played in the shadow of the elms when the heat of the summer was unendurable, and there I learnt my first lessons of life, and cried when I had my first fall."

She was moved by these reminiscences, but again mastered her feelings.

"When you have asked for the mistress of the château, an old servant will announce you— the nurse who guided my childish steps. If only she had remained with me to counsel me in my first experiences at court, as she did in my first experiences of life——" Her voice faltered.

Etienne, ashamed to be the witness of her emotion, begged that she would tell him what she wished to say another time. But she refused to let him go.

Summoning up all her courage, she controlled herself and instructed him to go to Maignelais, and to persuade her aunt to let Antoinette come and stay at Roberdeau. "Say to my cousin," she went on, " that I am longing to see her and to talk of the days that are past. She cannot refuse to grant my wish. As a pledge of my friendship and gratitude take this ring."

She pulled from her finger a valuable jewel and pressed it upon the king's secretary, and he promised to do her bidding even though the streams should turn to torrents and the oaks of Maignelais become giants ready to block his path to the entrance of the castle. Truly it was the day of chivalry.

The roads were unsafe for travellers. They were infested by brigands, and nobles rode abroad pillaging the homes of their own vassals and holding them captives for ransom. It was necessary to go fully armed. When Chevalier was knighted, Charles had said to him, " Etienne, notre Seigneur Dieu t'a fait naître chevalier, et je veux que tu meures chevalier de ma main." Now he donned his coat-of-mail, girded on his sword, fastened his gilded spurs, and seized his buckler, on which the legend ran :

" Tant elle vaut celle pour qui je meurs d'amour."

Flinging himself into the saddle, he rode forth as the drawbridge was let down. Turning to look back at the castle he was leaving, he saw Agnes watching him from a window. He waved his hand. She nodded and smiled her farewell.

Many months passed before she saw him again, but at last she received a letter from him by a special courier, which told her that her aunt was dead, that Antoinette was willing to accept her cousin's invitation to court, and that he expected to accompany her thither as soon after his letter as the state of the roads would permit.

And, in fact, a few days afterwards, when Agnes was looking out of the castle windows, she caught sight of some travellers arriving on horseback, who proved to be no other than Etienne himself and the twenty-year-old Antoinette.

Hastening to the courtyard Agnes greeted

her cousin right heartily as soon as she dismounted.

"My cousin," she cried, "dear cousin. It is really you—but you have grown beautiful, more beautiful than ever."

Mlle. de Maignelais withdrew from the warm embrace with which Agnes had welcomed her, and gazed into the honest blue eyes so near her own.

"No one could be half so lovely as you, Agnes," she said, and the envy in her voice proved the sincerity of her words.

But Agnes took no notice of her cousin's manner. She turned to Etienne and thanked him warmly for the care he had taken of Antoinette during the long journey, saying that the king would amply repay his fidelity and loyalty.

Then Etienne bent low and kissed her hand, saying, "Mademoiselle, I wish for no other approbation than yours. If I obtain your goodwill nothing else in the world makes any difference to me."

Then they entered the castle, and for many hours Agnes talked over the old days with Antoinette, recalling their games, their childish quarrels and the people they had known. She questioned her cousin until she could think of no more questions to ask, and then it was Antoinette's turn to speak. She began by praising Agnes for the clever use she had made of her time.

"Your career has been very different to mine," she said. "I am but a simple country girl, living on the land like the daughters of my own tenants, with hardly any interests in life. But with you things are very different. You pass your days in the lap of luxury, dressed in beautiful gowns, and going to magnificent parties every day. You are surrounded by homage and courtesy. Every one seeks you out to compliment and flatter you. Even the king——"

" Oh, the king——" Agnes grew red, then pale. How much did her cousin guess, she wondered.

Antoinette answered the unspoken thought. " I know," she murmured.

But Agnes had no intention of giving her her confidence. She passed off the awkward moment by saying, " The king will be very pleased to see you, my dear Antoinette. I have often spoken about you, and he said to me one day, ' You must send for her to come to court. We will find her a rich husband.' "

Antoinette glanced at her mischievously. " Can you tell me, Agnes," she said, " why the king should trouble to think about my marriage when he does not even know me, and yet allows you to remain without a husband ? It seems to me that he must be long-sighted. He sees things at a distance, but not those near at hand."

Agnes made no reply.

It was some weeks before the king met Mlle. de Maignelais.

Antoinette had a certain charm of manner, and she was beautifully dressed. The king thought her attractive. But when he spoke to her he was disappointed. She wished to please, but what she said was not pleasing. She was clever, but her cleverness was tinged with ill-nature and contrasted to her disadvantage with the gentle kindliness that Agnes invariably showed.

So the king's remarks were limited to a few cold compliments, and Agnes was disappointed that Charles did not appear to like her cousin as much as she had expected he would.

Antoinette, on her side, disgusted that she had failed to make a more satisfactory impression upon the king, soon announced to Agnes her intention of returning to the Château de Maigne-lais. Before she left she told her cousin that her aunt's dying wish had been that she, Agnes, " should find happiness in innocent desires and purity of soul."

" It is too late, alas," thought the king's mistress, and the cruel stab in her cousin's parting words caused her many a hidden tear.

This was not the real end of the acquaintance between Charles VII and Antoinette. She became a very dangerous rival to the Lady of Beauty. But that was later.

Agnes had little time to regret her ungrateful cousin's departure. Gaiety and festivity were in the air, and it was necessary for her to show a smiling face to the king and join heartily in every form of amusement that was proposed.

CHAPTER XVI

THE JOUST

In June, 1446, there was one of the most brilliant assemblies of princes that had forgathered at court for years. In consequence a number of tournaments and banquets were arranged to honour the guests. The particular joust in June was named " the great Emprise of the Dragon's Jaws," or the " Pass of the Perilous Rock." The originator was the most distinguished visitor, René d'Anjou, and he held the tourney in favour of the ladies.

The mode of procedure in these affairs was very ceremonious. The prince who wished to organise the joust sent secretly to the prince to whom he wished to present the sword to know if it were his intention to accept the challenge or not.

The king-of-arms who was honoured with the message presented himself before the prince his master desired to challenge, and said to him : " High and powerful Lord, my valorous master, knowing your courage, chivalry and prowess, sends me to you, in all loving-kindness and without malice, to challenge you to a combat, tourney and bout at arms, to take place in the presence of dames and damsels, and to offer you this sword."

If the challenged prince accepted, he took the sword from the king-of-arms stating that he did so without ill-feeling and to give pleasure to the challenger and entertainment to the ladies. He then handed to the king-of-arms a roll of parchment on which were inscribed the arms of eight knights and squires, so that four of them, two knights and two squires, should be chosen as umpires.

When the names had been selected certain formalities were gone through in informing the individuals that choice had fallen upon them. Two ells of cloth of gold, or of rich velvet or of crimson figured satin, to which was attached a parchment with the portraits of the two chief Lords of the Tourney represented on horseback, were worn as a cloak fastened on the right shoulder by the king-of-arms, who then departed on his mission to persuade the said gentlemen to act as judges.

The inducements held out to the young knight or squire to take part in the jousting were that he would gain knowledge and experience in arms, and acquire honour, valour, grace or augmentation of the love of the gentle lady whom he called his fair mistress, since ladies always love and favour valiant knights.

After these preliminaries the knights and squires met to fix the date and place of the joust, so that the king-of-arms might begin to cry and publish the said tourney in such districts as were

CHARLES VII

interested in the same. In this work he was
assisted by heralds and pursuivants, who called
in their most strident tones :

" Or ouëz, or ouëz, or ouëz ! "

followed by all the particulars of the affair,
regarding the arms to be used, the prizes to be
given by the ladies, the crests to be displayed,
the flags to be hung from the windows, the nature
of the armour to be worn, and even the manner
in which the legs were to be protected as in war
(or more carefully still, if possible), and the
length of the spurs, which were shorter than on
other occasions.

After instructions had been given as to the
dress of those who entered the lists, a careful
description of the lists themselves was formu-
lated, and then the caparison of the horses was
discussed, the four escutcheons of the prince's
arms being emblazoned on the four quarters of
the trappings.

The costumes of the knights in these jousts
were remarkable for their richness and colouring.

At Nancy, for instance, Jacques de Luxembourg had purple cloth of gold, bordered with
ermine, and was followed by four horses with
trappings of white and crimson velvet, embroidered with lions and other golden ornaments,
his pages and gentlemen being dressed in keeping.
Jacques de Lalaing's charger was caparisoned in
blue and crimson velvet, brocaded with gold,
and mottoes worked in gold, with a mantle of the
same. Three horses followed him, their blue

M

and crimson velvet striped and starred with gold, his gentlemen and pages dressed in satin of the same colours.

De Clermont's suite was a rainbow in itself. His own trappings were green velvet ornamented with gold, and he was followed by six horses; the first caparisoned in crimson cloth of gold, the second with white and blue velvet, the third in damask and golden embroidery *à grand feu,* the fourth in crimson velvet, with his motto " Espérance de Bourbon " embroidered in thread of gold, the fifth in black and violet velvet, and the sixth and last in ash-coloured velvet. The pages and gentlemen were attired to match, and the effect must have been remarkably like a circus.

At Châlons the same gentleman appeared for the sake of diversity in cloth of gold and violet velvet on a very fine Sicilian charger, and the six horses that followed him had all different trappings, one beautiful effect being obtained in blue velvet *semé* with golden fleurs-de-lis and barred with crimson velvet. The Comte de Clermont was betrothed to Jeanne de France early in 1447, an event which gave rise to fresh jousts at Tours, so perhaps all this splendour was intended to dazzle his future father-in-law. The expense of keeping these bejewelled and be-satined horses and retinue must have been enormous.

Pierre de Brézé was rather more modest in his apparel. His colours were blue and red velvet trimmed with a silver fringe, his motto was worked in gold. He was followed by three war-horses; the first caparisoned in white velvet and silver gilt, the others in damask trimmed with gold, and his six gentlemen wore blue and crimson satin.

The tournaments began an hour after noon, and the ladies who had assembled in the grand stands, attired in glowing colours to emulate the appearance of the knights, " of piteous heart and desirous of seeing the said joust," were called upon to choose a *chevalier d'honneur*. He, being appointed, saluted and thanked them for the honour done him.

This arduous task over, the ladies were bidden to partake of wine and dainties. Sometimes they danced while the finishing touches were given to the arrangements for the combat, and then they mounted to their places once more to see their lovers and brothers do battle on the field.

The glitter under the bright sun on the afternoon of the joust was dazzling, the noise was deafening. Agnes had seen these brilliant gatherings often, and felt proud to be one among that vast concourse of the highest in the land.

On the day when the joust of the Great Emprise of the Dragon's Jaws took place on the road between Chinon and Razilly, she sat watching the preparations from a pavilion specially assigned to her and decorated with the king's arms. As she leant upon the balustrade which protected her and her women from plunging unexpectedly into the crowd beneath them, she was overcome by uncontrollable excitement.

M 2

Flags waved in the air, the horses neighed and stamped their hoofs impatiently, the heralds shouted out the names of the knights about to enter the lists, and explained loudly that four gentlemen had undertaken to guard the pass between the two châteaux *à force d'armes*, a condition being that no lady should cross the square where they had taken their stand unless she were accompanied by a worthy knight or squire who should break two lances for love of her. Should any lady, however, attempt to pass the spot by herself she would be obliged to leave behind her some article in hostage, which she could not reclaim until she had brought with her a knight to take part in the joust. Above the heads of the four enterprising gentlemen towered a column on which was represented a furious dragon. This was the point of danger.

> " Dans le plus beau de la saison
>   Entre Razilly et Chinon
>   Devant la gueule du Dragon
>   N'alloit Dame ne Damoiselle,
>   Sans noble homme et de renom,
>   Qui d'armes n'acquittast le nom,
>   Gan de main, ou ploit de menton
>   D'elles prenoit pour querelle
>   Quatre nobles, lesquelles nouvelle
>   Emprise avoient d'armes telle,
>   Que nulle joyeuse ou belle
>   Ne passeroit sans son amy,
>   Bonne, loyalle, sans cautelle,
>   Par qui joye se renouvelle,
>   Sans rompre deux lances pour elle,
>   Contre son courtois ennemy."

The intentions were better than the poetry, and right merrily the combat began.

Every lady who advanced brought her true cavalier, and if he were successful in defeating the knight of the Perilous Rock with whom he did battle, the latter gave to the lady a diamond worth a hundred crowns or more, and begged her pardon for having detained her prisoner. On the other hand, if he vanquished her knight the said knight was obliged to take her *touret* [1] or her glove and attach it to the shield of the conqueror.

Everything being in readiness, the queen and the lords and ladies took their seats on the richly draped stands, and the king came forth from a castle built specially for the purpose, followed by two Turkish attendants clad in long gowns and turbans. These were followed in turn by mounted drummers, fife-players and trumpeters dressed in the king's colours, scarlet and white, two kings-of-arms, and nobles bearing banners on which were pictured brave feats and valorous combats, mounted ushers, and the judges.

Then came a dwarf, dressed *à la Turque*, riding a fine horse and bearing a shield on which were the arms of King René, and following him was a lady beautiful beyond compare and richly gowned. She led a second horse by a leading-rein, and its trappings swept the ground.

She wore a red gown, and her bosom was swathed in soft lace almost the colour of her clear white skin.

To her fell later the pleasant duty of bestowing

[1] A light fichu of gauze worn as a kerchief.

the prizes on the gallant knights—a war-horse
to Florigny, a golden casket covered with rich
diamonds and rubies to Ferry, Monsieur de
Lorraine. With each prize she declaimed verses,
standing before the king, the queen, and all the
princes, princesses and other distinguished personages who were assembled round her, awaiting
the sound of her clear voice in deep silence.

> " Ferry Monsieur fut là present
> Et la Damoiselle plaisante
> Luy dit Monsieur, ce present
> De par les Dames vous presente
> D'un fermaillet d'or reluisant,
> Reconnaissance vous faisant,"

and a good deal more about his valour, and his
loyalty, and his honour.

The prize for Ferry was worth many thousand
francs, and nearly a hundred valuable gems were
given to the ladies. After Ferry had received
his gift the Queen of Beauty bestowed the war-
horse on Florigny.

> " A la demoiselle s'avance
> Le Chevalier plein de scavance
> Humblement luy fait reverence
> Elle en grand honneur le baisa
> Puis luy dit d'humble contenance
> ' Chevalier, par votre vaillance
> Ce prix aurez par redevance.'
> Tres humblement la mercia."

The fun during the bouts had been fast and
furious.

First of all came the queen, Marie d'Anjou,
with her knight, the Sire de Saintrailles. He
fought with Gaston, Comte de Foix, who con-

quered him. " Upon which the good lady removed her velvet kerchief and commanded her knight to fasten it to the shield of the Comte de Foix." Then Marie was led to the ladies' stand, where she remained " to see what happened to the other ladies, some of whom would lose their gloves, and some their kerchiefs. . . ." She was quite ready to laugh at the unfortunate ones.

Even as she expressed this wish it was doomed to a first disappointment, for as the King of Sicily led out the Comtesse d'Evreux, he vanquished the Comte de Tancarville, who gave a diamond ring to the lady.

When the next damsel of high degree, Mlle. de Montberon, was obliged to leave behind her a glove, because her knight, the Comte de Laval, could not withstand the spirited attack of Claude de Chasteauneuf, the queen cried, " Put yourself in the same category as I am, you may just as well be honest about it. I left a kerchief behind me, and you left a glove. We shall not be alone; never fear."

The next lady had a fine cavalier, the Seigneur de Lohéac, who had behaved with great courage at Nancy. He won his partner, Mlle. de Touches, a golden ring.

Mlle. Marguerite de Villequier was not so fortunate, and " though it gave her great grief " she handed over her kerchief. The queen burst out laughing and said, " Don't blush, m'amie. We are already three here who have been badly cavaliered, but there will be others."

On the following day Marguerite's cousin, whose knight was Antoine d'Aubusson, Sieur de Montet, the *Petit Trignac*, won a beautiful diamond ring.

Antoine de Chabannes fought against the Marshal of Lorraine and lost, so he gave his lady a diamond and snatched a kiss from her lips, saying, " Madame, prenez, en gré."

Etienne Chevalier [1] entered the lists on a richly caparisoned horse; the words

" Exaltabitur sicut unicornis cornu meum "

and the E.C. bound by a knot were embroidered in gold on the crimson velvet.

When the Lady of Beauty entered the enclosure she was asked, " Who is your cavalier ? "

" Etienne Chevalier," she replied, gaily waving her hand towards him as he stood hoping to be the chosen knight.

He bowed low to his saddle, drew himself up again proudly and entered into combat with so much vigour that the knight who opposed him was vanquished in a trice.

Agnes received a lovely ring set with a priceless cut diamond as the result of his prowess.

She was smiling kindly upon her brave defender as she returned to the pavilion to show her treasure to the queen, who still watched the games with unflagging interest.

" Ah, ma fille," cried Marie d'Anjou, " you did well to win a ring, for there are some who say

---

[1] Cohen, *Chinon et Agnès Sorel.*

you are lacking in one." But Agnes knew well the taunt was meant in good humour, for the queen was never unkind.

Pierre de Brézé won his bout, but one of the queen's ladies, Annette de Guise, was obliged to pay a forfeit. She undid the tucker from her neck with a sigh, saying that when she was divested of it, she appeared " un peu brunette." But the queen on her approach said, " Çà ! çà ! brown lady, your colour and mine are much alike, come and sit beside me." Another young lady, Mlle. Gazelle, gave up her kerchief far more willingly than her glove, for " beneath the said kerchief there was nothing to be ashamed of nor anything that was not good to look upon."

At every fresh round Marie d'Anjou uttered a new quip. When Mlle. Jeanne Paulmarde came back to the grand stand with a ring, the queen, seeing her evident pleasure, remarked, " Ha dea ! Mlle. Paulmarde, you have been to the place where good servants are to be had, and you found one." " Madame," replied the young lady, " if you had pleaded with your knight-attendant as heartily as I did with mine, perhaps he would have won the day for you too."

To one lady Marie declared she must have said a good Ave Maria that morning for her cavalier, and with regard to another, who was in her household and who was not famed for her good looks, she seemed surprised that she should have succeeded where those who were more beautiful had failed. "Truly, Madame," was the reply, "I may not be beautiful, but I am clever enough to see that my knights don't fail me when I have need of them."

And so with much good-tempered raillery the joust came to a close at the end of three days.

King René had built a château at Launay, near to Saumur, which was completed in 1446, and festivities were arranged there as a kind of house-warming. This joust was called the "Pas du Géant à la blanche dame du Pavillon." Another tournament with a fantastic name took place about the same time, and was organised by six knights and squires of the Court of France, and called "L'Emprise du Cœur volant vermeil aux larmes blanches."

In this joust a new feature was arranged. The conqueror sent the vanquished adversary as a prisoner to some dame or damsel mentioned by him, and she alone was empowered to free him, which she did by unlocking with a small key a silver circlet which a herald had fastened to his leg as a sign of captivity. This little service was well repaid by a gift to her of a diamond worth a hundred crowns.

A month later another joust took place in the Forest de Thilley, in which many of the same combatants took part. Pierre de Brézé, Saint-railles, de Lohéac and de Clermont hardly ever failed to appear in the lists. It seemed as though these soldiers were spoiling for want of war, and that they found it necessary to expend their physical energy in some such martial exercises. No doubt the fact that the ladies played a prominent part in the mock-combats gave them an additional zest.

The year 1447 opened with new festivities at Montils-les-Tours, a residence which had been vastly improved during the preceding year, and which was becoming Charles VII's favourite château. Eleanor of Scotland and her retinue were present, and the occasion was the betrothal of Jeanne to the Comte de Clermont. The tournaments took place in the market-place at Tours " to pass the time pleasantly."

On February 5, a very sad event occurred, which proved that tournaments were not the safe amusement they might have been. There was at this time an embassy from England, Lord Dudley and Garter King-at-Arms were present when a young English squire, Jean Chalons, entered the lists against Louis de Bueil. The fight was really a duel, for Bueil had been made prisoner by the English at Château-Gonthier in 1448, and had made complaints of his captor, Chalons. The latter had demanded judiciary judgment, and Charles VII had given permission for a survival of the barbaric legislation which had almost fallen into disuse.

Accompanied by the queen, the two Scottish princesses, his mistress and the court ladies, he presided at the duel, which consisted of six rounds. At the fifth Louis de Bueil was wounded and his armour battered in. Saintrailles, who was umpire, begged that the fight should cease for that day. The king replied that it was necessary to consult the rules for these fights, and the outcome of the consultation was that the fight proceeded. The result was that Bueil received a fatal thrust.

An account of the fight was written by Fabyan.[1]

" A knyght of Fraunce called sir Lowys de Bueyll, chalengyd an esquyer of Englande named Rauffe Chalons, of certayn feetes of warre . . . but fortune to Chalons was so frendly that he ranne yᵉ Frenshe knyght thorugh with his spere, wherof the sayde sir Lowys shortly after dyed. Than this Chalons, lyke a cherytable Cristen man, mournyd for his enemy, and kept for him his obsequy as he had ben his carnall brother; for the whiche dede, of the Frenshe kynge he was greatly allowed, albeit, he was boûde so to do by yᵉ lawe of armys."

---

[1] *Chronicles of England and France*, 1811, p. 621. Fabyan gave an extraordinarily confused account of Agnes Sorel, making her mistress to Charles VI, and mother of Charles VII. " Of this Charlys sundrye wryters sunderly wryte, in so moche as some afferme hym to be yᵉ naturall sone of Charles the VII (Charles VI), some afferme hym to be the sone of the duke of Orlearne, and borne of the quene, and some there ben ꝩ name hym the sone of Charlys fore named, gotten in baast vpō his moost beauteuous paramoure named Agnes, the whiche, as testyfyeth Gagwynus, excellyd all other women in feture and beaute, and for the same to be surnamed yᵉ fayer Agnes. This in hyr myddell age dyed, and was so ryche, that hir testament amountyd to lx. M. scutjs of golde, the which in sterlyng money amountyth to the sūme of x M. li." *Op. cit.*, p. 640.

The misadventure of Bueil's death, although it caused great sorrow, did not interrupt the entertainments for more than a very short time.

The court was as gay as ever, and several marriages were arranged to take place. One of the *mignons*, François de Clermont, Siegneur de Dampierre,[1] was married to Mlle. de Montberon, who had lost her glove in the tournament between Razilly and Chinon.

The opportunity for lavishing handsome gifts upon the brides was taken by Charles, who also bestowed upon the queen and the Scottish princesses a large amount in cash " to be spent in gowns and other articles of attire."

A pugnacious cavalier of the type of Jacques de Lalaing arrived at court in the person of John Boniface. He belonged to the household of Alphonso V, and went from court to court holding *pas d'armes* and making a trade of jousting. About this time King René returned to court, and would no doubt have inaugurated more sports, but Charles was on the point of leaving Montils, and he had had enough of tournaments.

The king now installed his household at Mehun-sur-Yèvre near Bourges, and Agnes went to Bois-Trousseau.

The queen did not accompany Charles into Berry. She remained at Tours in order to make a pilgrimage to Mont-Saint Michel. Eleanor of

[1] The same referred to in Agnes Sorel's letter to Mlle. de Belleville as a messenger between them.

Scotland, the Comte de Nevers, the Comte de Laval and Marshal de Lohéac were in her train.

Bois-Trousseau is one of the most romantic of the châteaux connected with the Lady of Beauty.

CHAPTER XVII

THE LEGEND OF BOIS-TROUSSEAU

IN the reign of Charles VII Artault Trousseau, Seigneur de Mareuil et du Bois, married his son Jacquelin to Perrette Cœur, daughter of the celebrated Jacques Cœur, and her dowry was 10,000 livres tournois and jewels beyond compare. Seigneur Trousseau was then at the height of his fortune and had embellished and aggrandised his château, which became a residence worthy of a king. Charles VII often went there, either because the surrounding country was agreeable for hunting, or because this retreat, hidden in the midst of deep forests, offered a secret and mysterious home for his mistress. It was said that Agnes resided there still more frequently than Charles, and that lanterns arranged on the top of the principal tower gave easy means of communication to the lovers when the king was at the Castle of Mehun. The official deeds of the reign of Charles VII do not confirm the fact of his presence at Bois-Sire-Amé during the lifetime of Agnes, except on a single occasion, namely, in May, 1447, when his letters were dated from there. Possibly, however, when the king went to the Château du Bois he was otherwise occupied than in holding councils, drawing up contracts, or writing letters patent.

After the death of Agnes the king returned again and again to Bois-Trousseau. But it does not appear to be true that Charles bought the estate for the Lady of Beauty, because nearly a century later than the period in question a Trousseau still owned the castle and paid homage for it to Marguerite, sister of François I.

Either as recompense to Artault Trousseau for his kindness in lending the castle, or because he desired to have it made a more perfect royal residence, Charles had given the owner the sum of one thousand golden crowns, to be spent on alterations. Jacques Cœur was charged with the debt, and the catastrophe which ruined him prevented him from paying off the entire sum.

Although neither Charles VII's name nor that of the fair Agnes appears in the list of those who possessed the land, at least it owes to the king's visit there the title under which it is named in the contemporary documents. Perhaps the ingenious flattery may even be attributed to the sentimental tenderness of Agnes herself.

The château lay in the form of a parallelogram, surrounded by wide and deep moats crossed by a stone bridge. A huge block of buildings flanked by three strong round towers occupied one of the sides. Near one of the high and pointed gables was a square tower called the Tour du Nord, which was finished by a platform crenellated and with machicolations. Two more

[To face p. 176

AGNES SOREL

(*From an engraving by Petit*)

round towers occupied two angles of the enclosure. The entrance was defended by a drawbridge and placed between two towers less solid and less high. A very thick wall completed the enclosure and supported a crenellated gallery which served as a means of communication between the various parts of the castle.

Though simple and severe the castle was exceedingly strong. Paintings of religious subjects adorned the walls and vaults of the old chapel. By some the castle was called the Château de Dames, but this change in name did not in the least affect the romance which clung to its walls.

Every good legend leaves the historian sceptical, but gives him food for reverie. The story which connects the name of Agnes Sorel with Bois-Trousseau is of this character.

"This château," wrote Bengy-Puyvallée,[1] " is remarkable for the long visit made there by Agnes Sorel, mistress of Charles VII. When this prince stayed at the Château of Mehun, his mistress resided at the Château de Dames. The king joined her under the pretext of going hunting in the Forest of Dames and d'Allogny. My son, to whom this estate belongs, still preserves, in one of the rooms of the castle, the portrait of Charles VII, painted to represent Hercules, draped in a lion's skin, the portrait of the fair Agnes, her clothes-press, her toilet-table, the fire-dogs, an armchair and her table. This furniture is more interesting on account of its

[1] *Mémoire Historique sur le Berry*, Bourges, 1842, p. 88.

N

age rather than for the beauty of the workmanship. A remarkable thing is that in the interior
of the dressing-table a painting represents the
Passion of Our Lord."

"During my childhood in Berry," wrote
another author,[1] " I often heard tell of the pretty
little château which Charles VII gave to Agnes
Sorel. I believe that the ruins of it still exist
and can be seen in the environment of the cantons
of Levet, only it goes by another name than that
which M. de Bengy-Puyvallée gave to it. It is
called the Château de Bois-Sire-Amé, or, in the
Latin of the day, 'Boscius Senioris amati.' . . .
At that time, Charles VII was living in the
Château of Mehun-sur-Yèvre, where he died later
on. La Belle des Belles, as she was called, was
then living at Bois-Sire-Amé. There, every
evening, about nightfall, at an hour agreed upon
between them, the king and she each mounted
on a tower of their own dwelling-place and
greeted one another at a distance.

"It was their way of wishing each other good-
night.

"Those who are sceptical about such things,"
added this ingenuous author, " object that this
intercommunication could not have taken place,
because from Mehun it was impossible to per-
ceive the favourite's residence. As for myself
so much the worse for me, I cannot do otherwise
than believe in this playful fancy of two hearts
intensely devoted the one to the other; a

[1] Philibert Audebrand, *L'Intermediaire des Chercheurs et
Curieux*, Avril 80, 1908, col. 624–5.

practice which, moreover, is well in accordance with the chivalric manners of that day."

There is another version of the legend full of still more picturesque detail.[1]

Agnes, according to the king's will, had arrived at Bois-Sire-Amé, or to give it the title of its former owner, Bois-Trousseau. The king remained in Bourges busy with important affairs. She begged him " in the name of their gentle love, not to quit any great enterprise which God and France required." Charles obeyed her and remained at the post of duty.

One evening about this time Agnes was in the hall of the château, carelessly glancing through an illuminated manuscript which lay on her lap. She heard, as though in a dream, the striking of a church clock in the distance. Suddenly a servant entered to tell her that an unfortunate hunter, having missed his way and worn out with fatigue, had arrived, begging the lady of the house to give him some food and a night's rest. Hospitable and generous above all things, Agnes gave orders to have the man admitted at once. The Lady of Beauty, wearing a cap embroidered with gold, went out to meet him. The moon shone brightly and in a neighbouring wood the nightingale warbled the low notes of its love-song. The knight bowed low. The Lady of Beauty acknowledged his salute with a sweet dignity and grace peculiarly her own. Then he stepped forward, his head bent down, and two greyhounds

[1] Robert Duquesne, *Vie et Aventures Galantes de la Belle Sorel.*

N 2

which had followed him came sniffing round her. She peered through the darkness into his face.

" Agnes, Agnes, it is I ! " he cried, unable to keep silence longer. " Do you not know me ? "

" You, Sire ! Ah——"

She drew him quickly into the hall and he took her in his arms, showering caresses upon her. Dominated by his great love, Charles had left his castle and, in the disguise of a hunter, had sought out the mistress he had been pining to see.[1]

This incident must have occurred before Agnes was acknowledged by her royal lover.

There is yet another version of the legend which concerns a later time. In the historical records, as stated, there is no proof that Agnes stayed at Bois-Trousseau earlier than the spring of 1447, and by that time Charles had no need of disguise.

On the central tower of the fortified manor-house a huge pile of faggots, gathered from the surrounding woods, was heaped up and fire was set to it by a trusty attendant. The fair châtelaine herself climbed the narrow winding stairway to the top and came out to see that the flames mounted high and burnt clear, so that her beacon could be seen beyond the belt of trees that encircled the mansion. Had the light burnt low or been extinguished by heavy rains her heart would have grieved, for she would have

[1] There is a similar story told about Henry IV and Gabrielle d'Estrées, but the king was not so well received.

feared lest her lover should not come, and a night of love lost might be a night of love never recovered.

When the flare shone clear across to the big château, Charles quitted his pursuits, dismissed his guests, sent his soldiers about their business, said a curt " good-night " to his gentlemen of the chamber, and when he was left alone he listened until all was silent in the castle. Then he went out by a private passage-way, taking no retainer with him, but trusting to the dagger in his belt should danger lurk in the thick growth of forest that he had to traverse. Through the dark night he stumbled, sometimes tripping up against the spreading roots of the trees, scratching his cheek upon the twigs that swung against him in the wind, or even falling over a log that lay across his path. He cared little for such things. He was going to the one woman in all the world he loved, going to the home he had made for her, where he could spend a quiet hour by her fireside, playing with the babes that were his and hers.

The glow of the burning faggots grew clearer and clearer still to his sight, and soon he left the avenue of trees that led to the house behind him and was within the circle of light on the threshold of her mansion.

She stood in the entrance waiting for him, as she had stood many times already in her life, dressed in a long clinging robe of flimsy golden stuff which showed the slender lines of her figure. Her luxuriant hair was bound loosely round her·

head, her clear blue eyes were soft with the pleasure of his coming.

In another moment she had drawn him into the hall, where on a round table a simple supper was laid. He had eaten already, but she made him break bread afresh, for, said she, unless he ate with her, it would not be really their home. On stools near the fire, nodding sleepily, sat Marie and Charlotte. But they did not receive attention from their father until it was their turn.

There were other nights when Charles could not be at Mehun and had to stay at Bourges, five leagues away. And then the beacon at Bois-Trousseau shone out across the country and twinkled in the far distance like a star that had only a message of sadness and loneliness to give. For Agnes, separated from her lover, was alone indeed. No friend sat by her in that darkening hall, no kind hand was stretched out to meet hers in sympathy. For in all the world there is no loneliness so intense as the loneliness of the woman who is a king's mistress. That is her punishment.

Agnes's furniture from Bois-Trousseau was placed later in the museum at Bourges and has been fully described.[1] Among other items are several cabinets and chairs of carved wood as finely wrought as any of later date, and a sécrétaire which it would be difficult for modern ingenuity to surpass, either in design or execution. It is adorned with figures of singularly good proportion, and has panels painted in rich blue

---

[1] Louisa Costello, *Jacques Cœur and His Times*.

and gold, representing antique heads and armorial bearings. Another piece of furniture is a toilette table of cedar-wood, delicately put together, and having interior compartments in low-relief, showing groups representing scenes in the life of the Virgin Mother and her Son, admirably done. One cabinet has a cornice, supported by statuettes of Charles VII in the character of the god Mars, Agnes Sorel as Venus, and other figures. There are also some medallions which probably once graced the walls of a chamber. One of these is a portrait, in carved wood, of Agnes, and one of Charles VII as Hercules, surrounded by a group of warriors, who seem entreating him to leave Omphalium : beneath it, written in golden letters, is the inscription " Veritable portraicture de Herculé, emmaillotté de peau de lion : donné par le roy à la tendre Agnes, 1450."

Another treasure in the same museum is one of the vases which adorned the towers of Mehun-sur-Yèvre, and which, according to Louisa Costello's account, was filled with flowers and placed in the window as a signal from Charles to his lady-love. This vase was of china, high and large, and ornamented with open-work tracery which gave it a transparent effect.[1]

[1] The art of working in china had attained great perfection at this period, and Limoges was at the zenith of its fame. The same author mentions a plate of Limoges at Chenonceaux which bears a design representing Charles and Agnes riding the same horse. The king wears a costume similar to robe and cowl, and his mistress a tight-fitting gown, which by no means flattered the beauty of her form. The faces are not well designed, and the steed is a lumbering dray-horse with its tail tied in a knot.

The king and his mistress were not left i
seclusion at Bois-Trousseau. One day Jacque:
de Lalaing, the indefatigable squire, arrived tc
ask whether he might hold a new joust. The
king was pleased to receive him graciously, and
thinking highly of the young man, he advanced
towards him, took him by the hand, and said :
" Sire Jacques, we shall invite you to the royal
residence and wish that to pass the time you will
rest and banquet with our people."

He refused permission for the tournament to
be held, however, because at the latest event
instituted by King René several gentlemen had
been grievously wounded, and people were beginning to think such exercises too dangerous to life
and limb. As a matter of fact, however, a
tourney took place near Bourges in June, when
forty knights and squires fought forty others,
and in October there was another, probably in
honour of the young Burgundian squire.

After spending the summer at Bois-Sire-Amé
the king moved to Bourges, where he stayed
during the autumn and then returned to Touraine and spent Christmas at Chinon and Razilly.
It was at this moment that his thoughts were
turned from ease and pleasure to more serious
considerations, for the dauphin, his well-beloved
son, was plotting against the crown.

CHAPTER XVIII

THE INTRIGUES OF THE DAUPHIN

BORN in 1423 in the city of Bourges, Louis the dauphin was only twenty years younger than his father, and at an early age his overmastering nature led him to pit his strength against the king. Ready to throw himself into any adventure that offered peril and excitement, the prince had consented to join the rebel nobles in their onslaught upon the throne, known as the "Praguerie" in 1440. Naturally enough, for some time afterwards the relations between Charles and Louis were distinctly strained.

Du Fresne de Beaucourt declared that the dauphin left no stone unturned to remove the bad impression he had left upon his father's mind, to recover his favour, and to ingratiate himself with the great councillors of State. But the task he had set himself was a very difficult one, and the difficulty of it lay in his own temperament. Insatiably ambitious, he had not even tact enough to conceal the fact that he believed he could achieve more than his father were he on the throne. Comines said of him, " he seemed better fitted to rule a world than to govern a single kingdom." In his heart the dauphin considered this to be true, and he set

185

about proving it by opposing the king in everything he did.

Thus he became a real danger at court. His actions were not always openly hostile, and whilst he wore a smile on his lips, and spoke pleasant words, he was planning and scheming in his treacherous heart against those who were in power.

In 1444 the dauphin had been appointed to command the army sent against the Swiss. There were some who said the king had temporarily rid himself of his unruly son by these means. But Charles was for ever hoping for signs of grace which never came, and would have preferred to keep the dauphin by his side had Louis only showed promise of reform. When he was wounded at the siege of Saint-Hippolyte, Charles forgot all the rancour he had felt, and remembered only that his son was in danger. He sent courier after courier to recall him to court.

Once more installed at home, a new source of disagreement occurred between the dauphin and the king. Charles had been sincerely fond of his daughter-in-law, and did not fail to blame Louis for the neglect which brought about Margaret's suffering and death. This sad event was the occasion of a fresh outburst of bitter reproach on the part of the king; and Louis took his reprisals in bad part.

Although he had received liberality at the hands of the king, although he had been entrusted with confidential missions and placed at the head of the soldiers, he still felt that he had grievances against him, and though he found it hard to put a name to them, as he was bent on quarrelling, the merest pretext was enough to enable him to carry out his intentions.

A cause for complaint was all ready to his hand. On his return from Switzerland Louis found that his father had fallen greatly under the domination of Agnes and of her friends, of whom Pierre de Brézé was the most important.

Aware that he could not hope to gain his father's ear with others so privileged to speak into it, he at first tried to ingratiate himself with those who held the power he coveted. He looked with admiring eyes at the Lady of Beauty and presented her with some rich tapestries brought from the south. He had taken them during a successful expedition against the Comte d'Armagnac, and they represented the story of Susannah and the Elders.

To Brézé he gave forty-five casks of Rhine wine, and was instrumental in helping him to obtain the *comté* of Maulevrier in recognition of certain services done when negotiations had been entered into with the Duc de Savoie regarding the cession of Valentinois and Diois.

Margaret had possessed little influence for good over her careless spouse, but she was by nature a peacemaker, and with her death the only mediator " within the fleur-de-lis " was removed and the breach in the royal household widened perceptibly.

Louis borrowed money on every side. He had

extravagant tastes and little wherewith to satisfy them. He had no scruples in making enemies. He quarrelled with Dunois, with Louis de Bueil, who was afterwards to meet his death in the joust, and with several others. He was at daggers drawn with René d'Anjou, and before many years had passed he was to flee for shelter to his father's enemy, the Duc de Bourgogne.

In the meantime passive dislike and idle mischief-making did not satisfy the prince's impatient mood. He desired active measures, and very soon found an outlet for his love of intrigue in stirring up sedition and evolving a plot.

It was whilst the court was at Razilly and he was at Chinon that he was inspired by an evil plan.

Among the king's attendants was Antoine de Chabannes, who had been made councillor and chamberlain in spite of his support to the anti-royal party in the Praguerie. Taken into favour again, Chabannes had followed the dauphin in the Swiss campaign. He was a captain of the famous *écorcheurs*.

At Easter-time the dauphin sent for Chabannes, who was some ten years his senior, and led him to a window in the château which looked on to the meadows. One of the Scottish archers happened to be passing, in a magnificent uniform, wearing the king's colours.

Pointing to this man, Louis said, " See, there goes one of those who are keeping all France in subjection."

" Whom do you mean ? " inquired Chabannes.

" The Scottish Guard," replied the dauphin. " It would not be very difficult to prevent all that."

" It is a fine institution, that guard," said Chabannes thoughtfully, " and the king deserves special praise for organising it. Certes, it is a matter of honour that a noble monarch should be so protected when he rides through the town or in the country. It gives security to his person. Had he not had his guard, people might have attempted many things which, under the circumstances, they dare not do."

After this speech Chabannes tactfully changed the subject. He hinted amongst other things that he had been talking to one called Villars, who had said that whilst the king was at Châlons he had intended to give the dauphin more power, that he had confidence in him and wished to entrust him with important affairs.

But the dauphin interrupted impatiently. He declared that this was all talk and that he had never been treated fairly or given a chance to show what he could do.

There the matter ended for the time being. He sent Chabannes to Savoy on a special journey and promised him a large sum of money if he could carry out what was required of him.

A few months later Chabannes returned. Louis had been to see the king at Razilly and called up his messenger, whom he patted playfully on the shoulder.

" Come now," he cried. " There is nothing

else for it, but to send the king's people packing."

"How do you intend to do that?" asked Chabannes, surprised.

"Well! it is not difficult. I have fifteen or twenty arbalisters and thirty archers, or thereabouts. And you have some archers too, I hope. You will have to arrange to let me have five or six."

Negotiations proceeded between the two, and the names of one or two possible additions to the little company were mentioned.

"But, Monseigneur," said the astute Chabannes presently, "I assure you the matter cannot be done so easily, for the king has the soldiers under command and they are quartered round here."

"I have enough soldiers to subdue his," replied the dauphin.

"But how do you mean to do it?" continued Chabannes.

"You know," explained the dauphin, "that anybody has the right of entry at Razilly. We will enter one after the other, in such a way that we are not noticed and until there are enough of us inside to do the trick. I shall have my thirty archers and fifteen or twenty arbalisters, as well as the gentlemen of my household with me. I shall soon win over the king's gentlemen;" and then he proceeded to mention several men who were well disposed towards him and probably in his pay.

"When I have all those I have named on my

side," he boasted, " I cannot fail to be the stronger party. First of all we must make for the two small turrets and take our stand there."

Chabannes listened thoughtfully. " Monseigneur," he said at length, " the thing is not as easily done as said, because when you have taken Razilly as you suggest, the soldiers will march up from without and capture all those who are inside."

But the dauphin would not listen to this possibility of failure. He was quite certain he could count on enough men.

" But I must be there personally," he added, " because every one who sees the king fears him, and if I were not there myself my men's hearts might fail them when they set eyes on him. But in my presence every one will do what I bid them and all will go smoothly, for I shall put good men and true round him, and as for his guard I will make sure of them because I shall have three or four hundred lances out against them."

After that he began promising favours to all concerned. Chabannes was to be munificently rewarded, the *mignons* (Clermont among them) were to receive such moneys as would satisfy them, and as for Pierre de Brézé, " Well," said the dauphin, " he will go on governing as he has been doing, but it will be under me."

And with these significant words he turned away.

A few days later he inquired whether the archers had arrived.

" Send for them and do not be anxious," he said to Chabannes.

By that time his plots were almost ready and he felt certain of attaining the result he desired.

Before long the intrigue grew more and more complicated. M. de Bueil, who had been disgraced a little while before and removed from the dauphin's household, approached Brézé. There were constant journeys between Bueil's house and Chinon and Razilly. Jean de Daillon, another of the dauphin's men, was one of his agents. He was always in the company of Bueil. One day they met Chabannes and said to him half in joke that they thought he had two strings to his bow.

" I have only one," replied Chabannes, " but it is such a good one that I think there is no chance of its snapping."

Bueil was warned by one of his servants that his position was getting dangerous, but he would not listen. " I am not afraid," he replied, " of the seneschal, nor of the seneschal's lady, nor of any of their *seneschalleries*—not a jot. The king regards me with favour, and I stand better with Monseigneur than ever."

Another servant deposed that his master, Bueil, had declared : " This government cannot go on. Do you think the dauphin and all the nobles will suffer the things that they see happening to continue ? They are all on his side and have taken their oath of fidelity to him, and very soon we shall see a powerful cabal and a change of government, for this seneschal meddles in every-

[*To face* p. 192

LOUIS THE DAUPHIN

thing and destroys everything. He takes money on every hand. He has had four hundred thousand crowns since the truce. The Duc de Savoie gave him the *comté* of Maulevrier and another sum of money, because he got him off paying homage. He keeps the king under the influence of that Agnes who is in the queen's household. He sent Monseigneur to Germany to deliver the country of him. He left him without provisions and took away his soldiers. He'll be paid out for all that," and so forth, and so forth.

No sooner was the plot ready to burst over the heads of the king and the seneschal, than Charles, who had already grown suspicious of what was in the wind, ordered an inquiry to be made, and, by dint of bringing pressure to bear, obtained depositions by Antoine de Chabannes,[1] by Benoist, servant to de Bueil, as well as by some of the archers of the Scottish Guard and others.

It appeared from these statements that the dauphin had tried to win over the captains of the archers, and that he intended at all costs to rid the country of Brézé and, if possible, involve Agnes in his downfall.

Daillon and Louis de Bueil were accused of taking part in a plot to kill Brézé and they hastily fled from court. Chabannes was supposed to have received ten thousand crowns for his share in the affair, but, according to one account, he

---

[1] Duclos, *Recueil de Pièces pour servir de suite à l'histoire de Louis XI*, 1746.

o

gave back the money and saved his skin by turning king's evidence.

Charles, who was convinced at last of his son's guilt, ordered him into his presence and reproached him bitterly with his conduct.

" Louis," he said, " I am well aware of the ill-feeling you harbour against Brézé, who has served me well and loyally. You have plotted against his life." ·

" Sire," replied Louis boldly, " I have done nothing that Chabannes did not counsel me to do."

" By Saint-John," swore the king, " you lie."

He then sent for Chabannes, who contradicted what the prince had said.

Then Louis was very angry and rated him loudly.

At last Charles found it necessary to interfere.

" Louis," he said to his son, " I banish you for four months from the kingdom and you must go to the Dauphiné."

The prince removed the cap he was wearing. He went out uttering a savage oath between his teeth.

" By my bare head," he muttered, " I will revenge myself on those who have been instrumental in turning me out of my own house."

According to Du Fresne de Beaucourt, it is not true that the dauphin was exiled in this manner. Charles sent him to the Dauphiné on a political mission. Many causes were at work to bring about a definite breach between father and son, and some accounts blame the Lady of

' Beauty for the final parting between king and prince.

The relations between Louis and Agnes are not clearly defined. Was it the dauphin's intention to propitiate his father's mistress when he gave her the tapestries, or was it because he was moved by her grace and beauty to an expression of his regard for her ? The question is not an easy one to answer. Louis loved intrigue and mystery. A thousand motives surged in his intricate brain, a thousand purposes, most of them tinged with evil, led him into strange deeds.

Agnes was beautiful, Louis was young and at that time susceptible to feminine influences. But Agnes must have read the mind of her lover's son, have seen danger there and—if she listened even for a moment to his plausible flattery and insidious demands—disgrace.

Whatever relations he desired should exist between them, whatever the answer she gave to his advances, one thing is certain. Louis did not persist in his endeavours to ingratiate himself in her esteem. His interest turned to dislike, his dislike to hatred, and his actions led him to make that hatred visible to all.

Some have declared in his defence that it was love for his mother which led him into showing Agnes open scorn. Though Louis must be given the credit of loving his mother, even if he cared for no other soul, this proposition is not a sound one, for he knew his mother had been supplanted by Agnes in his father's affections early in 1444,

O 2

and in that year he gave her presents. It was not until 1446 that he first took up a hostile attitude.

Nor was it Marie d'Anjou who instigated her son to advocate her cause and, if possible, oust her rival from the high place she had reached at court. Marie had long since accepted the inevitable, and it cannot be imagined for a moment that she would do anything to widen the already gaping breach between her husband and her favourite son.

Louis had one motive in doing everything in his power to make things uncomfortable at court for his father's mistress. Agnes was in the king's confidence, Agnes had power, Agnes could sway all those who had a weighty say in affairs of government. Louis envied her this. All that he desired for himself was implied by those words—confidence, power, sway! He longed to be first in the kingdom and Agnes stood in his path.

"The king is behaving as badly as he can," said the dauphin to the familiar spirits who were at his beck and call in the Dauphiné. "But I intend to put matters to rights as far as he is concerned. When I am near him again, I will chase away Agnes and make it impossible for him to go on with his follies. Things will go on far better then than they have been doing." [1]

That was his avowed intention. He meant to make matters so thoroughly uncomfortable and difficult for the favourite that she would find it

---

[1] *Procès de Mariette*, p. 285: Preuves de M. Escouchy.

necessary to retire from the position at court she had filled with such grace and—when compared with others—even with modesty.

Duquesne declared that Louis opened his campaign by attacking the virtue of the Lady of Beauty and that Charles, taking this denunciation as coming from envious lips, and knowing the absolute loyalty which Agnes had invariably shown towards him, would not listen for a moment to his son's accusations.

But this method of slandering an enemy would appear far too direct for one who was noted for the devious paths in which he trod. One would expect something more subtle, more evil, and more in the nature of backbiting than this from the subtle prince.

The same author told a story of intrigue in which Chabannes took part.

Louis desired an incontrovertible proof of Agnes's perfidy and he sought for one. The Comte de Chabannes, whose good looks and witty tongue made him eminently suitable for such an attempt, according to one account offered his services to the dauphin in his secret plans, and assured him that he could not fail. Judging from the intrigue already described, in which Chabannes played a part, it is more likely that Louis pressed him into his service.

One afternoon in September when the afternoon light began to fail, Agnes was sitting alone in a corner of the park, listening dreamily to the splash of a fountain into its basin where floated languid odorous water-lilies. All of a sudden the count appeared in sight. Enchanted to have his company she smiled, and waving her hand pointed to the space beside her on the stone seat. Having greeted her respectfully he sat down, and they talked in a familiar strain.

He spoke of lovely flowers which withered even as earthly joys wither, of the sun over which cloud-shadows pass, as troubles come to dim the mind of kings at the height of their triumph. He continued in so mournful a strain that at length she inquired what it was that grieved him.

At first he would not reply, but moved by sudden passion, he fell at her feet and begged her to have pity on him; he was dying of love for her.

He seized her in his clasp and was about to press a burning kiss upon her lips, when, with an almost superhuman effort, Agnes broke away from him and fled crying and terrified towards the castle, pursued by her persecutor.

At the gateway she met the king. He soothed her as well as he was able and urged her to tell him the truth. What was it that had driven her crazy with fear ?

She pointed to Chabannes, who had not dared to make his escape, and cried, " He is to blame."

The king was very angry. He ordered the delinquent to follow him into his private apartments and threatened to throw him into the deepest dungeon of the castle.

Only the intervention of Agnes saved him from

this disgrace, and turned his punishment into one of exile. Chabannes bowed his head and went away.

Whilst the king was listening to the full account of the matter from the lips of Agnes the dauphin entered the apartment. He was in a very excitable mood and paced up and down the room, not listening to what was going on between his father and Agnes, yet throwing angry looks in their direction and muttering to himself.

At length Charles could bear his son's conduct no longer. He turned round sharply to ask what he meant by this interruption, and to his great surprise Louis broke out into angry invectives against the Lady of Beauty.

The king was so taken aback by this unexpected outburst that the dauphin was able to utter a number of disrespectful things before he could stop him.

" Par la Pâques-Dieu, Sire ! " almost shrieked the prince, working himself up into a furious passion. " This woman," pointing at Agnes, " is the cause of all our misfortunes. She it is who spreads discord between us. Her rashness deserves punishment."

And stepping in front of her as she rose in horror at his violent remarks, he struck her full in the face.

The historical accounts of this incident vary somewhat. Pius II [1] went so far as to declare that Louis threatened the defenceless woman

[1] Pii II. Pont. Max. Commentarii rerum memorabilium.

with his sword ! Another authority [1] said he boxed her ears.

There was, at any rate, a disgraceful scene of some kind. Charles threw himself upon Louis and forced him to his knees. Agnes fell at the king's feet begging pardon for his son. Her grandeur of soul touched both father and son. Charles VII's passion died out. The dauphin's cold and egoistic spirit stirred for a moment with better impulses. The king, beside himself at this latest exhibition of his son's incorrigible behaviour, ordered him sadly out of his presence.

Agnes considered seriously whether she should leave court and retire to one of her châteaux. To come between father and son was a great grief to her, almost a crime in her eyes, and she understood that it was impossible for both herself and the dauphin to remain near the king. She was quite ready to sacrifice herself if reconciliation could be brought about in that way.

But this was not to be. Whether Louis made the relations between his father and Agnes a pretext for refusing to countenance the immorality at court, or whether he endeavoured to rival the king in his amours and was actuated by personal jealousy will never be known. Alienor de Poitiers wrote in *Honneurs de la Cour :* [2] " I saw the King of France, packed off by his father King Charles on account of a quarrel of which the fair Agnes was the cause." Nor was

[1] Jean Bouchet, *Annales d'Aquitaine.*
[2] In Lacurne de Sainte Palaye, *Mémoires sur l'Ancienne Chevalerie.*

this the only reference to the fact that the Lady of Beauty had more to do with the rupture between Charles and Louis than his plots against the crown.

Vallet de Viriville [1] stated that since his return from the expedition in Armagnac, the dauphin paid court to the king's mistress. If that were so, disaster was a foregone conclusion.

The same author told an interesting story of an allegorical scene depicted in the hall of the Angelots in the house of Jacques Cœur at Bourges.

" The sculptured scene," he wrote, " occupied three faces of a capital. A grove or orchard was represented. On the right a young woman, clothed in prodigiously luxuriant clothes and furs, reposed calmly in a bed of flowers. At her feet a fountain played. From beyond its basin there advanced insidiously a young prince, his hand resting on his heart. He was accompanied by a jester who followed him in the guise of a guide. The lady, lifting her right hand to her forehead, was apparently indicating the crown [2] which encircled her brow. The prince, on the other hand, pointed out another crown, this time the royal crown, which was reflected in the basin of the fountain. Above, buried in the bushy leafage of a tree in the centre, a crowned king apparently took part in the conversation. Unfortunately the scroll which issued from his mouth was bare or defaced."

[1] *Histoire de Charles VII*, Vol. III. p. 282 *n.*
[2] The crown of a duchess perhaps.

Round the borders of the scene were inscribed the favourite mottoes of Jacques Cœur: " Dire, faire, taire " and " En bouche close n'entre mouche."

Vallet de Viriville was certain that in this representation he recognised Charles VII, Agnes and the indiscreet Louis.

How such a daring subject came to be placed in so prominent a position as the house of Jacques Cœur cannot be determined.

It was a thousand pities that Louis did not restrain his feelings and think twice before taking action in the matter of his father's love affairs. Such interference is rarely successful. In his case it was positively disastrous.

It resulted apparently in the final separation from his father, which, perhaps for Charles, was not the worst that might have happened.

Into the life of Agnes it brought deep unhappiness. Up to that point she had been gay and careless enough. Now she awakened to the fact that her position was untenable.

According to Cohen's account she decided to withdraw for a time to Beaulieu, near Loches.

Charles, reduced to despair by the thought of separation, endeavoured to turn her from her purpose.

" No, Sire," she replied to his pleading, " the years I have passed with you have given me too many enemies. Render to those who hate me a favour they greatly desire. The assurance that your heart remains mine is all I need, and I should have no other wish on this earth, if I could say to myself that your thoughts would some-times follow me into my retreat."

Far from the court she lived a retired and quiet life, busying herself with works of charity and acts of piety.

Her days were spent in visiting the poor, consoling the unfortunate, and encouraging those who found the burden of destiny too heavy. Many times she opened her purse when she heard a story of want or misery. Wherever there was sorrow to heal, anxiety to relieve and tears to wipe away, there she hastened with words of comfort. The greater part of her income was devoted to good works of this kind.

Delort [1] varied the story a little. When the quarrels between the dauphin and Agnes became more and more frequent, the Lady of Beauty, thinking she would be happier in Touraine, asked the king to let her return to her birthplace, Fromenteau, to see her daughters, from whom she had been separated for some time.

The least absence annoyed Charles, but he nevertheless gave his consent; and the queen, in bidding Agnes adieu, told her how pleased she would be to see the little girls on her return.

Agnes departed, accompanied by Etienne Chevalier, who was usually appointed to be her travelling companion. The joy of the children, when they saw their mother again, the clamorous reception of the inhabitants of the happy country of which she was the benefactress, roused in her

[1] *Essai critique sur l'Histoire de Charles VII, d'Agnès Sorelle et de Jeanne d'Arc,* 1824.

feeling heart a triumph far more satisfying than any derived from the vainglory of courts.

When he despatched an embassy across the Channel, Charles was unable to receive news of Agnes every day because Etienne Chevalier was in England. He then went to Tours with the queen and visited the charming retreat at Fromenteau. Agnes gave to their majesties the most pleasant and varied festivities, and her hospitality was enchanting. Marie d'Anjou treated the three daughters of Agnes as though they were her own children, and said she wished to have Charlotte [1] to stay with her.

The attachment which Marie d'Anjou showed towards Agnes's children increased the hatred of Louis for "La Belle des Belles." His antipathy changed to fury. He did everything he could to irritate his mother against Agnes, but the queen, who loved peace, was as moderate in her advice as in her conduct.

When the dauphin left the French court, any ambitious woman might have been pleased, continued Delort, but Agnes, on the other hand, was grieved. "She feared that she was the innocent cause of the conspiracy of this wicked son against his father, and although the love of the king was just as warm as ever for her, her life which had passed pleasantly and happily, was disturbed by the departure of the prince."

If it be true that Agnes voluntarily withdrew from court, the withdrawal was only temporary.

[1] Charlotte was supposed to be older than Marie (or Marguerite).

She could not immediately forget the dauphin's malice, and she was unhappy because, owning many houses and lands, she had been accused of avarice and greed. According to one account, the latter consideration weighed even more heavily than the former.[1]

Dunois, who was one of the most outspoken of men, was said to be guilty of remarking : " Cette douce colombe ne serait-elle point une pie effrontée ? "

This unjust remark reached her ears and her eyes grew moist with unshed tears. Terribly troubled she had thrown herself at the king's feet.

" Take back, Sire," she cried, " all the presents with which you have enriched me and allow me to leave this wicked court."

Unable to impose silence on his contemporaries, Charles VII hoped to deceive history. He sent for Jean Chartier, his historiographer, and ordered him to employ his skill in " contradicting the injurious rumours which besmirched the honour of la belle Agnes."

The manner in which the historiographer accomplished this difficult task has been mentioned. It was not altogether convincing. Chartier was silent concerning the part played by Agnes in the rupture between the king and his son.

[1] Gaboriau, *Les Cotillons Célèbres*. Paris, 1860.

CHAPTER XIX

PIERRE DE BRÉZÉ

THE dauphin left for the Dauphiné on January 1, 1447, and was soon installed in the province which he regarded as his own exclusive kingdom. He reigned there for ten years, and only left it when Charles, owing to his son's aggressive policy, was forced to send an army against him. Then the prince fled to Burgundy.

From the beginning of his exile Louis took an increasing interest in affairs at the French court, and never ceased to plot and plan, especially with a view to removing Pierre de Brézé and Agnes Sorel from court.

He had friends in the council, spies in the king's household, and confidential servants in other quarters to whom he promised all kinds of benefits if they would keep him informed of everything that went on.

He grew shameless, openly denouncing the king's immorality, threatening to bring about the banishment of Agnes, and urging the people to ask why Charles took no steps to recover Normandy, which was still in the hands of the English.

Brézé, it was said, paid no attention to any of the king's sins of omission, and only spoke what he was instructed to speak by the fair lips of the Lady of Beauty.

Against him, no doubt, the dauphin's worst enmity was levelled, and so well did he lay his plots that he managed at length to implicate the minister, and almost succeeded in bringing about his downfall.

In this intrigue a certain Guillaume Mariette was the central figure. This man, an agent of the dauphin's, played a double game, and sold himself to the highest bidder. Brézé begged him to communicate to the king certain information contained in a report which was worded as though it had been written to Brézé himself. He told Mariette the king was very clever, and as he did not know his ways he was to be careful to have his answers ready, and be assured in his tone about what he was going to say. He was to recite his story, and then beg the king to keep his own counsel about it. He might say as much evil as he liked about himself (Brézé), but he was to be silent about Agnes, or, as he put it, " il n'est jà besoin de parler de la Dagne."

Mariette did not bring himself at once to carry out this commission. He had seen Brézé at Bourges in June, 1447. Some time later Brézé, who had been dining with the Chancellor, encountered Mariette and asked him if he had had an interview with the king.

Mariette replied that he had presented himself at a time when the king had retired to his private apartments and could not see him.

" Monseigneur," he added, " you have a high

position and much wealth. It seems to me it would be better to conceal the things you wish me to say to the king. He may tell them to Monseigneur le Dauphin, and both you and I would be ruined."

" Stupid ! " replied Brézé, " do not speak so, for the king knows about it already, and will be very interested in what you tell him, because you are in the dauphin's household. Tell him what I have told you, for I assure you he will not repeat it to any one. The king has no intention of making his son come to face him, for he knows well he would only embroil matters if he were here."

Mariette sought out the king and told him of the dauphin's underhand dealings, the information he had managed to obtain and the means he employed.

The king listened very calmly.

" It is impossible that the dauphin should come here unless commanded to do so," he said.

Mariette told him that it was nevertheless the prince's intention to come, because he wished to remove from court all those who displeased him, the king's mistress amongst them, and to place those who were in his pay, like the Chancellor, the Comte du Maine, and several others in their place.

The king dismissed his informant, begging him to keep him aware of what was going on. He did not think it wise that communications should be addressed to him personally, but he asked him to send them to some one in his household.

Mariette requested him to name somebody. And he mentioned the seneschal.

"Ah," replied the spy, "there is no need for the seneschal to know anything of the matter. For he is the most double-faced scoundrel at court, and will not keep your secret."

"By Saint-John," replied the king, "I am not sure you are not wise," and he told him to write to the Comte de Tancarville instead.

A little while afterwards Mariette wrote to the Duc de Bourgogne, "Brézé has been much out of favour. He has been at the point of dismissal, but did everything he could to get reinstated. However, I should not be surprised if he were to get checkmated this time, for the dauphin is less and less pleased with him, and does all he can to put the king out of conceit with him too."

Charles turned over in his mind the possibility of dismissing the seneschal, but it was not easy to rid himself of a servant who was as useful as Brézé. The Comte du Maine, the Chancellor Jouvenel and Siegneur de Blainville all took his part, and the cloud passed over his head without his knowing how gravely he had been menaced.

Then a strange thing happened. Presently Mariette was arrested for certain defalcations in the capacity of king's notary, and was imprisoned at Loches, and then despatched to Lyons. There he managed to escape and made his way to the Dauphiné, where he expected to find a refuge. On the contrary, he was seized by the orders of Louis and incarcerated at Côte-Saint-André.

P

No doubt Louis desired to obtain from the lips of his victim certain information which would be useful in bringing about the downfall of the seneschal.

It was more than mere coincidence that the trial of Brézé and the trial of Mariette in the Dauphiné took place at exactly the same time, in the spring of 1448.

Mariette was tortured in prison, and in between barbarous punishment he received medical treatment in order to keep him alive, lest he should die without giving to the world the truth about certain matters.

He was proved guilty of more than one fraud, and it was said that he had the minister's ear, and that, unknown to the king, Brézé had received his confidences and used him as a tool. His revelations compromised the man who had thus employed him.

Mariette was sent to Chinon after his trial and from there to the Bastille. He was condemned to death and transferred to Tours, where he was decapitated.

The dauphin sacrificed his agent for carrying out his instructions too literally, but did not forget to recompense the Mariette family for its loss.

The prince's charges against Brézé accused him of having sacrificed the interests of the king to enrich himself, and of having deceived and injured numerous lords of the council who had confided in him. He denounced his enemy at the moment when Brézé had forced the English to cede Mans.

The seneschal was greatly amazed when he found himself thus attacked, and when he discovered that those who had appeared to be his sincerest friends were in reality his persecutors.

He appealed to the king demanding to be confronted by his accusers. He asked that judges might be appointed and his case inquired into. He offered to give himself up as prisoner if the king wished him to do so. Charles approved of his attitude, and while Parlement was busy discussing his case in April, 1448, Pierre de Brézé was exiled from court and deprived of his appointments. Matters looked very black indeed for him.

Then another strange thing happened. During the last weeks of April a certain young woman arrived in Paris apparently on a pilgrimage. She stayed in the capital until May 10.

Four days later Brézé was restored to favour.

He owed the king's clemency to Agnes Sorel.

P 2

CHAPTER XX

THE ENTRY INTO PARIS

In the reign of Charles VII Paris presented a very charming and varied character.

" The streets are narrow, it is true," wrote Capefigue,[1] " but each block of houses stands by itself with trim plots and gardens, vine trellises, and fine vegetable enclosures. The town is crowded with churches and convents, fine mansions, so elegant that one would say they might be carried in the hand, as the stone statues of saints, set under porches, carry the models of cathedrals on the tips of their fingers. There are only three bridges crossing the Seine, sheltered from the sun, rain and wind; the Pont aux Meuniers is in the form of the Bridge of Sighs at Venice. Every house, even those of the middle classes, is adorned with emblematic figures, with gables and strangely shaped water-spouts.

" In the extreme south stands Sainte-Geneviève with its shrine surrounded by charming cottages, the gardens of which, planted with vines, stretch to the Bièvre; on the Seine was Nôtre-Dame, the pride of the city, and, as if to present a contrast, the Châtelet, with its turrets, the bright Saint-Chapelle of Saint-Louis, with its lofty spire, and

[1] *Agnès Sorel et la Chevalerie*, 1860.

the vast convent of the Augustine monks, the Hôtel de Nesle; farther off there are seen the charming Pré aux Clercs and the buildings of the University.

"On the other bank of the river Seine, the Bastille, with its four towers, surrounded by a park and orchard, the royal residence of the Tournelles, with its small forests of cherry-trees, its vine trellises, where the muscatel grapes hang in beautiful clusters; the Rue Saint-Antoine, reserved for tournaments; Saint-Paul, Les Celestins, La Grève and the Louvre, from which, to the north, on the eminence that bordered on the beautiful factory of Venetian glazed tiles, could be seen the windmills that turned as the breeze shifted this way or that.

"Such was Paris under Charles VII, where were seen passing and repassing processions of lords and ladies on richly caparisoned horses, monks, black and white, armed men dressed in two colours, as they have been painted on cards and tarots, shopkeepers with their hoods, gypsies, pages, and varlets, long processions of pilgrims, walking to the sound of the peals of bells, ringing out joyously at the prospect of a festival, or full of sorrow and lamentation for the dead."

Such was the Paris, too, that Agnes saw on the day in 1448 when she arrived in the capital accompanied by Guillaume Gouffier [1] and de

[1] Guillaume Gouffier and Poncet de Rivière, squires; a sum for their expenses on a voyage which they made from Tours to Paris in company with Mlle. de Beauté, who was making a pilgrimage to Sainte-Geneviève.—Du Fresne de Beaucourt, *Histoire de Charles VII*, Vol. IV. p. 215.

Poncet de Rivière, ostensibly for the purpose of making a pilgrimage to Sainte-Geneviève, but, combining mercy with pity, also with the intention of interceding with the king on behalf of her friend, Pierre de Brézé.

"In the last week of April," wrote the chronicler,[1] "there came to Paris a young lady, whom it was said was publicly loved by the king, *sans foy, sans loy, et sans veristé,* towards the good queen his wife, and she bore as great estate as a countess or duchess. And she came and went very often with the good Queen of France, without any shame at her sin, on account of which the queen suffered much grief.

"And because the people of Paris did not show her as deep reverence as her great pride expected, she said when she left that they were villainous folk, and had she known that they would not show her more honour than they did, she would never have entered the city, nor put foot therein; which would have been no great loss. Thus departed the lovely Agnes on the 10th day of May back to her sins as before."

The reception given to Agnes was not a warm one, and she heard remarks which were not altogether complimentary. Several causes may have contributed to this.

A hard year had brought famine in its train, the war had reduced people to misery from which they were only recovering by degrees, and the sight of a lady who had no real right to the royal state in which she travelled, who was adorned

[1] *Journal d'un Bourgeois de Paris.*

with gold and diamonds, dressed in rich silks and furs, accompanied by a retinue and surrounded by luxury, aroused feelings of anger and jealousy in those whose hard-earned wages were barely enough to supply their daily bread.

Besides, she was not accompanied by the king. Had Charles been by her side a very different reception would have awaited her. In his presence no one would have dared to criticise her. One hundred and fifty years later the people cheered Gabrielle d'Estrées as she passed through the same streets.

" In September, 1597, Henri IV entered Paris in state. Mme. de Liancourt, as Gabrielle was called, preceded him in a magnificent open litter, loaded with pearls and jewels, which glittered so powerfully that the lights of the torches paled before them, and wearing a black satin robe all puffed with white." [1]

Agnes, bound on her mission of mercy, was more worthy of respect than the rival of Marguerite de Valois.

A fine house had been prepared for her near the river,[2] and there she remained during her short visit to the capital. When she left Paris it was to return to the sunny south, her well-beloved Touraine, where the people knew and understood her gentle character.

She had achieved her purpose, for the king had pardoned Pierre de Brézé.

In spite of her intervention in this matter

[1] L'Estoile, *Journal du règne de Henri IV*.
[2] Some say it was situated on the Quai Debilly.

never a word was breathed against her name and that of the seneschal, although hers was coupled with those of both Etienne Chevalier and Antoine de Chabannes.   Their friendship was admittedly pure.   They had probably known each other at the Angevin court long years before they had been brought into contact with the king.   Brézé may have been one of the " young men-at-arms and gentle companions " who, according to Olivier de la Marche, were introduced to Charles by his mistress and did him good service.   On the other hand, it is more likely that Brézé was at court long before Agnes, and he may have been instrumental in introducing her there.

Her letters to him [1] are friendly and intimate in tone.   She addressed him as Monsieur mon compère, which probably implied that she had been godmother to some infant to whom he was godfather.

Her first letter to Brézé was written about 1446 from Cussay, near La Guerche, on the last day of April.

" Receive, my dear compère, my special recommendations.   A certain Mathelin Tiery, father of one of the maids of my household, has complained to me that the rent which he used to receive on a butcher's shop in the town of Chinon, and which amounted to twenty-two sols, was hardly improved during the occasion of the war, and is now only worth sixteen sols, which, added to the small amount that has remained to him, makes

[1] See Appendix B.

it impossible for him to live, and he has fallen into great poverty. The said Mathelin begs that you will condescend to grant him an appointment which was promised to him by your squire Guionnet, which would come at a moment most convenient for his maintenance.

"Therefore I beg of you to grant this favour in order that the said Mathelin might be given an indemnity for being harshly treated in the matter of the said rent, and you will give me great pleasure if you hasten the affair.

"Praying God, monsieur mon compère, that He will grant your desires,

"Your servant and commère,

"AGNES."

The second letter was written from Amboise on August 18, probably also in 1446.

"Monsieur, my very dear friend and good compère, I commend myself to you most sincerely. I am sending you the letters of respite touching the homage of La Fresnoie, begging you to give me your kind counsel, and do me the service to complete the affair, as I cannot leave here, and because the king, however much I may appeal to him, likes to remain in this place, whither you will be able to return to see him, bringing an answer to the said matter.

"Monsieur mon compère, we have had an adventure with a man who was said to be a ruffian and scoundrel, and who made up to one of the women and entered the hôtel in the night, whence he took by means of tools with which he opened the cupboards, some jewels and reliquaries of which the said woman was in charge.   And when leaving the house he jumped into a ditch, where he was captured, and they say he was taken thus because of the reliquaries he had stolen.

" Monsieur mon compère, I send you my greetings and recommend you to God, who will, I hope, grant all your desires."

There is a simple and downright note in the character of Agnes which is very delightful. She must have been a good friend.   There is more honesty about her than about any other of the kings' mistresses, except Louise de la Vallière, and Louise was wanting in the kindly comradeship which Agnes knew well how to bestow.

When Fouquet, the superintendent of finances, approached the mistress of Louis XIV, even though he may have wished to do her a service, she suspected his motives at once and appealed in indignation to the king.

Not so in the case of Agnes.   She knew how to sustain amiable relations with Jacques Cœur, with Pierre de Brézé, and with Etienne Chevalier, without allowing any one of them to overstep the legitimate bounds of intimacy.   With every temptation to play the *cocotte*, to bid them do her will and derive advantages from their friendship, she refrained from all these things.   It was to her they owed much, rather than she to them.   Never was king's mistress less imperious or less exacting.

Her value to Charles lay at least in that; she knew how to conduct herself towards his most important councillors, how to be their true friend and to further the good feeling between them and the monarch.

In this she was a politieal help-mate, which the queen had never been and never could be.

Whatever Pierre de Brézé did for her she repaid amply; the reverence which Etienne Chevalier felt for her is one of the most charming incidents in her life-story, and the trust she reposed in the powerful Jacques Cœur was touching in its intensity. Had she lived, Jacques Cœur's fate might have been a far less cruel one, and his name might never have besmirched the memory of Charles VII with a stigma of base ingratitude.

CHAPTER XXI

JACQUES CŒUR

" SIRE," said Agnes Sorel to her lover, " receive Jacques Cœur well, for gold will be none the less necessary than steel when it comes to the reconquering of your kingdom." [1]

Jacques Cœur was born at Bourges, a few years before Charles VII. His father, Pierre Cœur, was a rich merchant, and Jacques felt himself called upon to carry on the traditions of his house, which he did with huge success. He founded not only his own commercial reputation, but that of the whole of France.

About 1418 Jacques Cœur married Macée de Leodepart, the daughter of an influential citizen of his native town. Ten years later he established a commercial partnership with two brothers of the name of Godard, and soon afterwards he extended his operations until they reached far and wide across the globe.

In the pursuit of his personal ambitions he travelled to many foreign countries, Damascus amongst them, and he put France on so sound a commercial footing that she was able to compete with Italy and other countries in the Mediterranean, then the centre of the world's trade.

[1] Gaboriau, *Les Cotillons Célèbres.*

In the course of twenty years he had established agents in as many as three hundred cities, and it is not surprising that his name was one to conjure with, that " as rich as Jacques Cœur " became a catchword, that the king was willing to place the financial affairs of the country in his capable hands, and that the Lady of Beauty reposed a great trust in him and looked to him to carry out her dying wishes.

His profession was one of great importance in the days before there was an official called " surintendant des finances."

The silversmith was an indispensable personage in the eyes of kings and nobles. He made large advances, and in exchange was allowed imposts, customs and revenues under fair conditions. His trade was not merely a craft, but an art. He had to do with the minting of money, the care of the coinage, and the testing and purification of precious metals.

When quite a young man Jacques Cœur was employed in the mint at Bourges. His wealth resulted from the sale of merchandise at the fairs of Paris, Lyons, Bourges, Toulouse and Albi.

When the royal house was strengthened by an alliance with the House of Anjou, Jacques Cœur received the official title of royal silversmith and keeper of the treasures.

Under the protection of the Queen of Sicily, mistress of Agnes Sorel, he procured considerable resources for the royal cause. He negotiated loans at Genoa, Milan and Venice with the Lombard merchants, to whom he offered his own fortune as security.

He was the first to introduce the cutting of diamonds into France, and brought workmen from Venice and Constantinople for this purpose. The first ornament in this new style was given to the Lady of Beauty, if we may believe the chroniclers.   Jacques Cœur made her a present of a clasp for her belt, which she constantly wore.

Owing to his vast influence he gained the confidence of the highest in the land.   He knew a great deal about the king's private affairs. The current expenses of princes and princesses of the blood were no secret from him.   In his papers, which he had kept in wonderful order, the names occurred of Mesdames Radegonde and Jeanne de France, of the Duchesse de Bourbon, of the Duc d'Orléans, and of all the favourites, *mignons* and other influential people.

He had in his possession a number of documents referring to the affairs of Agnes,[1] and in return she protected and encouraged him.[2]   He it was who furnished the king with the necessary money to allow him to prosecute the war against England.

When Charles desired to begin the conquest of Normandy, he said to his argentier, " What is the state of the finances ? "

[1] Soixante parties (titres, papiers) de feue Mademoiselle de Beaulté, avecques certaines cédules liées ensemble et subscriptes " Icy sont les parties et la dépense de feue Mademoiselle de Beaulté signées de sa main."—Vallet de Viriville, *Histoire de Charles VII*, Vol. III. p. 284 *n*.

[2] Capefigue, *Agnès Sorel et la Chevalerie*.

"Sire," replied Jacques Cœur, "all I have is yours," and he produced some two hundred thousand golden crowns.

When the time came to maintain the advantages gained by the French the argentier opened his purse once more.

Bouchet described his methods of raising money. "Having gone carefully into the question of finances," he wrote, "he found that there were in the kingdom of France seventeen hundred thousand belfries, taking one in every town. He allowed for those towns that were ruined seven hundred thousand, leaving a million of belfries. Thus by taking, one with the other, twenty livres tournois a year for aids and taxes, etc., a sum was produced every year of twenty millions, which were employed in the following manner :

"Firstly, for the expenses of the king's household each day one thousand livres tournois, which is yearly, three hundred and sixty-five thousand livres tournois.

"The same was allowed to the queen and her ladies, and the same for the royal children.

"A million went to the upkeep of towns, fortresses and castles.

"Seven millions two hundred thousand livres went in soldiers' pay, and one million for officials.

"A million was reserved for gifts to knights, squires and others for rewards and services, whilst for gifts to ambassadors and those engaged in public business there was another million. Three hundred thousand livres a year went in engines of war, and for the maintenance of persons at sea two millions. In all, this made fourteen millions five hundred and eighty-five thousand livres tournois."

Five million four hundred and fifteen thousand livres remained at the disposal of the king, a part of which was perhaps used for increasing the army, but most of it was expended on pampered favourites.

Three thousand livres, as we know, was the annual allowance of the Lady of Beauty, but how much more she owed to the services of her good friend, Jacques Cœur, does not stand on record.

The argentier was as willing to help by his counsel as by the large sums he procured for those who asked his advice, and his astute judgment and foresight had gained for him the honour of carrying out several missions of importance on the king's behalf.

In 1446 he went to Genoa with Tanneguy du Chastel, the seneschal of Provence.

Two years later he was sent on an embassy to Pope Nicholas V, in company with Jean Juvenal des Ursins and Tanneguy du Chastel. They departed in ships equipped at Jacques Cœur's expense. This journey had far-reaching effects for the financier, because the Pope became his staunch friend, and it was to him he fled after losing the favour of Charles VII. Nicholas was, moreover, well-disposed to the Lady of Beauty, and on the 3rd of the nones of April, 1448, the year of the visit, he wrote her a letter, still in

[To face p. 224

JACQUES CŒUR

existence, conceding to her demand for a portable altar. " We incline favourably towards your devout supplications," he informed her, " because of the great devotion you have testified to us in the affairs of the Roman Church," and he granted to her confessor the power to absolve her from any sins, crimes and excesses, reserved for absolution by the apostolic see, at the hour of her death.

At the entry of the French into Rouen, in 1449, Jacques Cœur rode beside Dunois and Brézé. All three wore coats of violet velvet trimmed with fine fur, and hats of black velvet. The trappings of their horses were crimson satin embroidered with fine gold and silk. This splendour of apparel and presumption of conduct appear to have been one of the first causes of complaint against the financier by envious enemies, who began to murmur about the luxury in which he lived and the large possessions he boasted.

The argentier's house in Bourges has for many centuries been a landmark, renowned for its beauty and costliness. On a site bought from Jacques Belin he built an hôtel in 1442 at the cost of one hundred and thirty-five thousand livres, and by these means obtained one of the most remarkable mansions of his day. When Agnes came into favour his luxurious projects were no doubt already under consideration. Perhaps he consulted her as to the style of adornment and furniture his new mansion was to contain. It was the day of mottoes and devices cunningly introduced into the sculptures and paintings.

Q

The phrase "A vaillants cœurs rien impossible" appeared on many of the walls and windows. Another was "Faire, dire, taire de ma joie." A third, which implies that Jacques Cœur was a man of deeds and not of words, was "En bouche close n'entre mouche."

The main buildings surround a spacious court-yard. The chief entrance-tower, octagonal in form, is encrusted with stone pictures. In the central pavilion is a small but singularly beautiful chapel, reached by a fine spiral staircase.

The roofs are covered with sculpture, and open lacework stone parapets bear the mottoes. Every pipe is wrought and ornamented. The chimneys are decorated, and indeed every separate part of the building is in its way a work of art.

The large dining-room was adorned with fine tapestries, furnished with carved benches, chairs and coffers, upholstered in velvet and gilded leather. On reception days the apartment glittered with the light of many torches, and was the scene of gay banquet after banquet at which the king and the Lady of Beauty took part. There the troubadours sang praises of "la belle des belles" and of the military heroes who were winning conquests for France. No food was served to these exalted visitors that had not been cooked in silver vessels and transferred to platters of gold. There were beautiful silver mirrors in which Agnes saw her fresh loveliness reflected, and vases from which she picked delicately scented blossoms to wear on her white bosom.

In the centre of the floor of the dining-room

was a flat stone which served as a trap-door, and led to the vaults used for the purpose of storing the argentier's great treasures, and some belonging to Agnes as well. It was said that these subterranean passages led as far as Sancerre, and that wine from the vineyards came in by this route.

The house was said to be full of surprises and unexpected beauties of all kinds, and Michelet called it a house of mystery and considered it symbolic of the owner's life. At all events in this superb abode he was able to indulge his luxurious tastes. Nor was it his only residence, for he had an equally magnificent house at Montpellier, called " Le Loge," which was the chief depot of his merchandise, another at Lyons, another at Marseilles, a fourth at Beaucaire, and between thirty or forty other estates in different parts of the country.

All this worldly wealth did not suffice to save the richest commoner in the kingdom from an undeserved and wretched fate. All his sacrifices and kind deeds had been done in vain. They were soon forgotten. Had Agnes lived longer this catastrophe to her friend would have been averted. She would have pleaded for him, have proved to the satisfaction of all that his motives had been pure.

But when she was dead the jealousy and envy of others grew and increased till they broke all bounds. Through the machinations of his enemies, who were afraid because he knew so much about them and their affairs, he was cast down

Q 2

from his high estate. In vain he looked to his natural protector, the king, for pardon. There was no mercy for him in Charles's heart, and no mediator to take the place of the Lady of Beauty.

CHAPTER XXII

ETIENNE CHEVALIER

JACQUES CŒUR was Agnes Sorel's friend and adviser in all practical matters concerning her finances, her possessions, and even her jewels and clothes, but Etienne Chevalier was her friend in the romantic and artistic affairs of her life. Those who spin legends have given him a charming part to play. He accompanied her on her journeys, acted as her right-hand man in the king's absence, kept Charles informed of everything that happened to her, and smoothed any crumpled leaf he could from her scented bed of roses.

In spite of the suggestions of one or two chroniclers to the contrary, he was a chevalier *sans peur et sans reproche.*

It was Dreux du Radier [1] who tried to prove that he shared with Charles the heart of the Lady of Beauty, and that from being her friend he became her lover; but if he loved her it was with a sincere and honest esteem that had nothing in it to dim his respect.

The circumstances which gave rise to suspicions

---

[1] *Mémoires historiques, critiques et anecdotes des Reines et Régentes de France,* 1776.

of the contrary were enumerated by the same author. " After the death of Agnes," he wrote, " Chevalier had himself painted with a scroll issuing from his lips on which was inscribed a rebus. First came the word *Tant*, which was followed by the wing of a bird (aile), after that came the word *vaut*, then a saddle (selle) succeeded by *pour qui je*, a horse's bit (mors) and *d'amour*. According to Etienne Chevalier and the manners of the day this represented:

" *Tant elle vaut celle pour qui je meurs d'amour.*"

" That," said Dreux du Radier, " appears to be the sentiment of a tender lover who is deeply afflicted by the death of a beloved mistress."

Further supposed evidence of an unwise intimacy was a rebus, or hieroglyphic motto, inscribed over the door of a small court which led into the garden of Etienne Chevalier's house in the Rue de la Verrerie, Paris. Engraved in the stone and interlaced with golden leaves were the words " Rien sur elle n'a regard," or " Rien sur L n'a regard," in which, of course, there is a play on the name of Sorel or Surelle.[1]

These are, after all, small matters on which to base a daring assumption.

There is in existence a more convincing proof—

[1] It is interesting to note that the motto " Rien sur L n'a regard " was found on Fouquet's *Boccace*, which was thought to have been painted for Etienne Chevalier, but that Durrieu in " La Légende et l'Histoire de Jean Foucquet " (Extrait de l'*Annuaire Bulletin de la Société de l'Histoire de France*, 1907), declared the owner of the MS. was one Laurens Gyrard, and the motto was an anagram on his name.

not of any ignoble passion, but of reverence and humble worship offered by a good man to a fair yet frail woman, to one he wished to shield from every unpleasantness her equivocal position might have caused her. This was a painting executed by the great artist Jean Fouquet representing Agnes as the Madonna, with Etienne Chevalier kneeling before her in prayer and supplication.

How came such a daring piece of work into being ?

Chevalier was essentially French in character and culture, and his tastes were inherently artistic. He possessed a library which included the works of the best authors, translated into his own language, written by good copyists and ornamented by celebrated artists. His house was full of sculpture and decoration, his chapel was adorned with stained-glass windows, and in all his surroundings were traces of his predilection for beauty and good workmanship.

Chevalier did not lack means wherewith to indulge his love of art. He held the appointment of Secretary in Charles VII's household, as his father, Jean Chevalier, had done before him. Agnes Sorel gave him her protection, and no doubt advised him how to win the king's esteem and confidence. Perhaps he owed to her his entrance into the favour which he kept by his own talents, his devotion, and his probity. He occupied high positions, fulfilled important missions, and acquired great benefits. He was Lord of Eprunes, of

Grigny, of Vignau, of Plessis les Comte and other estates. In 1445 he was sent to England with the title of Ambassador to negotiate peace, and in 1452 he became Treasurer of France and Secretary of State.

In his desire to protect the arts Chevalier allied himself with Jean Fouquet, who was the master of a new school of illumination.

Fouquet was born at Tours between 1415 and 1420. At the age of about twenty-five he went to Rome to paint the portrait of the Pope, Eugenius IV. He returned to France about 1447, and it is probable that soon after that date he was commissioned by Chevalier to do certain work for him.

The great masterpiece which he executed for his patron was a wonderful "Book of Hours" containing a number of miniatures exquisitely painted.

The artist was famous both for his landscape effects and portraiture, and Chevalier asked him to paint a scene representing himself in company with his patron saint, St. Stephen, on his knees before the Virgin, saying he wished to implore the intervention of Heaven for his protectress, Agnes Sorel.

Fouquet, thinking he read the mind of a grateful and reverent worshipper, and wishing to pay a compliment to one who was a power in the land, was struck by the brilliant idea, as he considered it, of taking Agnes Sorel herself as the model for his Madonna.

Perhaps he confounded, as Etienne Chevalier may have done himself, the aim of his prayer and its object. Fouquet did not disguise the resemblance in any way. The portrait was said to be a speaking likeness of the Lady of Beauty, revealing her delicate features and the charms of her neck and bosom, of which, if Georges Chastellain is to be believed, she was too proud.

About 1450 the artists, having repeated conventional types to satiety, introduced realism into the arts. It was thought no disrespect, especially by Italian painters, to represent living people in holy groups. Fouquet had acquired this practice when in Rome, and his paintings for Etienne Chevalier and others repeatedly introduced the portraits of famous individuals, who sometimes had no real business in the scene.[1]

In the Virgin of Nôtre-Dame de Melun the purity and chastity of the subject are beyond question, whilst the luminous brilliancy of the complexion and the touching expression of maternal tenderness were those for which Agnes was well known.

At that date no objection was taken to this licence so long as the Holy Virgin gained in elegance, beauty and distinction from her model.

[1] In the *Boccace* of Munich Fouquet painted " Le Lit de Justice tenu par le Roi Charles VII en 1458 à Vendôme pour le Jugement de Jean Duc d'Alençon," in which almost all the well-known people were represented, among them Geoffrey Soreau, cousin of Agnes. Pierre de Brézé was absent.

Moreover, the French loved sincerely the woman who was said to have roused the Kinglet of Bourges from his sadness, and who urged him not to belittle his defenders against the valiant attacks of English chivalry. She had shown energy in public life, and for this she deserved glorification.

Vallet de Viriville attempted to verify the reality of the likeness of the painting to Agnes from internal evidence, but he was not entirely successful. He pointed out that Agnes was born not far from Tours, the home of Fouquet. In the works of the artist a type of women figured who were distinctive and peculiar. This type, gracious and gentle, eminently French, seems to have been furnished by the femininity of his native province.

The panels representing Agnes and Etienne Chevalier were of similar dimensions, and formed a diptych which was placed in the Church of Nôtre-Dame at Melun, probably after the death of the donor in 1474.

They were removed in 1775, as an inscription written at the back of Agnes's portrait proves.

La Sainte Vierge
Sous les traits d'Agnès Sorel
Maîtresse de Charles VII, roi de France
Morte en 1450

This picture which was in the choir of Nôtre-Dame de Melun was done by the wish of Maître Etienne Chevalier, one of the testamentary executors of Agnes Sorel, 1775. (Signed) Gaulthier, avocat.

From Melun the portrait of Agnes went to Antwerp, and that of Etienne Chevalier to Frankfort, and then to the Berlin Museum. There they remain respectively, separated by a ruthless destiny even as the originals were parted by an insurmountable barrier in life.

The description of the portrait of Agnes in the catalogue of the Museum at Antwerp is as follows:

" The Virgin and the Infant Jesus. Seated on a throne ornamented with precious stones, Mary, her head encircled with a crown enriched with pearls, from which hangs a diaphanous veil. An ermine mantle covers her arms and shoulders. The top of the corsage of her gown is unlaced, and leaves the left breast uncovered. She keeps her eyes lowered upon her divine Son seated on her knees. Blue angels and red archangels press round them in veneration."

" There is to us something shocking," wrote Bouchot,[1] on the subject of this painting, " in thus showing, under the name of the Madonna, the Mother of God, the Lady de la Beauté seated devoutly, crowned with pearls, as are the Flemish Madonnas. At the request of Etienne Chevalier, the financier, his Mæcenas and friend, he painted this picture, and on the leaf of a diptych, facing her, Chevalier himself, kneeling, whom his patron St. Stephen presents to the Mother of God."

[1] *Cosmopolitan*, New York, Vol. XVIII., 1894-95, pp. 85-48.

It is not difficult to understand why the church at Melun was chosen as the resting-place for Chevalier's beautiful gift. It was his native town, and he was buried there in 1474 beside his wife Catherine, who had died more than twenty years earlier in August, 1452. Agnes was also known in the town of Melun. She left thirty golden crowns to the Church of Saint-Aspais.

Originally the diptych had borders of blue velvet adorned with embroidery of gold and silver, which gave it a very rich appearance. Taking into account the beauty of the subject, the skill of the artist and the generosity of the donor, the recipients must have regarded the gift not only as priceless in itself, but as embodying a gracious thought on the part of their patron.

The date of the painting is uncertain. It may have been executed in the lifetime of Agnes, and perhaps even with her knowledge. But it is more probable that Chevalier had the work done soon after her death, in memory of one of whom he retained the kindliest thoughts.

Henry IV, it is said, seeing the original painting in the church at Melun, was charmed with it, and offered to buy it for a sum of ten thousand livres.

The portrait was later included in the collection of celebrated personages. The figure of Agnes was reproduced without the babe and without the angels. This mutilation gave a bizarre effect to the picture, which appears to represent an individual in part Madonna, in part courtesan.

Interesting as is the diptych at Melun, the work is nothing in comparison with the famous " Book of Hours " painted by the same artist for his patron. The miniatures prove that Fouquet was a painter of the first rank, and that the French school at that time equalled those of Italy and the North.

Whether it too was a memorial in honour of the Lady of Beauty, or whether the authorities who suggested this were carried away by their own love of the romantic, it is not easy to say.

Chevalier's initials [1] or full name are repeated in most of the miniatures, and in many were portraits of himself and other well-known people, and it is difficult indeed not to believe that representations of Agnes are introduced on almost every page among the various female figures.

Forty-four detached leaves of this wonderful work are in existence. Of these forty are in the Musée Condé at Chantilly, two are in the Louvre, one in the Bibliothèque Nationale, and one in the British Museum.[2]

The best portrait of Chevalier himself is one similar in character though different in design to the diptych. Assisted by angels and in company with his patron saint he renders homage to the Virgin and the Infant Jesus. The painting represents him in the prime of his manhood

[1] The " E. C." device appears in a charming little " Book of Hours " now in the British Museum. Add. MS. 16997.

[2] Add. MS. 37421.

and the fulness of his power. Fortune smiles on him and offers her best gifts. He kneels reverently on a tessellated pavement of marble and gold, his hands clasped, his attitude confident, his faith burning brightly. He is dressed in a long red robe adorned neither with embroidery nor fur, and falling about his feet in long plain folds.

In one of the miniatures Fouquet represented the king in the guise of one of the wise men from the East. Charles is surrounded by the Scottish Guard, and kneels on a cushion in the centre of a carpet strewn with fleur-de-lis. All the authorities, Du Fresne de Beaucourt included, concede that this is an authentic portrait. The author of the *Histoire de Charles VII* did not believe that the painting at Antwerp was by the same artist as the series of miniatures adorning Chevalier's "Book of Hours." He felt convinced that if Fouquet had painted Agnes Sorel he would have been named amongst King Charles VII's artists, but royal patronage did not come to him until the reign of Louis XI. In spite of the fact that he had painted the Pope as early as 1447, his reputation was not thoroughly established until nearly twenty years later. Louis loaded him with benefits and even visited him in his hôtel.

One thing might explain Charles's reluctance to reward Fouquet for honour shown to Agnes Sorel. If the painting was not executed till the time of her death, Antoinette would have already become official favourite when the king knew of the work. He would scarcely have cared to see the miniatures, which would naturally recall things better buried and forgotten.

Henri Bouchot believed that in Chevalier's "Book of Hours" he saw the greatest compliment the faithful secretary could pay to the Lady of Beauty. "In it," he wrote, "the king, Agnes and Chevalier constantly appear in the guise of saints, in the mystic communion of devout companionship." He thought this fact confirmed the legend which represented the treasurer as a very humble and secret lover of the fair lady. "Chevalier alone used this book," he continued, "the king cannot even have known of it. On each leaf Agnes appears; sometimes as a Madonna, in the porch of a Gothic cathedral; sometimes in the adoration of the Magi, in which ceremony one of the kings from the East is represented by Charles VII, surrounded by his Scottish Guards, with the Castle of Loches in the background; sometimes in the shape of some saint, St. Apollina undergoing martyrdom, St. Catherine of Sienna, St. Solange. Notice the singular coincidence that St. Catherine wears the gown and surcoat of a duchess, the very dress that the king in his sorrow was to bestow on the statue of his lost sweetheart."

Another writer [1] saw in these wonderful drawings of saints and Madonnas the features of the Lady of Beauty. "In all the scenes of the Virgin's life," she wrote, "we find her bearing the features of Agnes until an older and sadder

[1] Alice Kemp-Welch in *The Nineteenth Century*, Sept., 1905, pp. 416–26.

type becomes necessary in the 'Crucifixion,' the 'Entombment' and the 'Announcement of the Death' and the 'Death' of the Virgin. When, however, death has transfigured age and sorrow, the likeness of Agnes reappears in the 'Assumption,' the 'Coronation,' and, the crowning glory, the 'Enthronement of the Virgin.'"

"In the 'Enthronement of the Virgin,' for instance," wrote Mr. Herbert,[1] describing this artist's beautiful painting, "his instinct for majestic composition and his skill in perspective are finely exemplified. We seem to be looking down the nave of a vast cathedral, built up not of stones but of saints and angels, rising tier on tier to the key of the vault. Far away in this living temple the Three Persons of the Trinity all exactly alike sit clothed in white on three Gothic canopied thrones; and the Virgin is seated on a fourth throne, placed like a bishop's at the side of the choir."

Another of the miniatures which has been thought to represent the Lady of Beauty is "The Martyrdom of Saint Catherine." The saintly figure is kneeling tranquilly, her hands clasped and eyes raised to heaven, thanking God for His protection. She is dressed in a short mantle of purple velvet trimmed with ermine and drawn in at the waist with a golden girdle. Her long skirt of blue velvet sweeps the ground. "An attempt has been made to see in her a grand lady contemporary of the King Victorious,"

[1] *Illuminated Manuscripts*, 1911.

[*To face p.* 240

A PORTRAIT OF CHARLES VII

(*From a miniature by Fouquet in Etienne Chevalier's "Book of Hours"*)

wrote Gruyer,[1] " and it was thought that, owing to her almost royal gown, the lady was Agnes Sorel."

In yet another painting Etienne is represented kneeling opposite another kneeling figure, which may or may not be Agnes. His short, dark hair is cut close over the temple, but forms a crown about his head. His austere features, his broad brow, fine eyes and strong jaw give him a mona-chal appearance. He wears a purple robe, and his physiognomy bespeaks a lofty soul and high intelligence.

It is strange how little is known of this man in real life, how difficult it is to get at the truth about his feelings towards the Lady of Beauty. And yet if these marvellously life-like paintings really represented her, what memories must have been stirred in the later years of his life by the pages which reproduced the death and funeral of the Madonna, and even the joyous crowning in heaven, which must have seemed to him emblematic of forgiveness for the earthly frailty of Agnes.

In the monument at Loches Agnes was represented holding her hour-book in her hands. " When she was dying," said Bouchot, " she called for the hour-book which Fouquet had so magnificently illuminated, read an orison to Saint Bernard written in her own handwriting, and, leaf by leaf, reviewed her past life."

No doubt the author's love of romance led him

[1] *Les Quarante Fouquet.*

R

astray, but it adds to the interest of this remarkable manuscript to think that it was in the possession of the Lady of Beauty, and that during her lifetime the compliment which Chevalier and Fouquet intended was appreciated by the one who inspired it.

CHAPTER XXIII

THE CONQUEST OF NORMANDY

AGNES was stimulated to greater heights of fortitude by the knowledge that these friends believed in the purity of her ideals. After the rupture with the dauphin her one impulse had been to leave the court for ever, to break away definitely from the king. Yet, knowing how great was her influence over him, she felt she had no right to consider only her own wishes if she could aid him by her advice and counsel. She consulted Chevalier on this point, and he told her where her duty lay.

"The king needs you and the country needs a *king*," he said. "Do not leave him at the moment of crisis."

He referred to the unrest that was in the air.

The relations between France and England were getting more and more strained every day in spite of the truce. That the English should be firmly quartered in Normandy was a serious blemish on the otherwise prosperous reign of Charles VII. Throughout the province, pillagers and brigands carried on raids which the English seemed unable or unwilling to quell.

Owing to the unsettled state of affairs pirates flourished in large numbers in the Channel, a menace to both countries. The French frontiers were constantly being harried by bands of armed men, who ravaged the villages at night and in the day carried on their nefarious pursuits wearing masks. They were known by the name of *les faux visages*.

The French and English governments were both aware that it was necessary to take steps to remedy this state of things. Neither life nor property was safe, owing to the lawlessness which obtained.

A large number of despatches passed between the two countries at this date, and from 1445 to 1449 a constant succession of ambassadors travelled backwards and forwards between the two courts.

A clause in the treaty of marriage between Marguerite d'Anjou and Henry VI stipulated that the town of Mans should be immediately restored to France. Great difficulties and delay attended the execution of this clause.

After four years of negotiations Charles grew weary of the enemy's dilatory proceedings, and in March 1448 commanded an army to march upon the town. The king took up his position at the Château de Lavardin, whence he super-intended operations. Dunois, de Lohéac, de Clermont and Jean Bureau were among the leaders, and on the 16th of the month the English retired, leaving the French to occupy the town.

Under the roof of Lavardin, said one authority, " the Court of France flourished in all its splendour. Agnes Sorel had followed her royal lover thither, and love-songs mingled with the clash of arms." [1]

After the siege was over the king accompanied by Brézé and Agnes went to Tours, where Easter was celebrated. There they remained until the trial of Brézé took them to Paris.

By the siege of Mans Charles VII made it clear to the English that he was not prepared to allow them to have their own way any longer. A fresh series of embassies took place between the two great Powers, and, although in appearance the negotiations pre-supposed a desire for peace, in reality the King of France was preparing for war. He strengthened his alliances, he improved the newly organised army and regulated its discipline. He only awaited a pretext for aggression.

Immediately after the affair at Le Mans a new truce was entered into, but it was obvious that it would not be of long duration.

The French king wrote to the people of Rheims in September, 1448, saying that he planned to march into Normandy, and asking for their support. He attempted to bridge over the differences which existed between himself and the Duc de Bourgogne at the beginning of 1449.

On February 16 Pierre de Brézé, whose military tactics were likely to prove indispensable, was appointed Captain of Châtillon-sur-Indre. The garrison expelled from Le Mans sought a new abode on the frontiers of Normandy. The garrison of Verneuil attacked the town of Fou-

[1] Pétigny, *Histoire du Vendômois*, 1849, p. 880.

gères in Brittany. The English repudiated this breach of peace and refused to give recompense for it.

It was the moment for the French to draw the sword. No time had been wasted during the five years' truce. Charles had concentrated his troops at Evreux, Louviers, Dieppe, Pontoise, Beauvais and Ailly-sur-Noye.

The king was eager enough, it must be supposed, to chase the English from his kingdom. But it was not an easy matter to take a decisive step. Agnes spurred him on.

The scene from *Le Jouvencel*, already referred to, contained, according to Lavisse and other authorities, an allusion to her conduct, and related a story well known to the contemporaries. It indicated the attitude she took at the time when the projected invasion of Normandy was being discussed, and described her efforts to combat the king's doubts.

When Bueil [1] wrote *Le Jouvencel* Agnes was dead and her royal lover had followed her to the grave. Louis XI, enemy to Agnes and enemy to Bueil, was on the throne. The author cannot therefore be accused of wishing to insert in his romance a flattery addressed to those in power, and it is probable that in this instance he adhered to historical accuracy.

After dinner, he wrote, the king rose from table and withdrew to his own apartments. The queen went also, accompanied by her ladies, who

---

[1] His son Antoine married Jeanne, third daughter of Agnes and Charles.

made good cheer and much entertainment as was the custom. They gave way to unrestrained rejoicing. Among the number a very beautiful lady spoke, saying to the king, "Sire, I hear you have just heard good news. God be praised! Take us with you to war; we shall inspire you with courage and all your company as well. The luck we shall bring you will be of greater value than you imagine."

And the king replied, "If all had not been practically won by now it would be well to go and take you, for I know quite well that you and the other fair ladies who are here could vanquish all. But Jouvencel[1] has conquered already! It would be no honour to us now."

And the lady answered, "You do not distress yourself about anything. Do you think you can be a great king without affairs? Never! There are none. Great kings must have great affairs of State. You will have plenty of other opportunities of enjoying the society of fair ladies when you wish to do so."

The king saw the justice of her rebuke. The courage Agnes showed in thus openly attempting to overcome his reluctance to set forth was worthy of her, but it did not suffice to exert it only once. Charles looked upon the plans of his captains with a more favourable eye, but he could not come to a final resolution in a day.

While Agnes remained at his side he saw the path he ought to tread clearly, but when she

[1] A flattering allusion to the military advance in Normandy made by the French since May.

left him, even for a short time, his faith wavered. When the court moved northward Agnes obtained permission to stay for a while at the Château de Beauté—the possession which was dear to her heart, because she took her name from it.

Charles had granted her request unwillingly enough. He could not bear to be separated from his mistress at any time, but when stirring matters were in the wind he felt more than ever the need of her presence.

Agnes was wise, however, in carrying out her purpose. She found that continuous life at court made great demands on her strength, and that she could not do justice to herself or to the king unless she was in good health. She knew, moreover, that after a short separation from him he appreciated her all the more, and so she made the excuse that her tenants at Vincennes required the presence of their châtelaine, and she refused to disappoint them.

She had not left court for more than a few weeks when Charles saw that the moment for taking a decisive step had arrived, and still he found it difficult to make up his mind what to do.

CHAPTER XXIV

WHAT HAPPENED AT THE CHÂTEAU DE BEAUTÉ

THE fate of France was trembling in the balance. Should the king reopen war against the English or should he not?

The army had been reorganised. The soldiers were ready. They only waited the word. But this Charles did not give. He did not dare to put his luck to the test.

Up and down the apartments of the palace he paced deep in thought. Then he called a gentleman of the chamber and sent him—not for his best captains, for he knew the military side of the question by heart,—but for his secretary, Etienne Chevalier, who had proved his loyalty a thousand times in as many ways.

"What can I do, Sire?" cried Chevalier, seeing the king's perturbation.

"Do?" inquired the harassed king; "there is everything to be done. I have only to raise my little finger and my men will set forth to battle. But——"

"But—you hesitate, Sire?" stammered Chevalier. "Why not make the movement you suggest?"

Charles came close to him and spoke in his ear.

249

"Is the moment propitious, think you?" Without waiting for an answer, he continued, "I do not mean to question our position or the strength of our armies. But are the Saints with us? Answer me that."

Etienne Chevalier shook his head gravely. "I dare not respond for the Saints, Sire. That is a question for one who is more closely in touch with them than I. What does our demoiselle de Beauté say to it?"

"Agnes? I have not put the matter to her," explained Charles hurriedly, being astonished that Etienne should suggest his mistress was more saintly than himself. "But I know what she would counsel. She has ever urged me to take the harder path when it came to a matter of duty."

"Then ask her now, Sire," was the secretary's prompt reply, and he respectfully withdrew.

Charles was not satisfied with the turn the conversation had taken, but he decided to act on Etienne Chevalier's advice. He ordered his horse and set out for the Forest of Vincennes.

On a hillside surrounded by a wide belt of sturdy oaks stood the Château de Beauté, where Agnes was staying.

Charles reached the castle wearied from the pace he had come.

"Where is your lady?" he cried to those who met him at the drawbridge.

As the words left his lips he caught sight of Agnes in the gardens, and hastened to her side.

She was wearing a rich brocade gown trimmed with furs, which became her well. The king thought he had never seen his mistress looking more lovely.

But her cheeks were paler than usual, for Agnes had suffered of late from regret. She had fought the good fight until she had grown strong enough to put her own happiness in the background and the king's duty first.

" I have come to you to-day, fairest one," began Charles, as he stooped to kiss her hand, " to tell you——" But she stayed his words with her fingers on his lips.

" Tell me nothing, for my heart has told me already why you are here, Sire. I can read the question in your mind before you speak it."

" And your answer ? " he asked anxiously, having kissed the fingers which she speedily withdrew.

" Those who put their trust in God never fail," she said simply. " That is my answer."

A tiny sigh escaped her. She had not learnt to put her trust in God without taking pains.

" I believe you are right," cried the king, after a short pause for reflection. " But you condemn me to leave you."

" Nay, Sire, it is not I who decree it, but the fates that made you a king."

" You are always right, ma belle," went on Charles. " I have never known you otherwise. In the trouble with my ingrate son you saw what I should do, though it pained you to tell me, as it pained me to do it. It was you who warned me that he plotted against the seneschal, and your coming to Paris when you did saved me from a grave error. May you be spared to me for many years, that I may always be guided by your good judgment and your generous mercy."

He sighed deeply. He wished that Agnes's influence had come into his life sooner, at the time when the trial of Jeanne d'Arc—witch as she had seemed to him then—had taken place. Agnes, he felt sure, would have advised toleration. Ever since those days he had suffered grave doubts about the Maid; she had answered her judges so fearlessly, she had always been modest and pure.

The Lady of Beauty was speaking. Her voice broke in on his thoughts.

" I, too, hope I may be spared, Sire, and that my poor council may profit you; but I fear——" For a moment her vision had grown clouded, her heart faint. She made an effort to be brave.

" Nay," she went on. " To-night we will not speak of fears. One thing is sure; I shall warn you once again."

" Only once—Agnes ? "

She nodded but did not speak.

The king was ever ready with personal fears. " Do you foreshadow danger to me in Normandy ? " His voice trembled with emotion.

She turned to him smiling bravely. " I cannot see what the danger is, or for whom it lurks in wait, but your duty is clear. In Normandy your path will be one of success. You will conquer and deserve the name Victorious. But beyond that all fades—all is dark—there is another———" Her voice trailed off into silence.

The king shuddered. He was very imaginative.

"Come, Sire," said Agnes, with an effort chasing away her gloomy forebodings, "the troubadours await us with love-songs; we will tell them to sing of war and battle instead. They shall give us the clash of arms on the cymbals, and their trumpets shall bray of triumph."

They left the gardens and found a great banquet being prepared in the large hall of the castle.

"You counsel me to ride, but you tempt me to feast," cried the king, amazed.

"Nay, Sire, not so; for he who rides fasting is a worse enemy to himself than any he may be called upon to face in the field. Let us eat and be merry so that you set forth in good heart."

So cleverly did she ply him with food and entertainment that never once that evening did he show signs of weariness or indecision. His doubts were forgotten, his confidence assured. The responsibilities of him who wears a crown can only be lightened by one who loves him and understands how to bring peace and fresh courage to the tired brain. Only one woman can perform this part in a man's life, as Agnes did for Charles VII in the best and truest way, by putting aside her own will to do his and that of the people.

Before he retired that night Charles had paid

his mistress the greatest compliment a king **can** pay.

" I have worn the crown, ma belle," he **said,** " all these long and often weary years, but you and you only have kept its gold untarnished. God, who understands human weakness, will reward the strength and love you have shown me, and if for no other reason He will pardon your faults."

At these solemn words Agnes bent low and kissed the king's hand.

" May He guard you and bring you good fortune, Sire. For myself I ask nothing. I rejoice in your coming greatness, and all I pray for is that the people when they praise you will think not unkindly of me."

She smiled and bade the king good-night. There was an added tenderness in her voice, a sweet light in her eyes. Her love had become purified, and from being merely personal had grown solely patriotic. Something told her that her work was nearly done and that soon she would rest.

As the king rode forth the next morning to begin the campaign his thoughts were of her, and he remembered her wish that the people might not think harshly of her, and he vowed that all he could do to bring about this result should be done.

That day he proclaimed in public that the Lady of Beauty had urged him to set forth to fight the English, and every one who heard him spread the news, and the rejoicings were general.

Because Agnes had been instrumental in bringing about the fulfilment of their wish to wage war against the enemy, the people forgave her her wrongdoing, and, when France became once more a free land, her name was spoken with gratitude and her memory was revered with love.

Charles declared the truce officially broken at an assembly held at Roches-Tranchelion, near Chinon, in July, 1449, and acquiesced in the desire of the French nobles to march against the English at once.

He left Chinon on August 6, and advanced upon Normandy, leading his men to the capital. Passing through Verneuil and Evreux he took up his quarters at Louviers, where he remained throughout September.

At the end of the month he besieged Château Gaillard, one of the most strongly fortified castles of Normandy. After six weeks the English were reduced by famine and obliged to capitulate.

Early in October Charles was stationed at Pont de l'Arche. The armies under Dunois, d'Alençon and Saint-Pol were converging on Rouen. The king and the brilliant company in his train were received by the people with ovations. On October 9 a military demonstration was made before the city, and, encouraged by the sight of their king and his men, the townsfolk of Rouen decided to take the offensive against the enemy.

A week later a more serious attack was made, which resulted in the fall of Rouen in November, and the triumphal entry of Charles VII into that city on the 10th of the month, the account of which is familiar to every one.

After a stay of ten days Charles left Rouen and went to Jumièges, where he spent the first week of December, leaving for Caudebec en Caux with fourteen or fifteen thousand men.

From there the army moved to Montvilliers, where Charles directed the operations preliminary to the siege of Harfleur. The king was very active. Every day he went personally amongst his men to encourage them, inspected the entrenchments and organised the plan of attack. In a fortnight Harfleur had capitulated.

The greater part of Normandy was now in the hands of the French. The year 1450 opened under favourable auspices.

On January 5 the king left Montvilliers and returned to Jumièges, whilst the army marched down the Seine to attack Honfleur.

At Jumièges a great grief awaited him. In his personal distress military operations were temporarily forgotten.

At the last Agnes had begged for permission to accompany the king to the seat of battle, but he had refused. Some authorities said that during the campaign she had remained with the queen at Chinon. Others believed that after she retired from court she crept as close to the

ESTIENNE CHEVALIER, *Seigneur du Vignau, du Plessis le Comte et autres lieux, Conseiller et Secretaire du Commandemens des Roys CHARLES VII et LOVIS XI et leur Ambassadeur en Angleterre et en Italie, Decede le 3 Septembre 1474.*

[*To face p.* 256

ETIENNE CHEVALIER

operations of war · as expediency permitted,
namely, to her own estate of Vernon-sur-Seine in
Normandy.   There she waited in great anxiety.

It was then that rumours of a plot against the
king's life reached her ears, and she set forth on
the perilous journey which was to be her last.

s

CHAPTER XXV

JUMIÈGES

" IN this Abbey of Jumièges," wrote Jean Chartier, " the king found a young lady called ' la belle Agnès,' who had come there, as she said, to warn the king and to tell him that some of his servants were about to betray him and deliver him into the hands of his former enemies, the English, concerning which news the king was incredulous and only laughed at it."

The chronicler's words imply that Agnes had heard of a plot against the king's life, possibly emanating from the dauphin, but no authentic account of any intrigue at this time exists in history. Perhaps the Lady of Beauty was urged by jealousy to attempt the long and perilous journey to Normandy at a time of the year and in a state of health which hardly warranted such an undertaking.

Whatever her reasons for following the king to the scenes of war in Normandy, they must have been weighty, and she paid for her temerity with her life.

Charles had re-conquered many of the strongholds of the neighbourhood, only a few of which remained in the hands of the English. Having placed the command of Harfleur in the charge

of Dunois, he returned through Caudebec to
Jumièges, which he reached on January 16.
There he stayed in an edifice consecrated to the
use of kings and princes adjoining the Abbey of
Jumièges, a retreat visited by members of royalty
intent on the pleasures of the chase. He had
ordered certain improvements to be made in
the apartments which he occupied, wishing to
receive Agnes there.[1]

The famous abbey stands where the river
Seine makes an abrupt but magnificent sweep
between Rouen and Caudebec, on a peninsula
about a league by a league and a half in extent.

To-day a picturesque mass of roofless walls
and arches, of broken towers and foliage-covered
windows, its floors open to the sky and spread
with a tapestry of grass and ivy, in the time of
Charles VII it was one of the richest and most
solid monasteries of France.

Peopled chiefly by monks and learned men,
its strongly fortified walls resounded not only
to chant and prayer but ofttimes to the noise
of revelry and banqueting; for the kings of
France held court there, and soldiers do not hush
the voice like priests.

The origin of the strange name of the abbey is
unknown.

" D'ou vient ton nom, Jumièges ? ils ne sauraient le dire
  O vanité de l'homme et surtout du savant !
  Gemitus ou *gemma*, ' douleur ' ou ' Diamant ' ?

---

[1] Du Gard, *L'Abbaye de Jumièges*, 1909, p. 45. This
throws a new light upon her visit. Perhaps the improvements were suggested after her arrival at Mesnil.

S 2

Choississez : tous les deux me plairaient davantage
L'histoire de ce cloître et de ces monuments
Montre autant de trésors que de gémissements."

Besides those who derive the name of the abbey from *gemitus*, meaning a place of groans, or from *gemma*, because Jumièges was the pearl of monasteries, some take the word as coming from *guen* or marsh, and imagine that the monastery was built on a piece of unreclaimed land which owed its fertility to the efforts of the holy brethren who congregated there.

The history of the abbey is well known to the general reader. It was founded in the seventh century by Saint Philibert, who left the Court of King Dagobert to turn monk. Having superintended the completion of the building he drew some seventy monks to the new monastery from those in the neighbourhood, and installed them at Jumièges under the rule of Saint Benedict.

The first dramatic tradition connected with the abbey was the death there of two young princes called " les énervés de Jumièges." Having rebelled against the authorities they were subjected to torture and abandoned in an open boat. Found by the monks they were taken to the abbey, all too late to restore them to health. This legend was borrowed by Ronsard in the fourth book of his *Franciade*.

But the real interest of the abbey is centred in the figure of the Lady of Beauty, whose sincere repentance for her past and whose sad death in the immediate vicinity have tinged the neighbourhood for all time with a spirit of romance and a tragic memory.

Dibdin,[1] one of the most prosaic of mortals, who said stoutly, " we will eat our cold fowl and drink our *vin ordinaire* upon the grass within the walls of the abbey," suffered from " a sort of romantic twinge," which made him very uncomfortable, as he munched his luncheon beside the grave of Agnes Sorel.

On one hand lies the Forest of Brotonne, on the other the Forest of Mauny; behind are the woods and precipices of Duclair, and the range of hills which follows the curve of the river is crowned with trees and fortified with natural buttresses of rock. This is a spot to dream in and see peopled with historic figures. Agnes, in the last extremity of dread and anguish, pressing on from the south in mid-winter, Charles hastening from the north to meet her, the ring and cry of battle still in his ears, form a picture of human struggle against difficulties full of the torture and the hope, the weakness and the strength, of love and life. Both were impelled by forces stronger than themselves; she to undertake so perilous a journey, he to leave the spot where his brave soldiers were fighting to regain their country.

Though history in this case is grim, tradition is more kind, and says that Agnes and Charles paid many visits to the neighbourhood, and saw it under fairer conditions than in those painful

[1] Tho. Frognall Dibdin, *A Bibliographical, Antiquarian and Picturesque Tour in France and Germany,* 1821, Vol. I. p. 198.

last weeks of the lady's life; and truly the abbey is so smiling a spot that it is difficult to connect it with death or sorrow; it seems more typical of youth and promise, of happy love, of gentle peace and the blessed rest which undoubtedly were found there by the Lady of Beauty at the last.

Thus Leitch Ritchie pictured her when he wrote of the places which Turner had immortalised with his brush :

" But who is she," he wrote, " this lady of the past, who, gliding away from the ruins, seems to take the path towards the little Château of Mesnil in the neighbourhood ? Flowers spring up beneath her feet—sweet phantom flowers, which fade when she is gone by; the air around her is rich with fragrance; the very shrubs, as they wave back their branches to let her pass, appear conscious of the queenly step of beauty. It is Agnes Sorel, the noble, the high-hearted—ay, the honourable, ay, the virtuous Agnes Sorel, the *mistress* of Charles VII. This admirable woman, unambitious of acting the part of a heroine herself, was satisfied with making her lover a hero. ' If honour,' said she, ' cannot lead you from love, love at least shall lead you to honour ! ' "

She was the loveliest of the lovely, and of a sweet, gentle, meek and holy disposition; charitable to excess, kind, generous and forgiving.

Her heart was peculiarly open to religious impressions, and when summoned by the angel of death in her mid-career—in the flush of prosperity, the pride of place, the full glow of a beauty without comparison—the single error of her life presented itself in the aspect of a mortal sin, and she wept tears of remorse for that heroic love to which, perhaps, her country owed its freedom.

In vain had the Maid of Orleans been burnt on the stake, in vain had her saintly spirit ascended to paradise, had not Agnes remained, the guardian angel of her royal friend, to inspire him with honour through the vehicle of passion and infuse the enthusiasm of kingly virtue.

This radiant being was to vanish from the eyes of her royal worshipper all too soon.

In a spirit of sacrifice, to save the king, she made the fatal journey. If she had been staying at Vernon, as some suggest, the undertaking was not so great, but if she came from Touraine she must have suffered severely from the adverse conditions under which she travelled.

Her manor at Mesnil was ready to receive her—a charming residence, nestling in a fertile orchard country, with a wide sweep of the river visible from the windows.

Deshayes[1] described a small house, said to be occupied by the mistress of Charles VII, as so simple and unpretentious in comparison with neighbouring edifices of the same date that it could only have been a dependency of a more considerable castle in which she might have lived; or it may have been the chapel of the castle. There was also another building which

[1] Deshayes, C. A., *Histoire de l'Abbaye Royale de Jumièges.* Rouen, 1829.

was more imposing, but which Deshayes still thought was not the main residence. Traces remained in it of a spacious chimney, which appeared to indicate that it was a kitchen. But the monks declared that this apartment served the fair Agnes as a dining-room.

A large vault in this building served as an entrance to the manor, which indicated that the original château was of considerable size and importance. Confusion arose because the attached house was at one time occupied by a certain beauty, Mme. Laguerchois, who died there, and the furniture she left was supposed to belong to Agnes Sorel.

Nodier[1] gave a somewhat similar description of " la jolie maison du Mesnil-la-Belle." He said her initials were engraved upon the outer walls. " The Lady of Beauty," he wrote, " often visited the saintly monastery, for her love, although guilty, had not turned her heart away from God, and did not cause her to neglect the ministers of the altar. Thus the good monks were lenient towards a fault which perhaps contributed to save France and still more to enrich the monastery. They showed a tender predilection for the gentle sinner, seeking her friendship in life and giving room to her ashes, which rested in their church under the gracious and pitiful gaze of the Madonna."

Usually, no doubt, Agnes stayed at the manor whilst Charles was at the monastery. The distance between the two was about two and a

[1] *Voyages Pittoresques et Romantiques dans l'Ancienne France : Normandie,* Vol. I. pp. 49–53. Paris, 1820.

half miles. Part of the way led through a gate and a beautiful avenue of trees, which now bears the name of the Allée d'Agnès Sorel.

One of the owners put a new gate in the place of the original one, bearing the inscription :

"Agnès par cette porte arrivait du manoir;
Un page la guidait vers le royal dortoir.
Agnès de Charles VII ranima le courage.
Son nom cher à la France a passé d'âge en âge :
Belle était son surnom,
Et de la belle Agnès cette porte a le nom."

According to another legend a subterranean passage led from the monastery to the manor, and the vaults from which it sprang may still be seen. Deshayes was probably right when he refused to believe that any of these subterranean passages extended for more than a league. One led down to the river, and that way came smuggled treasure which helped to swell the money in the coffers of the monks. A toll was taken of all the fish caught in the sea, and a share of all the wine pressed from the vineyards round about the abbey added substance to the revenue.

Probably there was not a passage leading all the way to Mesnil, but one that led out of the king's residence so that Charles was able to leave Jumièges without his attendants knowing that he was absent. His horse would be waiting for him at the gate which guarded the entrance to the vaults, and from that point he could ride through the avenue and so to the manor.

And Agnes awaited him anxiously enough. As the evening grew darker she listened for the distant sound of hoofs. Did he come or did he make merry that night in the abbey, she wondered.

She pictured the scene in the guard-room, and heard in imagination the clatter of spurs, and then the sound of laughter and good cheer. Or was it the sound of the wind shrieking in the trees, for the clouds had gathered and a storm come up. But nothing deterred the king, who meant to ride that night, and he drank a last cup, and, beckoning to a single guard, he marched down the stone steps to the subterranean passage, jesting even as he went. And so love met love.

In after years there was something eerie in the obscure chambers of the isolated manor-house when the hour came that brought spectres abroad to visit the closed door and peer in at the shut windows. The February nights were dark and gusty, and, as the wind dropped suddenly and rain pattered quickly on to the thick foliage, a long piercing cry struck on the ear, and when it died away there came the noise of sobbing, and all who heard trembled—for Agnes was no more—and it was Charles who had wept.

In the abbey itself she had her nooks, where she spent quiet hours before her death.

In the upper room of the abbey dependencies, where the museum now is, is the window from which she gazed out upon the main building, and before it stands the *prie-dieu* on which she knelt to pray. She would sit for hours in this corner, while the king attended to affairs of State, and ponder over the past and wonder what the future

—the future that seemed so uncertain—had still to bring.

But there were other times when she was gay and fearless and her dark forebodings vanished. Then she sat by her window and worked at a piece of tapestry, and with her nimble fingers fashioned the figures of a holy group, meaning the work to be a present to the monks who loved her.

And all the time she prayed that her daughters might be happy when she was no longer there to care for them, and that they might grow into noble, virtuous women, and be married to good men who would guard them and keep them from all the dangers through which she herself had passed. She wished each one of them a far better fate than to be a king's mistress.

And sometimes her thoughts would stray to a less pleasant topic, and the face of her cousin Antoinette would rise before her as in a vision; and then she would shudder, because she had seen the king's eyes turn that way, and she knew that Antoinette would do her best to fill the place she was leaving, and to fill it in a manner unworthy. But how could she warn her lover against the designs of a scheming woman ? She had never spoken ill of any one, how could she say what was evil of one of her own family ? That was impossible.

And then her face took on lines of pain again, for she remembered how much she had suffered from the things that had been said against her by vile tongues.

Jean Chartier wrote of her meekness in bearing with this indignity, " The publication of evil reports and scandal having come to the ears of the said Agnes, she was so saddened and displeased that she showed great contrition and repentance for her sins. She thought often of Mary Magdalen, who was a great sinner of sins of the flesh."

Soon she fell ill.

Her fourth baby had been born at Mesnil, and not long afterwards she was stricken with a mortal disease, probably typhoid, or another which left equally little chance of her recovery.

She had not been mistaken then.   Her end was near.

Charles hastened to her bedside, but it was not he who could bring her the comfort she needed.

" When falling ill," wrote Chartier, " she called devoutly on God and the Virgin Mary to come to her aid.   Then, like a good Catholic, after receiving the Sacrament, she asked for her ' Book of Hours ' so that she might read the verses of Saint Bernard, which she had written with her own hand.   She afterwards made her will and testament, in which were many bequests, and she appointed the noble Jacques Cœur her executor, in company with Robert Poictevin and Etienne Chevalier, the king's treasurer. She desired that the king alone should be the first, and in every way have the control of these three persons."

Having accomplished which, Agnes, seeing and

realising that her malady was hourly gaining in force, and that she could no longer master it but must succumb under its influence, called to her bedside Monsieur de Tancarville, Madame de Brézé, the seneschal's wife, and Gouffier, the same squire who had accompanied her from Tours to Paris, as well as all the ladies who usually attended upon her. To them she said—much in the tone that Margaret of Scotland had used only five years earlier when she cried " Out upon this life," only with even more sincerity, for she had experienced more wickedness—" How frail is our flesh, how abject and vile a thing, and truly of what little worth."

Afterwards she called to her confessor, praying him to absolve her from all her faults and sins, in virtue of an indulgence from Loches. And this he did at her request.

Then after giving a loud cry, demanding the mercy and grace of God and the Holy Virgin, her soul departed from her body, and she passed away on Monday, February 9, about six o'clock in the evening.

Her heart was removed from her body and buried in the said abbey to which she had given her bequests. Her body was taken to Loches and buried there in the collegiate chapel of Nôtre-Dame, upon which she had also bestowed donations.

The Lady of Beauty was no more.

The monks of Jumièges declared that the fair Agnes died in sentiments of penitence, full of regrets for what she had done amiss. In dying she bequeathed to them a large sum, charging them to say masses for her every day and to celebrate one solemn service every year for the repose of her soul.

The canons of Loches voluntarily accorded her similar services in recognition of two thousand golden crowns which she gave them to buy the lands of Fromenteau and Bigorne. Besides she gave them a tapestry of great price and many pictures and jewels.

King Charles issued letters to this effect in December, 1451, concerning the last wishes of " our late cherished and well-beloved in her lifetime, demoiselle et dame de Beaulté, de Rocquesezière, d'Issoudon et de Vernon-sur-Seine."

They did not scruple at Loches to accept her donations, but after the death of Charles VII, one day when Louis XI was in their church, they showed him the tomb of their benefactress, and thinking to flatter him, believing the hate which he had felt for her during her lifetime was still centred in her ashes, they begged him to have her monument removed from their midst, for they pretended that scandal attached to it.

" I agree," said the monarch, angered by their ingratitude, " but you must render up all you received from her."

The demand was frequently renewed in the succeeding reigns,[1] and in 1777 the tomb was

[1] In 1772 a request was presented to Louis XV, giving good reasons for moving the tomb, which was so massive that it left only three feet of passage on each side of it,

placed in the aisle of the church. They opened the sarcophagus, in which was found an outer coffin of wood, a second of lead, and a third of wood inside all.

The pearly teeth of the Lady of Beauty and a strand of her lovely fair hair were well preserved. The rest was ashes. The hair is treasured at the abbey to this day, and M. Duquesne in his work on the Lady of Beauty printed a letter from M. Lepel-Cointet dated July 7, 1908, vouching for its authenticity.

The ashes were collected in an urn and placed in the tomb, but at the time of the Revolution the violation of the tomb was completed and the monument was broken up. The pieces were taken to Paris in 1805 to be restored, and afterwards placed in the tower of the Château of Loches, which is called by the name of Agnes.

The tomb has often been described as one of the most beautiful ornaments at Loches. Henry James,[1] writing of it, said, " She has always, I know not with what justice, enjoyed a fairer fame than most ladies who have occupied her position, and this fairness is expressed in the delicate statue that surmounts her tomb. It represents her lying there in lovely demureness, her hands folded with the best modesty, a little

---

which prevented the officiating priest and the deacons from walking abreast, and made them risk spoiling their robes by rubbing them against the tomb. Probably the king consulted Mme. du Barry, who was naturally interested in the point raised, and he wrote the answer across the report, " In spite of everything, leave the tomb where it is."

[1] *A Little Tour in France*, 1885.

kneeling angel at either side of her head, and her feet, hidden in the folds of her decent robe, resting upon a pair of couchant lambs."

At the moment when Agnes died Charles had been about to make her a duchess. The coronet was engraved on the monument at Loches.

He ordered the funeral himself, and when the monks inquired what were to be the burial rites, he answered proudly, " She must be buried like a duchess." The carrying out of the arrangements was left to Etienne Chevalier, who accompanied the mortal remains to Loches.

Those who followed her body to the grave wept when they thought of her love. Even in death she was beautiful, her golden hair lying in long tresses about her pale face. Nine hundred monks of Jumièges chanted by her grave-side. The king and all his court were in the Chapel of the Virgin, the crowd knelt, and tears coursed from the eyes of the poor whom Agnes had loved and who had given their love in return for hers.

Her heart was buried in the north transept of the great church at Jumièges, and now an ivy-grown hollow marks the spot. A marble tomb was placed upon it, the huge slab of black marble being raised some three feet from the ground. Formerly it was surmounted by a white marble statue, representing her kneeling and holding in her hands a heart which she offered to the Virgin, praying her to make her peace with God. At the foot of the tomb was another heart in white marble.

Four epitaphs were written to her, two in

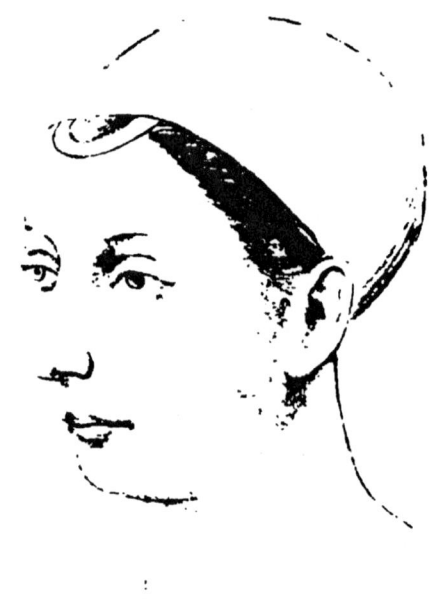

La Belle amps

Adieu de louange soy amour En anergie
Et tout cesos de france Recomvisss...
que nyst tout fe qua olaytre petouuser
oleuse namuyy ory d andsest vuuyte

[To face p. 272

LA BELLE AGNÈS

(*From the portrait in the album of Mme. de Boisy*)

Latin and two in French. The Latin ones were similar to those at Loches, beginning :

"Hic jacet in tumba mitis simplexque columba."

["Here lies in peace a dove whiter than swans, more sparkling with wit than a bright fire. Agnes was too fair. She is now under the sod, she whose face was like unto the flowers of spring. . . . Do not wonder if her effigy appears clad in princely robes. This honour was due to her for her virtues and meritorious graces."]

The black marble slab served for some time as the balcony of a house in Rouen, but has long since been restored to Jumièges, and is now in the museum there. It bears the following inscription :

"CY GIST NOBLE DAYMOSELE AGNÈS SEURELLE, en son vivant DAME DE BEAULTÉ DE [RO]QUESSERIÈRE, D'ISSOUDUN E[T] DE VERNON SUR SEINE, PITEUSE ENTRE TO [UTES G]ENS, ET QUI LARGEM[EN]T AUMOSNOIT [S]ES BIENS AUX EGLYSES E[T] AUX POUVRES, LAQUELLE TRESPASSA L'AN DE GRACE M CCCC E[T] XLIX."

A column built out of the old stones about her grave was raised above the spot where rested her heart. Beside it grew a weeping willow.

One of the inscriptions on the column was :

"Agnès, cet être objet des royales amours,
Près du vieux monastère a terminé ses jours;
Sur sa tombe élevée en la sainte chapelle,
De nombreux pèlerins venaient prier pour elle;"

and beneath :

"Passants, ne priez plus,
L'Eternel a fait grâce :
Agnès a trouvé place
Au séjour des élus."

T

No sooner was Agnes dead and buried than there arose a cry that she had been poisoned. Some said the dauphin was at the root of the tragedy; others blamed Jacques Cœur, who was sentenced to be tried for the crime. In similar cases foul play was often suspected, and a parallel instance is that of Gabrielle d'Estrées, who was seized with convulsions on her return from Tenebræ, and expired two days later in fearful agony. Henri IV had been on the verge of making her his queen. She, too, died as a consequence of child-birth.

A few months after the death of the Lady of Beauty a woman named Jeanne de Vendôme, wife of François de Montberon, Lord of Mortagne-sur-Gironde, was drawn into a plot of which Chabannes and probably the new favourite, Antoinette, were instigators. The Dame de Mortagne was influenced to make the assertion that Agnes had died in consequence of poison administered to her by Jacques Cœur.

He was also accused of conspiring against the king, of coining money of false weight, of furnishing arms to the Saracens, of exporting precious metals to the Orient, and a number of minor charges.

He was at Tailleburg with the king, all unaware of the tragic fate that awaited him, and utterly unsuspicious of the king's intentions, when he was struck as by a thunderbolt from the blue.

On July 31, 1451, he was arrested and cast into prison on the extraordinary charges enumerated, of which murder and theft were the most criminal.

The accusations began in the following candid manner, utterly ignoring the fact that it was not eighteen months since the accused had been appointed chief executor of Agnes Sorel's will:

" Charles, by the grace of God, King of France, to all by whom these present letters shall be seen, greeting.

" Whereas after the death of the late Agnes Sorelle, Damoiselle, the common report was that she was poisoned : and by the same common report, suspicion was entertained of Jacques Cœur, then our counsellor and silversmith, and also that he had sent armour to the Saracens, our ancient enemies, and enemies of the Christian faith : and as many of our subjects have made great complaints and clamours of the said Jacques Cœur, accusing him of having made great extortions and exactions in our province of Languedoc on our subjects, and of having transported, or caused to be transported to the said Saracens, by his people, factors and servants, in his vessels, great quantities of silver, so that it was said that our whole province of Languedoc was emptied of its treasure :

" We did therefore order information to be laid on the subject of the death by poison of the said Damoiselle Agnes, and reports to be made to us in our castle of Tailleburg, where we were staying for the conquest of our duchy of Guienne, and caused the charges to be seen by all, as also the

T 2

deposition of Mme. de Montberon, who, touching the case of the said death and poisoning of the said Agnes, had deposed against the said Jacques Cœur.

" By the advice and after the deliberations of our Grand Council we did order and appoint that Jacques Cœur should be arrested and his goods put into our hands by inventory," etc., etc.

Jacques Cœur was cited to appear before a commission, at the head of which were Antoine de Chabannes and Guillaume Gouffier.

He was exculpated of conspiring with the dauphin and of poisoning Agnes Sorel, but he had thousands of enemies all ready to profit by his downfall, and one hundred and fifty witnesses gave evidence against him. One of them was the Etienne de Manné already mentioned, who had stolen many of Jacques Cœur's goods, Agnes Sorel's furs amongst them. He had been dismissed at the time, but generously saved from prosecution by the employer he had cheated. He was now given letters of remission for his fault by the authorities in order that he might bear witness.

Jacques Cœur languished in prison for months, was subjected to torture, was transferred from dungeon to dungeon, and finally was sentenced at Lusignan, May 19, 1453.

He was declared worthy of death, was loaded with humiliations, his goods were confiscated, his offices taken from him, and it was decreed that he should make the *amende honorable* without hood or belt, which typified the fact that he had been stripped of all his worldly goods.

"I cannot speak falsely in reporting," said Etienne Pasquier of this trial, "that it was the jealousy of the great men of Charles VII's court which concocted this tragedy."

There was only one redeeming feature in the scandalous affair. Not only was the victim entirely cleared of any suspicion as to the death of the Lady of Beauty, but his accuser, the Dame de Mortagne, was condemned to the *amende honorable* towards him she had sought to injure, and was ordered to keep ten leagues away from court. Her life was granted because her ancestors and her husband had rendered services to the State.

Bereft of his possessions, Jacques Cœur was no longer worth keeping a prisoner. He was allowed to remove from his dungeon at Poitiers to a monastery at Beaucaire. He remained there for some eighteen months " under the safeguard of the king."

Escaping from this life of inaction he made his way to Rome, shaking the dust of his native land for ever from his feet. The Pope offered him an asylum in his own palace, and nursed him through a dangerous illness. At the time of the trial Nicholas V had written to Charles to plead in the financier's favour, but without avail.

Among those who derived benefit from the division of the great man's property were Chabannes, Gouffier, and Antoinette de Villequier. Agnes's brother Jean shared in the spoils, receiving jointly with his mother[1] the estate of Geran de Vaux.

Pope Nicholas died on March 25, 1455, only a few days after tardy reparation had been done to Jacques Cœur in the shape of letters exculpating him from the charges against him. But justice had come too late. He died, probably at Rome, in the following year.

Two centuries later in the reign of Louis XIV, the *surintendant des finances*, Nicolas Fouquet, fell under almost parallel circumstances. Both were betrayed by the kings they had served.

Had Agnes remained alive Charles must have acted differently. Yet it is not certain that he did not desert his mistress before her death, as he did the man who was accused of causing it. The ways of such a king fall far below the highest standards of honour.

As though the irony of Jacques Cœur being accused of poisoning the woman who had befriended him were not enough, a grim fate arranged that his daughter, married to the Lord of Bois-Trousseau, should live on in the home where once the beacon lights of the Lady of Beauty had shone from the battlements to welcome the king, her lover.

With Agnes there passed away a beautiful woman, and all that remained of her physical perfection was a feeble image on her tomb representing what she had been in life. The

---

[1] According to Anselme's account. It must not be forgotten that a doubt exists as to whether Catherine Soreau was alive at this date.

pompous titles to which she had laid claim were the sole signs of her perishable grandeur. Soon even they passed into other hands. But she left behind her a beautiful tradition, if not of virtue, then of patriotism; and patriotism inspired the French poets to sing her praises and extol her charms.

Jean Antoine de Baïf wrote verses on her death at the manor-house not far from Jumièges. They have been rendered into English :

" This then is Mesnil called from her whose charms
Above all other themes the poet warms.
Agnes, the star of Charles, whose grievous fate
Left his heart torn, forlorn and desolate.
Here perfumed airs amidst each secret shade
Tell of their early loves that cannot fade;
These ruined walls seem mourning in decay
That worth and beauty should be swept away;
The wind moans round them sad and heavily,
An echo of fair Agnes' dying sigh.

'Twas when, with conquer'd Normandy his prize,
The lover from dread battles turned his eyes,
And midst the shadows of lone Jumièges sought
The darling object of his tenderest thought.
Then Agnes came—she heard of treachery
And flew to warn him of the danger nigh,
For Fate had led her to this holy fane,
And doom'd her ne'er to quit those walls again.

Alas ! fond lover, after all thy care,
Thy toil, thy valour, was thy hope but air ?
All thy heart promised void ? The trial past,
Is death and sorrow thy reward at last !

O Death ! has beauty then, no power to move ?
Deaf art thou thus to constancy and love ?
But great although thy power, and fell thy sway,
And in her youthful prime she fell thy prey,
The wrong is less than if, as Fortune willed
The days by Nature granted had been filled

And those fair features and those eyes so bright
In dim and fading age had lost their light:
And that renown of Beauty's Queen no more
The world would give her, since its power was o'er.

No! to the end so lovely and so dear,
The peerless star shone ever bright and clear:
Agnes will live ' fair Agnes ' in her fame
So long as Beauty shall bear Beauty's name."

CHAPTER XXVI

ANTOINETTE BECOMES MME. DE VILLEQUIER

In October, 1450, nine months after the death of Agnes, the king arranged a marriage between her cousin and his *mignon*, André de Villequier. Antoinette was by that time his mistress. Both she and her husband received lands and money liberally. Among the estates that had belonged to Agnes which were given to Mme. de Villequier were La Guerche and Issoudun.

At first, perhaps, the king's motives in his treatment of Antoinette had been pure, and his attentions only a consequence of his attachment to her cousin. The de Maignelais family had lost some of its lands in a great law-suit with the Bourbons, and in August, 1449, six months before Agnes died, Charles had withdrawn the estate of Maignelais from the ownership of Charles, Duc de Bourbon, and restored it, not as might have been expected to its rightful owner, Jean de Maignelais, but to his daughter Antoinette.

In April, 1454, André de Villequier died, and Charles spent that summer between the Châteaux of Pressigny and Preuilly, close by La Guerche where the widow was staying.

During 1454 and 1455 Antoinette had an annual pension of two thousand livres " to help her to keep up a good estate," and the chroniclers said, as they had said of Agnes before her, that she was as rich as a princess, and her household equalled, if it did not surpass, that of the queen.

Antoinette, then, had won the place for which she had schemed, just as two centuries later Mme. de Montespan reached the goal she had aimed at during the lifetime of Louise de la Vallière. After the honest, modest and faithful mistress, who tried her best to keep her royal lover in the path of well-doing if not of rectitude, came the grasping, ambitious, dangerous woman who plunged her paramour into extravagance and excess, pandered to his vices and brought about his moral downfall.

Like Mme. de Pompadour for Louis XV, Antoinette arranged for Charles VII a kind of *Parc aux cerfs.*

" After the said Fair Agnes was dead," wrote Jacques du Clercq, " King Charles put in her place the niece of the said Fair Agnes, who was the wife of the Duc de Villequier,[1] and she was as beautiful as her aunt, and she always had in her company five or six of the most lovely women in the kingdom, who followed the king wherever he went, and were dressed as richly as possible like queens, and held great and extravagant estate, and all this was at the king's expense; they made a greater show than any queens."

In 1455, when Antoinette was at the height of

---

[1] For niece, Du Clercq should, of course, have written cousin, and he seems to have ignored the fact that the favour of Antoinette began before her marriage.

her favour, and was able to do whatever she pleased with the king, she made the acquaintance of a young beauty whose name was Blanche Retreuves. Blanche lived with one Mme. de Jenly, and the Duchesse de Villequier, seeing her beauty, desired that she should come to court as one of the charming ladies in her train. Mme. de Jenly refused to allow this without the consent of Blanche's father. But he, being avaricious, gave his permission to the nefarious design of the duchess, and Blanche and her brother Jaquet were sent to join Antoinette's household. "The said Blanche," wrote Du Clercq, "when she left the house of her father at Arras, wept bitterly, and I was told that she said she would rather have remained with her father and have lived on bread and water. But she was obliged to go . . . and soon after she had been with Mme. de Villequier, report said that she stood as high in the king's graces as Mme. de Villequier herself."

The circumstances which governed such conditions in the fifteenth century are not easy to grasp, and the proof of it lies in the fact that Marie d'Anjou not only willingly gave presents [1] to the *maîtresse en titre*, but concerned herself with the moneys due to the " filles joyeuses qui suivent la court."

The reigning beauty then, with her two thou-

---

[1] In the accounts occurs an item " for gold ornaments on a crystal fountain of fine workmanship on which were chased foliage, gargoyles and *quatre leons d'or bien gentemens faix donné en estraines à Mlle. de Villequier.*"

sand livres income, and her name appearing in
State documents of importance, held her own
until the end of Charles VII's days. She had
more political power, perhaps, than her cousin,
because Charles was more easily governed in his
old age, and the woman who governed him was
more self-seeking.

The dauphin Louis was better disposed towards
her than he had been to Agnes, in spite of the
fact that he attempted to justify his conduct in
fleeing to Burgundy in 1456 by citing the dis-
orders which went on at the French court. He
kept up a secret correspondence with the favourite, and learnt from her much that happened.
Nor did he scruple to avail himself of a base and
clumsy trick in allowing a letter written by him
to Antoinette from Genappe purposely to fall
into the hands of one of Charles's attendants.
The letter implicated Chabannes, who was forth-
with exiled, although speedily recalled when the
intrigue was discovered. The rebellious prince
and the shameless mistress were in league, and
Antoinette received a pension of six thousand
livres from Louis after he became king.

Before the death of Charles VII she had
deserted him for François II, Duc de Bretagne,
and after 1461 she lived with the duke openly
and gave birth to five of his children.

Compared to her Agnes is indeed a lovable
figure, far above the sordid meanness, the disloyalty and vulgar intrigue of which her cousin
was capable. Nor could Charles ever have shown
for Antoinette the genuine affection which he

felt for Agnes. To the latter he had given the passion of his life, a passion he had never felt for the bride to whom he had been affianced at the age of nine. To his last mistress he gave only the dregs of his better self, and with Mme. de Montespan she might have said, " The king does not love me, but he desires to have the most beautiful woman in his kingdom for his mistress."

Charles lived ten years after the death of Agnes. The rapid conquest of Normandy was followed by the more difficult task of bringing Guienne to submission—a province which for three centuries had been partly in the hands of the English.

At the close of July, 1458, Charles, leading a fourth section of the army (three sections having gone before him), arrived at Bordeaux, round which the French attack had been centred, and on October 19, 1453, the banner of France was flying in the city.

When he became victorious Charles bethought him of Jeanne d'Arc. He wished the Church to proclaim her sanctity. No sooner had he taken Rouen than he charged Guillaume Bouillé, a doctor of theology, to make an inquiry into her trial, and after many delays and much discussion, well known to the general reader, at length on July 7, 1456, her sentence was revoked by the Pope. Six years had passed since the first step to this end had been taken, and it seems probable that it was Agnes herself who had in the first instance inspired her royal lover with the idea of doing a tardy justice.

When this achievement was completed the

best of the king's years were over. In 1455 the insidious disease which was to carry him to the grave made its appearance. From 1457 onwards he suffered from an incurable malady. The last four years of his life were embittered by the cold-blooded behaviour of the dauphin, who grew daily more anxious to mount the throne.

At the beginning of July, 1461, Charles's health broke down utterly, and he was unable to take nourishment. The historians declared that he refused to eat because of his fear that his son was trying to poison him, but it is more probable that the morbid conditions were the result of a disease of the maxillary glands. On the 22nd of the month he died, and, if we may judge by the care with which he had provided for the future of Agnes Sorel's daughters, it is probable that in spite of the intervening distractions he had never forgotten the years he had spent in happiness with the Lady of Beauty.

CHAPTER XXVII

THE CHILDREN OF AGNES SOREL

AGNES SOREL left four daughters, the youngest of whom died at the age of six months, soon after her mother. After the Lady of Beauty's death it was necessary to find homes for the other three children, who were all of a tender age, and practically orphans, since their father did not as yet openly acknowledge them.

Marie, the eldest, was placed in the charge of Admiral de Coëtivy, and brought up at the Château of Tailleburg. Her guardian was killed at Cherburg in 1450, and his brother Olivier became the head of his house and guardian of Marie. In 1451, when Charles was staying at Tailleburg, he gave a present to his natural daughter, and now and again sent money for her requirements.

Olivier de Coëtivy was made prisoner by the English when they invaded Guienne, and no sooner was he set free than he demanded his ward's hand in marriage. To this the· king assented, and he gave Marie a dowry of twelve thousand golden crowns, to be paid within six years. The letters patent concerning the marriage were dated October 28, 1458, and in the following November Charles acknowledged .

Marie to be his daughter, gave her the name of Valois, and allowed her to use the arms of France with the bar sinister. He presented her with one thousand six hundred and fifty livres for new gowns " à son plaisir le jour et fête de ses noces." The contract of marriage was signed on November 25.

The marriage was a happy one, and Marie was a loving and loyal wife. Her letters, collected by M. Marchegay,[1] are taken as intensely typical of a certain class of life of that day. " This exquisite and precious collection introduces us to the hearth of a united and faithful couple," wrote one author.[2] " Under the reign of her brother, who detested in her the memory of Agnes, she suffered in company with her husband many hardships, and was even made to leave her dear Castle of Tailleburg, where she had been brought up.

" The miserable trials of her existence, the fatigue of numerous confinements, which carried her to the tomb at the age of thirty-seven, could not sadden the delicious letters written to Olivier de Coëtivy during the long absences which separated them."

She lived a country life in the midst of nature and surrounded by her little ones, of whom she wrote in a charming manner. Surely her simple courage, her pretty ways and her happy affections were inherited from her mother. No one has

[1] *Lettres de Marie de Valois, fille de Charles VII et d'Agnès Sorel*, 1875.
[2] Lavisse : *Histoire de France*, Vol. IV. pt. ii. p. 169.

for a moment cast a doubt on the authenticity of these letters, which were found by Marchegay in the Archives of the Duc de la Tremoille.

"You will please to know," she wrote on the last day of February, 1464, when announcing the birth of a second son to his father, "that the first Friday in Lent it pleased God to deliver me of ε fine son, at about eight o'clock in the evening, which infant is so beautiful that you would be astonished. But, Monseigneur, as you know, it is impossible to be surprised that he is good-looking, for every one says he resembles you very much indeed, and it could not therefore be otherwise. It seems to me that you ought to praise me very heartily, because I have given you two such fine sons one after the other. If it had been a girl, I should have said everything bad in the world about it, on account of the trouble I had, but because it is a son, I should be ashamed to complain of that. . . ."

Whatever her hardships may have been the life of Marie was happier than that of her sister Charlotte, who was married in 1462 to Jacques de Brézé, son of Agnes's friend Pierre. By this marriage Charlotte became mother of that Louis de Brézé who, early in the sixteenth century, married the fair Diane de Poitiers.

On May 18, 1462, Louis XI wrote a letter "in favour of the marriage which has recently been arranged between our dear and well-beloved natural sister, Charlotte de France, and the son of our beloved and loyal knight, Pierre de Brézé, Comte de Maulevrier."

U

The marriage was regarded as a reconciliation between Pierre de Brézé and the new king, and it must also have seemed as though Louis buried his animosity towards the bride's dead mother.

Unfortunately the alliance, from which five children were born, was terminated by a tragedy. The Comte de Maulevrier was of a harsh and sullen disposition. He was jealous of his wife and his chief huntsman, Pierre de la Vergne.

One evening in June, 1475, some meddlesome friend informed him that Pierre de la Vergne was closeted in his wife's apartments, and that his honour was endangered. He rushed to the room, and discovered the huntsman with the countess.

Without waiting for explanations he struck the man dead, and followed his wife into the nursery, where she had taken refuge in her terror behind the beds in which the children lay asleep. He drew her from the place in which she was concealed, and thrust a dagger into her heart.

He was tried and found guilty, but released from prison in 1481. Before his trial he had erected a magnificent tomb to his wife's memory, and eventually he was buried in this tomb by his own instructions, which appears to prove that he repented of his rash act, and gave the countess at length the credit of being innocent.

The third and youngest living daughter of Agnes was Jeanne, who was brought up by Prégent Frotier, Baron de Preuilly, and promised to him as his bride. The arrangement, however, came to nothing, and she was married on December 23,

1461, to Antoine de Bueil, son of the admiral Jean de Bueil who wrote *Le Jouvencel,* in which reference is made to Agnes's influence over the king at the time of the Conquest of Normandy.

The doubt that hangs over the date of birth of the Lady of Beauty is extended to the births of her three daughters. According to Anselme Charlotte was born in 1434, Marie in 1436, and Jeanne in 1445; but these dates are not based on authentic documents, and, if it be true that Agnes did not meet Charles till early in the forties, they are obviously erroneous.

It may be taken for certain that Marie was older than Charlotte, and that the latter cannot have been twenty-seven when she was married and forty-two when she was taken in adultery. It is also more probable that Marie was fourteen or fifteen when affianced to Olivier de Coëtivy, and not twenty-two when Charles described her as " of an age to be married " in his letters of October, 1458. Her first son was born three years later, probably when she was seventeen.

It is also more likely that when Agnes died the children were quite young. Had they then been grown up it would hardly have been necessary to place them in the hands of various guardians.

Perhaps it may also be regarded as more probable that Agnes Sorel's four children were born within the space of six or seven years, than over the longer period of sixteen years, which was given by the earlier historians.

U 2

CHAPTER XXVIII

CONCLUSION

THE CONTROVERSY ABOUT AGNES

THE French have always been keen disputants in their literary and historical controversies. They enlist in separate camps, and do battle royal with words for weapons in the most spirited fashion.

From the days of the war between Ancients and Moderns, when epigrams fell like hailstones upon the heads of the literary men engaged in it, a thousand questions have raised the interest of authors and historians, and given them the opportunity of expounding their theories and endeavouring to prove their points.

Round the sunny brow of the fair Agnes discussion has raged with no stint of phrases. Chroniclers have been quoted and requoted, their careless sentences have been pulled into shreds in the hope of discovering some hidden meaning, their facts have been submitted to a dozen tests, and their inaccuracies exposed by the ruthless hand of the expert.

Although much had been written about the Lady of Beauty before 1855, no one had been bold enough to give the whole case in its chief lights, and to collect all the scattered theories was by no means a small undertaking. On the publication of M. Vallet de Viriville's *Agnès Sorel, étude morale et politique sur le XVe siècle*, however, M. Ludovic Lalanne entered the arena against him, and the resulting argument put forth the pros and cons of the whole question so clearly that it may be regarded as representing a very large proportion indeed of the evidence available.

M. Lalanne was the forerunner of M. du Fresne de Beaucourt in his doubt as to the birth-date of Agnes being correctly given by Anselme, and to him must be accorded the original credit of unmasking an historical bogey.

"I agree willingly," wrote M. Lalanne, "although there is no proof of it, that Agnes exercised a happy influence over her royal lover, but I am in complete disagreement with M. Vallet as to the epoch and consequently as to the importance of this influence, because I cannot admit the dates on which they are based."

He then proceeded to quote the two important points of evidence in the chronicles of Thomas Basin. First that Agnes died in the flower of her youth, which implies she had not reached the age of forty, and secondly that he placed the commencement of the relations between her and Charles VII about the time of the truce between France and England, namely 1444.

M. Lalanne considered that all the documents cited by M. Vallet de Viriville supported the theory of the later date. He mentioned the accounts of the household expenses of Isabelle in which Agnes appeared in receipt of payment;

pointed out that the letters were written according to M. Vallet de Viriville's opinion between 1446 and 1449; and that she received the Château of Beauté in 1444, of Rocquecezière in 1446, a pension of three thousand livres the following year, and of Vernon in 1449. He noted that it is impossible to explain why from 1434 to 1444 history is completely silent, and no documents relate to Agnes if she was the king's mistress during those ten years.

According to Delort, said M. Lalanne, her eldest daughter was born in 1434, and the fourth sixteen years later, just before her death. At the last confinement she would then be forty years old.

Charlotte, who was not married until the reign of Louis XI, was killed in 1476 by her husband, Jacques de Brézé, who surprised her in adultery. She was then forty-two.

These facts, concluded M. Lalanne, were possible, but not very probable.

M. Vallet de Viriville replied to M. Lalanne as follows:

He sent him an extract by the Prior Marye from *l'Histoire de l'Abbaye de Jumièges* in which the author said Agnes died " aged only forty years," which he considered conclusive, adding that the most esteemed biographers had given the date of 1409 without contesting it.

He thought Basin deserved the palm for being the worst historian of the reign of Charles VII without exception, and quoted one or two of his misstatements. As for the fact that Agnes was at court in 1444 this was attested by many documents, but that did not prove that the *liaison* began precisely at that date. M. Vallet de Viriville considered that there was a secret understanding for some time before Agnes was acknowledged *maîtresse en titre*.

" The flower of youth," M. Vallet de Viriville thought, belonged rather to the calendar of the poets than the Gregorian calendar. On the cheeks of Ninon that flower did not fade at forty, nor indeed until some ninety spring-times had passed.

The author entered into a discussion of Isabelle's departure for Naples in 1435, which was said by Pius II to be the date when Agnes remained behind in the queen's household. He also stated that the rupture between king and dauphin in 1440, at the time of the Praguerie, had for its cause a lady who was much in favour with the king, though he does not name her until the later episode when Louis retired to the Dauphiné in 1446.

The question of Jacques du Clercq, who wrote " Agnes was one of the most beautiful women of the realm, but she did not last long, and died," was not important because M. Vallet de Viriville considered a woman who died at forty had come to a premature end.

M. Vallet de Viriville then entered into a complicated discussion as to the ages of the daughters, which did not prove much.

After again mentioning the fact of the name of Agnes appearing on the pay-list of the House of

Anjou, M. Vallet de Viriville concluded by remarking that the lack of documents concerning Agnes before 1444 was not confined to her case, and since, before the truce, Charles had neither land nor money to give away, and some of the places he gave to Agnes were still in the hands of the English, it is hardly surprising that there were no earlier deeds of transfer of property.

M. Lalanne again stepped in to argue that any competent person who consulted the *Histoire de l'Abbaye Jumièges*, in which Marye wrote, found it bristling with errors of all kinds. He quoted Jean Chartier, who said that the king loved Agnes for the *folies de la jeunesse*. He replied he could find no trace of Isabelle's visit to Charles VII in 1485; that Pius II was uncertain whether the first or second quarrel between Charles and Louis was due to Agnes; that Olivier de la Marche described the sympathy between the queen and the Duchesse de Bourgogne owing to their husbands' infidelity in 1444, when the king had *recently* taken unto himself a lady of low birth, Agnes Sorel; that Chartier said Agnes was in the queen's service for five years, and that if the eldest daughter, Marie, was born in 1445 she would have been about fourteen at the time of her marriage, which was quite a usual age.

M. Vallet de Viriville then allowed the argument to drop.

" The date of 1485," wrote Du Fresne de Beaucourt,[1] considering the date of the *liaison*,

---

[1] *Histoire de Charles VII*, Vol. III. p. 287.

" cannot be reconciled with the age of Agnes, who, according to the most authentic data, must have been born not in 1409 or in 1415, as her biographers state, but not earlier than 1422. Otherwise it would be necessary to erase from the chroniclers the   ̧es in which they insist with concerted unan: on the youth of Agnes, the follies of youth w.   captivated the heart of the king, her premat.   death in the flower of youth," etc., etc.

This criticism is the same as that of M. Lalanne already answered by M. Vallet de Viriville. The language of compliment permitted of such statements, and Diane de Poitiers, whose years mounted to seventy, was still known as a fair young damsel in poetical language.

Beautiful ladies, like Agnes, have no more years behind them than those they do not succeed in concealing, was the opinion of one author.

M. Vallet de Viriville suggested three solutions of the problem. The first was to allow the legend full sway as did M. Delort.

The second consisted in denying all or rejecting all that happened before 1444, and in believing that at this date Charles VII began his acquaintance with Agnes.

The third hypothesis was to place the birth of Agnes in 1415, that of Marie in 1486, that of Charlotte in 1488, and keep all the other dates named in history, thus making the following table of events possible : [1]

[1] *Histoire de Charles VII*, Vol. III. pp. 28–24.

1430 (?) Given by Charles de Bourbon (?) to Isabelle,
        wife of his ally, René, at the age of 15.
1435–44 (20 to 29). With the queen, but still dependent
        on Isabelle's bounty.
1436. Mother of Marie at the age of 21.
1438. Mother of Charlotte at the age of 23.
1444. Dowered by the king; at court, etc.
1445. Mother of Jeanne at the age of 30.
1450. Dies at the age of 35.

But M. du Fresne de Beaucourt [1] contended
in his latest work that:

> Marie de Valois was born about October, 1444.
> Charlotte about September, 1446.
> Jeanne about February, 1448.

The same author gave the following account of
the movements of Charles, Marie d'Anjou and
Isabelle.

In 1441 the queen was in the east with the
king. During the campaign of Guienne she went
to the south. On March 28, 1443, they made
an entry into Limoges with a brilliant cortège,
and then she went to Tours, where a daughter
was born on December 1, 1443.

Charles joined the queen at Montauban, where
he arrived on December 23, 1442. From there
he went with her to Toulouse on February 28,
1443. At that date Isabelle de Lorraine appeared
for the first time at court. Having left Naples
during the disasters of her husband (August, 1440)
she stayed first at Provence, then at Lorraine,
and went to meet René when, being forced
to leave Naples, he disembarked in Provence.

---

[1] *Histoire de Charles VII*, 1881–90, Vol. V. p. 75.

René hastened to salute the king at Toulouse (March 19). He went with him to Poitiers (April 8 to May 25). Isabelle went to Anjou. On April 16 she was at Saumur. In September Charles arrived at Saumur, where he stayed till the middle of February, 1444. From there he went to Angers and then to Tours. At that moment the Treaty of Tours was signed, and the marriage of Marguerite d'Anjou was celebrated.

There could, therefore, be no question of a *liaison* between Agnes and the king during Isabelle's absence between 1435 and 1442.

The author suggested that Agnes made her first appearance at court in March, 1443, if she was still among Isabelle's maids-of-honour, and that the relations began no earlier than at Toulouse at the end of March, 1443, and were not established until the following September. She went into the queen's household at the end of 1444, being then already a mother.

Of the controversy between M. Vallet de Viriville and M. Ludovic Lalanne, M. du Fresne de Beaucourt [1] declared that it lifted the whole question definitely out of the clouds in which it had remained enveloped.

He then mentioned the existing documents in the following order, and reiterated and summarised the whole position :

In the accounts of the Queen of Sicily's household from January 1 to July 31, 1444, Agnes Sorel appears as being recipient of x livres.

The same year she was designated Dame de

<hr>

[1] *Revue des Questions Historiques*, Vol. I. p. 210, 1866.

Beauté and received the Castle of Beauté near Paris as a gift.

In 1446 Roquecezière in Rouergue was added.

In 1447 she had a pension of 3,000 livres.

Between 1447 and 1449 she was given the Seigneuries of Bois-Trousseau and of Anneville, the Châtellainies of Issoudun and of Vernon-sur-Seine.

Her name figured again as partaking of royal liberalities at the end of 1449.

These facts were confirmed by the official chronicler Jean Chartier, monk of Saint-Denis and historiographer of France, who wrote of Agnes's death after she had been in the service of the queen five years or thereabouts.

By Thomas Basin, who referred to the Truces with the English, the first of which was signed May 28, 1444.

By Olivier de la Marche, who stated that when the Duchesse de Bourgogne was at Châlons the king had *recently* taken up Agnes Sorel.

These statements practically closed the evidence as to the date of Agnes's *public* acknowledgment.

M. du Fresne de Beaucourt then proceeded to question the dates of the birth of the daughters, in order to discover the length of time before 1444 in which Agnes had relations with Charles. "For," he remarked, "in our eyes it is as impossible to admit that the public favour of Agnes was anterior to 1444 as to pretend that her *liaison* with the king did not go back further."

Jacques du Clercq made his evidence that the

king was acquainted with a young lady named Agnes date from the Treaty of Arras, concluded September 21, 1435, with the Duc de Bourgogne, and said that until that date Charles had lived a *moult saincte vie*.

The evidence of Æneas Sylvius (Pius II) seems to refer to the same date, and Jean Chartier, who denied culpable relations, declared that if there were any they must have been carried on secretly, " as she was then in the service of the Queen of Sicily, before she was exchanged into the service of the Queen of France."

M. du Fresne de Beaucourt admitted the probability of a *liaison occulte*, but could not determine its duration definitely. He put no weight on the statements of Du Clercq and Pius II.

With regard to the age of the daughters, he supposed with Griffet that Marie (sometimes wrongly called Marguerite) was the eldest, and was about fifteen at the time of her marriage with Coëtivy in 1458, thus giving as her birth 1443.

This would presume that Charlotte was born in 1444 or 1445, was sixteen or seventeen when she married Jacques de Brézé, and thirty-one or two when she was murdered.

Jeanne was a minor when she was married to Antoine de Bueil in 1461. Perhaps 1446 would be the year of her birth.

Having placed the date of Agnes's relations with Charles between 1441 and 1443, M. du Fresne de Beaucourt drew conclusions as follows :

In 1433 Charles, he said, thanks to the influence of his mother-in-law Yolande and his wife

Marie d'Anjou, had sent away La Trémouille and commenced a rule of wise and clever ministers and councillors. In 1435 he concluded the Treaty of Arras, and five years later the awakening or transformation in his character was complete. Before Agnes and without Agnes the Kinglet of Bourges had disappeared and the King of France existed in all his glory and power.

In M. du Fresne de Beaucourt's eyes, then, the influence the Lady of Beauty possessed, and which he does not deny, was revealed only in court intrigues, in domestic quarrels occasioned by the dauphin's intractability, in certain favours and rapid advancements noticed by the contemporaries. She did good in giving alms, numerous donations and foundations, but she had little ascendancy in political affairs.

She had learnt the emptiness of pomp and show and earthly grandeur; she knew the value of things spiritual and unseen.

" How frail is our flesh, how abject and vile a thing, and truly of what little worth ! "

APPENDIX A

A PORTRAIT OF AGNES SOREL

CHARLES SOREL, the author of *La Solitude*, who claimed descent from Agnes, wrote thus of King François I's verse on her. "She merited that he should use his poetical vein for her as well as for Laura and Petrarch, and others for whom he did so. Having found a book of drawings at the house of Catherine [1] d'Hangest, wife of Artus de Boisy, grand master of France, who pleased himself with painting, he made mottoes or verses for each one, and for that of the lovely Agnes he made a quatrain which he wrote in his own hand, and which is still to be seen in this precious book.

> 'Plus de louange et d'honneur tu merite,
> La cause estant de France recouvrer
> Que n'est tout ce, qu'au Cloistre peut ouvrer
> Close nonnain, ou au desert hermite.'

"They say that if she had lived far from the pomps of court she could not have rendered so great a service to France."

Gouffier was one of the "gentle companions" who won the favour of Agnes, and after her death he inherited (March, 1450) the revenue

[1] This should be Hélène.

of Roqueceziére in Rouergue. In the following December he received more lands, he took part in the trial of Jacques Cœur, and inherited the Seigneurie of Boisy when the victim's goods were confiscated. His son was Artus de Boisy, who married Hélène d'Hangest.

The de Boisys made a valuable collection of contemporary portraits. Amongst them they placed a drawing of Agnes. She had been dead a long time, and they had not known her. But Jean d'Hangest, grandfather of Mme. de Boisy, had also been one of the " gentle companions." It is not surprising, then, that they had interest enough in consecrating a page of their album to the graceful image of the fair Agnes.

" From all these links, from all these facts," wrote Niel,[1] " is it not easy to conclude that this likeness of Agnes Sorel, thus preserved in pious and affectionate hands, causes to live again before our eyes in the most authentic manner and pure reality the charming woman who, at one of the most unfortunate and critical epochs of our history, only employed her ascendancy over the king's mind to recall to him what he owed to himself and to his people ? We do not doubt that the drawing was a copy of a painting executed probably by a master of the fifteenth century from the original. Duclos mentions a painting of Charles VII and one of Agnes Sorel in the same style."

[1] *Portraits des personnages français les plus illustres du XVI° siècle*, 1848.

[To face p. 304

CHARLES SOREL

APPENDIX B

IN his *Notes Supplémentaires*, M. du Fresne de Beaucourt [1] devoted some space to "Les prétendues lettres d'Agnès Sorel." In the *Revue des Questions Historiques*, t. xiv. p. 118 *et suiv.*, he cited these letters as authentic. Since then, however, certain circumstances arose which made him change his opinion.

M. Pierre Clément,[2] in his book *Jacques Cœur et Charles VII*, wrote of " some letters of Agnes Sorel, happily preserved to us, and giving precious indications of her character."

"All these letters, to the number of five," he said, " are previously unpublished. Two of them, the first and the fourth, form part of the rich and curious collection of M. Chambry, former mayor of the third arrondissement, who was kind enough to place these two pieces at my disposal. . . . The text of the second of the two letters addressed to the Sire de la Varenne has been communicated to me in an extremely obliging manner by M. Vallet de Viriville. The two others belong to M. le Baron de Trémont. Four of these letters are in the handwriting of

---

[1] *Histoire de Charles VII*, Vol. IV. p. 440.
[2] *Jacques Cœur et Charles VII*, p. 241, 1853.

Agnes Sorel; the main portion of the one addressed from Candes to Mlle. de Belleville, in which is mentioned the accident to little Robin, is not in the writing of Agnes, who only added the words ' la toute vostre bonne amye ' and her signature."

There was some doubt, it appears, as to the authenticity of these letters, but it was set at rest about 1846 by M. Teulet, paleographic archivist of the École des Chartes, who compared the handwriting of the letters with some at the Bibliothèque Nationale, known to be by Agnes Sorel.

M. Vallet de Viriville reprinted the letters in the *Revue de Paris*, and again in his *Nouvelles Recherches sur Agnès Sorel*, 1856, in which he wrote : " Some original autograph letters of la belle Agnes have been preserved. They are the source of the most direct and profound information which we can have in order to set our curiosity at rest on certain points. The letters reveal a fine soul, French wit, an alert, gracious and amusing intelligence." In his *Histoire de Charles VII* the same author wrote, " they show quite uncommon, intellectual culture on her part. . . . They reveal sentiments of generous and delicate charity, as much removed from the casual almsgiving of great ladies as from the matter-of-course, egoistical and imperious pride of heartless favourites."

On these grounds, the letters were for a time accepted as historical documents, and it must be confessed that, on the face of them, they appear authentic enough in purport; indeed, if they were forged, the inquisitive student asks immediately why they did not contain information of more importance, or were not addressed to more significant people.

M. du Fresne de Beaucourt based his opinion on that of M. Etienne Charavay, paleographic archivist, who declared that the letters came " from the too famous source, Letellier."

" I am assured," wrote M. Charavay, " that the three letters coming through this impure channel are no less false than all the other documents I have had occasion to examine, and which I have withdrawn from circulation or annulled by a special stamp. . . . The collection Chambry, of which I edited the catalogue in 1881, includes a certain number of the forged Letelliers, and among them was a letter from Agnes Sorel to Mlle. de Belleville. This document was a very poor forgery. . . . I therefore consider the four letters which have circulated as not genuine."

INDEX

ÆNEAS SYLVIUS. *See* Pius II

Albret, Jeanne d', 118

Alençon, Duc d', 26, 94, 96, 255

Alphonso V, 173

Angoulême, Comte d', 99, 107 *n*.

Anjou, Louis d', 21

Anjou, Marguerite d'. *See* Marguerite

Anjou, René d'. *See* René

Anselme (quoted), 3, 7, 10 *n*.

Arc, Jeanne d', 4, 5, 23, 27, 33, 62, 71, 72, 75, 77, 79, 252, 263, 285

Armagnac, Comte d', 187

Aubusson, Antoine d', 126, 168

Baif, Jean Antoine de (quoted), 279

Barbeline, 90

Barry, Mme. du, 61, 271 *n*.

Basin, Thomas, Bishop of Lisieux (quoted), 83, 300

Baude, Henri (quoted), 103, 137

Bavière, Isabeau de, 29, 30

Bavière, Marguerite de, 15, 20

Beauvau, Bertrand de, 96 *n*., 100–101, 106, 119

Belin, Jacques, 225

Belleville, Mlle. de, 135–8, 144, 306–7

Benoist, 193

Bigot, Guillaume, 130

Blainville, Seigneur de (Jean d'Estouteville), 101, 121, 209

Boisy, Artus de, 303–4

Boisy, Mme. de (Hangest, Hélène d'), 74 *n*., 303

Boniface, John, 173

Bouillé, Guillaume, 285

Bourbon, Charles, Duc de, 26, 84, 109, 281

Bourdigné (quoted), 14

Bourgogne, Duc de (Jean-sans-Peur), 31, 33

Bourgogne, Duc de (Philippe le Bon), 20, 77, 89, 94, 96, 112, 116, 188, 209, 245, 301

Bourgogne, Duchesse de (Isabelle), 112, 119, 222, 296

Brantôme (quoted), 67

Bretagne, Duc de (François II), 94, 96, 284

Brézé, Jacques de, 289, 294, 301

Brézé, Louis de, 171, 188, 192–3, 289

Brézé, Mme. de, 269

Brézé, Pierre de, Sire de la Varenne, 44, 95, 96 *n*., 99–101, 106–7, 110, 118–19, 122, 162, 169–70, 187, 191–2, 194, 206, 209–11, 213, 218–19, 225, 245, 289, 305

Bueil, Antoine de, 291, 301

Bueil, Jean de, 92, 99, 100, 119, 246, 291

Bureau, Jean, 101, 244

Bussy-Rabutin (quoted), 131

Calabre, Duc de (Jean d'Anjou), 94, 101, 106, 119

Calabre, Duchesse de, 97, 109, 117

Carpet (greyhound), 136

Chabannes, Antoine de, 168, 188–90, 193, 197–8, 216, 274, 276–7

Chalons, Jean, 171–2

Chambre, Christy, 126

Chambre, Nicole, 126

Chambry, M., 305

Champdivers, Odette de, 135 *n*.

Chanteur, Jacquette, 90

Charavay, Etienne de, 307

Charles VI, 30–1, 135 *n*.

Charles VII, 1, 2, 5, 7, 21, 23, 50–2 *et passim*; his temperament, 5–6, 24, 28–9, 30, 33–4; receives Isabelle de Lorraine, 23, 36; meets Agnes, 23, 27; birth, 29; early struggles, 31; ironical verses about, 32; Kinglet of Bourges, 32; loves Agnes Sorel, 38–9, 41, 46; his piety, 48, 120; parts from Marguerite d'Anjou, 109–10; at Sarry-les-Châlons, 111–15; grief at the dauphine's death, 123; his bodyguard, 126–7; influence of Agnes on, 127–8, 219; his love of horses, 137; his gifts to Agnes, 147; and Antoinette de Maignelais, 158, 281–4; at Mehun-sur-Yèvre, 173; at Bois-Trousseau, 177–82, 184; relations with his son Louis, 185–6, 197, 199; and Brézé, 208–9, 211; his ingratitude, 219; portrait of, by Fouquet, 238–9; at war with England, 243–6, 251–8, 285; at Jumièges, 261, 264–8; accuses Jacques Cœur, 275; his malady and death, 286

Charlotte (daughter of Agnes Sorel), 182, 204, 289, 291, 294, 297–8, 301

Charno, Phelice, 90

Charolais, Comte de (afterwards Duc de Bourgogne), 96

Chartier, Alain, 104

Chartier, Jean, 25, 47, 84–5, 205, 258, 268, 296, 300

Chartres, Regnault de, 96 n.

Chasteauneuf, Claude de, 167

Chastel, Tanneguy du, 224

Chastellain, Georges, 87, 106, 233

Chateaubriand, Mme. de, 27

Châteauroux, Mme. de, 61

Chevalier, Etienne, 24, 37, 68, 115, 119, 148, 152–3, 156, 168, 204, 216, 218–19, 229, 232, 234–5, 237, 241, 249, 268, 272

Chevalier, Jean, 231

Chissay, Monseigneur de, 149

Clément, Pierre (quoted), 305

Clermont, Comte de, 70, 112, 118, 162, 170–1, 191, 244

Clermont, François de (Seigneur de Dampierre), 137, 173

Clèves, Adolphe de, 112

Clifford, Lord, 106

Coëtivy, Admiral de, 99, 100–1, 106, 287

Coëtivy, Olivier de, 287, 291, 301

Cœur, Jacques, 62, 73, 119, 135, 176, 201–2, 218, 220, 223, 225, 229, 268, 274–6, 304

Cœur, Perrette, 175

Cœur, Pierre, 220

Cohen, A. (quoted), 11, 68, 148, 152, 168, 202

Cokesey, Sir Hugh, 106

Coudray, Mme. de, 90

Créquy, Seigneur de, 112

Cristofle, 136

Dagobert, King, 260

Daillon, Jean de, 192–3

Delort (quoted), 11, 203–4

Dreux du Radier, 229

Dubout, Alfred (quoted), 70

Du Clercq, Jacques, 89, 282, 295, 301

Duclos (quoted), 193

Dudley, Lord, 171

Du Fresne de Beaucourt (quoted), 3, 34, 41, 128, 131, 185, 194, 213 n., 293, 296, 305, 307

Dunois, Comte de, 26, 94, 132, 188, 205, 225, 244, 255, 259

Duquesne (quoted), 179, 197, 271

Eleanor of Scotland, 130, 171, 173

Elliott, Grace, 65

Estrées, Gabrielle d', 60, 180 n., 215, 274

Étampes, Comte d', 94

Étampes, Duchesse d', 61, 66

Evreux, Comtesse d', 167

Eugenius IV, Pope, 232

Fabyan (quoted), 172

Filleul, Jeanne, 104

Florigny, 166

Foix, Gaston, Comte de, 118, 166

Fouquet, Jean, 25, 231–3, 237–8

Fouquet, Nicolas, 218, 278

François I, 27, 74, 303
Fromenteau, Mlle. de. *See* Sorel, Agnes
Frotier, Prégent, Baron de Preuilly, 290

Garelle, Goffeline, 90
Gaucourt, Monseigneur de, 149
Gazeau, Guillaume, 126
Gazelle, Mlle., 169
Girante, Jehanne, 90
Girard, Bernard de, 66
Gouffier, 125–6, 213, 269, 276–7, 303
Grey, Lady Elizabeth, 106
Greystock, Lord, 106
Guienne, Duc de, 31
Guienne, Duchesse de, 118
Guise, Annette de, 169

Hall, Lady Elizabeth, 106
Hangest, Jean d', 304
Harancourt, Louis de, 106
Harcourt, Sir Robert, 106
Harpedenne, Jean de, 135 n.
Havart, Jean, 99
Henri IV, 180 n., 213, 236, 274
Henry V, King of England, 31–2
Henry VI, King of England, 31, 70, 91, 93, 96, 100, 110, 115, 244
Hervée, 90

Isabelle de Lorraine, 13–24, 36–7, 90, 95–7, 105, 107, 109, 117, 221, 295–6, 298–9

James, Henry (quoted), 72, 271
Jane of Scotland, 130
Jean, Duc de Touraine, 31
Jeanne (daughter of Agnes Sorel), 246 n., 290–1, 298, 301
Jeanne de France, 162, 171, 222
Jeanne II, 18
Jenly, Mme. de, 283
Jouvenal, Jean, 115
Jouy, Marie de, 10 n.
Juvenal des Ursins, Jean, 224

Lacurne de Sainte-Palaye (quoted), 16

Lady of Beauty, the. *See* Sorel, Agnes
La Fayette, 101
La Hire, 132
La Trémouille, 43, 100, 302
Lalaing, Jacques de, 107 *and note*, 116–17, 142, 161, 184
Lalanne, Ludovic (quoted), 293–4, 296–7, 299
Laval, André de, 101, 106, 115, 167, 174
Lecoy de la Marche (quoted), 21
Lenclos, Ninon de, 295
Lenoure, Isabeau de, 90
Leodepart, Macée de, 220
Leroux, Nicholas, 78–80
Lohéac, de, 167, 170, 174, 244
Lorraine, Duc de (Charles le Hardi), 15, 18
Lorraine, Ferry de, 108, 166
Lorraine, Isabelle de. *See* Isabelle
Louis the dauphin (afterwards Louis XI), 53, 97, 104, 114, 144, 185, 194–5, 197, 200, 204, 206, 246, 270, 284, 289, 295
Louis XIV, 41, 65
Louis XV, 41
Louis, Duc de Guienne, 31
Luxembourg, Catherine de, 118
Luxembourg, Isabelle de, 95
Luxembourg, Jacques de, 161
Lyonne, 90

Madelaine de France, 104, 114
Maignelais, Antoinette de (afterwards Villequier, A. de), 10 n., 11–14, 66, 125, 147, 152–8, 267, 277, 281–5
Maignelais, Catherine de (afterwards Soreau), 7, 278 n.
Maignelais, Jean de, 10 n., 281
Mailly, Mme. Marie de, 90
Maine, Comte du (Charles d'Anjou), 94–5, 97, 101, 106, 116–19, 125, 208–9
Manné, Etienne de, 135 n., 276
Manonville, Mme. Jehanne de, 90
Marche, Olivier de la (quoted), 25, 83, 103, 108, 113, 296, 300
Margaret of Scotland (the dauphine), 94, 104, 114, 117, 120, 186–7

Marguerite d'Anjou (afterwards Queen of England), 22, 91, 93, 95, 97, 100, 104, 107 n., 110, 244, 299

Marguerite, Mme. (sister of François I), 176

Marguerite de Valois, 135 n.

Marie d'Anjou, Queen of France, 15, 18, 31, 36, 40, 43, 48, 84, 94, 97, 104, 107, 109, 112–13, 117, 123, 166, 169, 196, 204, 283, 298, 302

Marie de Valois (daughter of Agnes Sorel, sometimes called Marguerite), 182, 204 n., 287–9, 291, 297–8, 301

Mariette, Guillaume, 207–10

Maupas, Jean de, 99

Melun, Prégente de, 104, 121, 131

Milan, Duc de, 115

Montberon, François de, Sieur de Mortagne, 274

Montberon, Jeanne de, Dame de Mortagne, 274, 276–7

Montespan, Mme. de, 61, 66, 131

Moreau, 106

Nevers, Comte de, 96, 174

Nicholas V, Pope, 224, 277–8

Odille, 90

Orléans, Duc d', 93, 96 n., 222

Orléans, Duchesse d', 117

Orléans, Louis d', 30

Pasquier, Etienne (quoted), 20, 277

Paulmarde, Mlle., 169

Philibert, Saint, 260

Pius II, Pope (quoted), 21, 64, 89, 199, 295–6, 301

Poictevin, Robert, 268

Poitiers, Alienor de, 200

Poitiers, Diane de, 61

Pompadour, Mme. de, 61

Radegonde de France, 107 n., 111, 222

Razilly, Jean de, 124

René d'Anjou, King of Sicily, etc., 15, 18–19, 21, 93–4, 96, 99, 101, 103, 106–7, 109, 116, 119, 159, 165, 167, 170, 173, 184, 188, 298–9

Retruves, Blanche, 283

Retruves, Jean, 283

Richemont, Comte de, 84, 94, 101, 118–19

Rivière, Poncet de, 213

Ronsard, 260

Roos, Sir Richard, 106

Saint-Pol, Comte de, 95–6, 106–7, 116–19, 255

Saintrailles, Poton de, 106, 118, 166, 172

Salignac, Marguerite de, 104

Savoie, Duc de, 115, 187

Scales, Lady Emma, 106

Serancourt, Catherine de, 90

Serrière, Catherine de, 90

Sevigné, Mme. de, 131

Sicily, King of. See René d'Anjou

Sicily, Queen of. See Isabelle de Lorraine

Soreau, André, 7

Soreau, Charles, 7

Soreau, Geoffrey (or Floreau), 8, 233 n.

Soreau, Jean (father of Agnes Sorel), 7

Soreau, Jean (brother of Agnes Sorel), 7–8, 277–8

Soreau, Louis, 7

Sorel, Agnes, date of her birth, 3–4, 7, 293, 297; commencement of her relations with Charles VII, 4–5; and Jeanne d'Arc, 6, 70–5, 252; her brothers, 7–8, 126; her girlhood, 9–14; her beauty, 11, 25–6, 46; described by Voltaire, 76; and Antoinette de Maignelais, 11–14, 152–8; at the Court of Lorraine, 14–15, 90; first meeting with Charles, 23, 27; her character, 26, 218, 262; urges the king to do his duty, 32, 70–2, 132, 247, 251–4; falls ill, 37, 268; compared with Louise de la Vallière, 42, 64; compared with Grace Elliott,

65; has her fortune told, 67–70; verses on her by François I, 74–5, 303; receives the Château de Beauté, 84; and the chroniclers, 83–90, 300; and Pierre de Brézé, 99, 211, 215; letters to him, 216–19; in the queen's household, 103; and the dauphine, 105; at the joust, 107, 163, 168; her growing power, 122; her love of justice and mercy, 129; her style of dressing, 134–5; her letters, 136–8, 145–6, 216–19, 294, 305–7; hunts with the king, 137; her residences, 144–50; at Bois-Trousseau, 176–82; and dauphin Louis, 53, 187, 195–201, 203–4; her pious works, 203; makes a pilgrimage to Saint-Geneviève, 211, 214; at Paris, 214–16; and Jacques Cœur, 220, 222, 227; and Étienne Chevalier, 229, 231–3, 241; portraits of, 234–7, 239–41, 304; at Jumièges, 258, 261, 267; at Mesnil, 263, 265–6; her penitence, 268–9; her death, 269; her last will and testament, 268, 270; burial, 269; her tomb, 271–3; epitaphs, 273; cause of her death, 274–6; verses of de Baïf, 279–80; her children, 287–91; controversy as to dates, 292–302

Sorel, Charles, 303
Stanislas, King of Poland, 17
Suffolk, Lady, 106, 109
Suffolk, Lord, 93–9, 108–9

Talbot, Lady Beatrice, 106
Tancarville, Comte de, 167, 209, 269
Teulet, M., 306
Tiery, Mathelin, 216
Tillay, Jamet du, 99, 101, 121, 130–1
Touches, Mlle. de, 167
Tour, Bertrand de la, 106
Trémont, Baron de, 305
Trousseau, Artault, 175
Trousseau, Jacquelin, 175

Vallet de Viriville (quoted), 3, 10, 16, 20, 30, 33, 76, 129, 135, 201–2, 222, 234, 293, 305–6
Vallière, Louise de la, 41–2, 54, 60, 64–5, 218
Varenne, Sire de la. See Brézé, Pierre de
Vaudémont, Antoine de, 19–20, 108
Vendôme, Comte de, 94, 96 n., 101, 115, 119
Vendôme, Jeanne de. See Montberon
Vergne, Pierre de la, 290
Villars, 189
Villequier, André de, 125, 281
Villequier, Antoinette de. See Maignelais, A. de
Villequier, Marguerite de, 121, 126, 131, 167
Voltaire, 75

Yolande d'Aragon, 15, 18, 43, 96, 100, 109, 301
York, Richard, Duke of, 115–16

Richard Clay & Sons, Limited, London and Bungay.

Lightning Source UK Ltd.
Milton Keynes UK
24 May 2010

154649UK00004BA/3/P

9 781142 019464